O9-AHU-596

Research in Principles of Life

BASIC SEMINAR

TEXTBOOK

INSTRUCTOR: BILL GOTHARD

All Scripture references are from the King James Version of the Bible, unless otherwise noted.

Printed in the United States of America.

Twelfth Printing, Revised March, 1987

ISBN 0-916888-05-3

Library of Congress
Catalog Card Number: 79-92142

HOW TO USE THIS TEXTBOOK

- ✻ This textbook is only an incomplete supplement to the 32 hours of lectures, diagrams and charts which make up the Basic Seminar.

- ✻ The textbook is designed to be studied along with the many pages of notes which are to be written during the Seminar.

- ✻ The purpose of both the Seminar and this textbook is to encourage a much deeper study and application of Scripture.

- ✻ Each time a Seminar is attended, different areas of personal need usually stand out. Steps of action in these areas should be worked out first. In preparation for this, a time of personal study in the Scriptures should be engaged in. The textbook and lecture notes may become useful in suggesting areas of Scripture to study.

- ✻ This textbook is only a beginning. There are many more truths from the inexhaustible pages of Scripture which can be added. We encourage you to join us in the deeply rewarding process of doing this.

NOTES

6 AREAS OF CONFLICT

1. ASSURANCE OF SALVATION

Scripture assures us that it is possible to know beyond all doubt that we do possess eternal life (I John 5:13). However, in the minds of many, there are distracting doubts about whether or not they really are Christians. They have gone forward or raised their hand in meetings to receive Christ. They have also prayed and asked Him to come into their lives, but the doubts still persist.

2. SELF-IMAGE

Scripture teaches that we are intricately designed and that each of our basic physical characteristics was prescribed by God and developed according to His plan. (Psalm 139:14-16). However, today the vast majority of people are extremely self-conscious about physical "deficiencies" in themselves, and an overwhelming majority of individuals would change inborn features if they had the power to do so. By this they are saying that God's workmanship is inferior to their desired self-image, and, therefore, He cannot be trusted in other areas of life.

3. PURPOSE IN LIFE

Scripture directs us not to be vague but to firmly grasp what we know to be the will of God (Ephesians 5:15-17). Today, however, both youth and adults are without clearly-defined goals around which they can relate their activities and the direction of their lives. Someone has well said that if we do not have something worth dying for, we do not have something worth living for either.

4. HARMONY AT HOME

Scripture attaches significant benefit and reward to the one who submits to the authority and direction of his parents as those who are set over him by the Lord (Ephesians 6:1,2). However, in today's society the father has not assumed his role of spiritual leadership; thus, his discipline is without Scriptural foundation. The mother has tried to fill the gap, and the children are in a struggle for independence to conform to the fast-changing standards of their society.

5. MORAL PURITY

Scripture warns us to flee youthful lusts and to avoid them like the plague (I Thessalonians 4:4; I Corinthians 6:18). Yet absence of clearly defined Scriptural standards is resulting in an acceptance of immoral activities which are producing guilt, frustration and an inability or fear to think clearly about the future.

6. GENUINE FRIENDSHIPS

One of the most basic human needs is intimate fellowship with others. When we try to fulfill this need without knowing or following the freedoms and responsibilities on each level of friendship, a host of life-long conflicts results, and we miss the necessary experience of developing genuine friendships.

NOTES

PRINCIPLES IN APPLYING SCRIPTURE

• It is essential that all Scripture be diligently studied and accurately applied. Each application must be in harmony with the total meaning and message of Scripture—not from an isolated verse taken out of context.

• We are to "study to show ourselves approved unto God" as workmen who do not need to be ashamed, knowing how to "rightly divide" the Word of truth.
II Timothy 2:15.

A. **WORKING THROUGH THE TEXT:** Before any application of Scripture can be made, there must be a thorough understanding of what the text is actually saying.

Why was it written?
To whom was it written?
What were the conditions at the time?
What is the precise meaning in the original language?
What related Scriptures explain it further?

• Studying to show ourselves "approved unto God" goes far deeper than learning all the facts of the text.

B. **MEDITATING ON THE TEXT:** Only as we meditate on large sections of Scripture will we begin to see the underlying principles of application to daily living. David testified, "I have more understanding than all my teachers: for thy testimonies are my meditation." (Psalm 119:99; John 5:39; Acts 17:11)

• There is only one interpretation of Scripture but there are many applications. These open up worlds of meaning in life.

C. **DISCOVERING PRINCIPLES IN THE TEXT:** After a section of Scripture becomes a living part of our thinking and we put related passages together, we begin to see underlying principles within that Scripture which can be applied to our lives.

A good illustration of this is found in I Timothy 5:18 and I Corinthians 9:7-14. Paul was emphasizing the right which ministers of the Gospel have to expect a living wage. To support this he used what first appears to be a verse out of context (Deuteronomy 25:4), but he goes on to explain the underlying principle in it which has universal application (verse 10).

NOTES

TRACING PROBLEMS TO ROOT CAUSES

ILLUSTRATION:

SURFACE PROBLEMS These problems are visible to other people. Sometimes it is clear what the deeper problems are, and sometimes the visible manifestation is very deceiving.	**Resulting illnesses, wrong priorities, financial problems, lying, stealing, cheating, arguing.** The visible results of inward conflicts. ↑	"From whence come wars and fightings among you? Come they not hence, even of your lusts that war in your members?" James 4:1
SURFACE CAUSES These problems are experienced within the emotions and feelings. Often they are not revealed to others or are revealed in confusing ways.	**Insecurity, worry, anger, envy, jealousy, tension.** The inward results of building our lives and affections around that which is only temporal. ↑	"But they that (desire to) be rich fall into temptation and a snare, and into many foolish and hurtful lusts, which drown men in destruction and perdition." I Timothy 6:9
ROOT PROBLEMS These problems are actually at the source of multitudes of surface problems and surface causes. When these are solved many surface problems and causes are also resolved.	**Greed for money and possessions.** Believing that a man's life consists in the things which he possesses. ↑	"The love of money is the (a) root of all evil." I Timothy 6:10 "He that hasteth to be rich hath an evil eye, and considereth not that poverty shall come upon him." Proverbs 28:22
ROOT CAUSES These problems are the result of resisting the power of God's grace. This is the power which God gives to follow His principles of life—both temporal and eternal.	**Refusing to dedicate personal rights and possessions to God.** Believing that these rights and possessions belong to us, and that we have the final right to use them as we choose.	**..."if any man will come after me, let him deny himself, and take up his cross daily, and follow me...for whosoever will save his life shall lose it...what is a man advantaged, if he gain the whole world, and lose himself..."** **Luke 9:23-25**

NOTES

BUILDING MATURITY THROUGH PRINCIPLES

4 STEPS TO MATURITY		RELATED SCRIPTURE
SCRIPTURE **1. PRINCIPLES OF LIFE** Underlying all the basic teachings of Christ there are significant principles which are essential for successful living.	**WISDOM**	". . . the words that I speak unto you, they are spirit, and they are life." John 6:63 "My son, attend to my words; incline thine ear unto my sayings. For they are life unto those that find them and health to all their flesh." Proverbs 4:20,22 "According as his divine power hath given unto us all things that pertain unto life and godliness, through the knowledge of him that hath called us. . ." II Peter 1:3
2. RELATIONSHIPS AFFECTED BY PRINCIPLES When a principle of life is violated or neglected, breakdowns result in one or more of these basic relationships of life: Response to God Acceptance of self Family harmony Purpose for the future Effectiveness in friendships Harmony in dating and marriage Management of financial affairs	**CONFLICTS**	"The ear that heareth the reproof of life abideth among the wise." Proverbs 15:31 "He is in the way of life that keepeth instruction: but he that refuseth reproof erreth." Proverbs 10:17 "For the commandment is a lamp: and the law is light: and the reproofs of instruction are the way of life." Proverbs 6:23
3. STEPS TO CORRECT VIOLATIONS Once a breakdown in a life relationship has been traced to a violation of a principle of life, clear and logical steps of action are required to reconstruct thinking and direction.	**DECISIONS**	"Turn you at my reproof: behold I will pour out my spirit unto you. I will make known my words unto you." Proverbs 1:23 "But let a man examine himself. . . for if we would judge ourselves, we should not be judged." I Corinthians 11:28,31
4. INSTRUCTION BASED ON CORRECTION Correction may produce an immediate solution, but further guidance of discipline in Scripture is essential to strengthen and reaffirm the importance of the steps which were taken.	**PROJECTS**	"All Scripture is given by inspiration of God, and is profitable for doctrine, for reproof, for correction, for instruction in righteousness: That the man of God may be perfect, thoroughly furnished unto all good works." II Timothy 3:16,17

NOTES

HOW TO GET THE GREATEST BENEFIT FROM YOUR PROBLEMS

• Most of us want quick solutions to our problems, but God wants to make sure that all His disciplines for character development in us and those around us are accomplished before He removes the problems.

• He is also more concerned that the right procedure be followed in solving the problems than that the problems are actually resolved. It is the process of solving our problems that constitutes the most meaningful chapters of our life message and becomes the greatest help to other people.

• We want to get out from under the pressure of our problems, but God wants to use that pressure to motivate us to a greater level of spiritual maturity than we would otherwise have achieved.

• Often our present problems are the results of past disobedience to the initial promptings of the Holy Spirit. Now God is using these problems to apply the pressures we need for complete obedience. If we fail to gain these benefits from our present problems He will only have to raise up new problems.

1. THE BENEFIT OF GETTING MORE "GRACE" FROM GOD

The success of our lives is entirely related to how much grace God gives us. Grace is the desire and power to do God's will. (Philippians 2:13) Paul's prayer was that grace would be multiplied to every Christian. How then do we receive this grace? There is only one way — by being humbled.

"God resists the proud but gives grace to the humble." (James 4:6) Nothing is more humbling than experiencing conflicts we cannot solve, especially when others know about our problems. But it is this very experience that God uses to break our pride and give us grace. That grace will be the prompting of God's spirit to accomplish the next four benefits God intends for our problems.

2. THE BENEFIT OF SELF-EXAMINATION

God requires that each of us maintain a periodic program of self-examination. "If we would judge ourselves we should not be judged. But when we are judged we are chastened of the Lord. (I Corinthians 11:31 & 32) "For whom the Lord loves He chastens." (Hebrews 12:6)

When things are going well for us we are not easily motivated to this activity. But when a major conflict arises and our spirit is grieved, we have the most effective motivation to search out the inner motives, actions, words and attitudes of our hearts. "The spirit of man is the candle of the Lord searching out the innermost parts of his being." (Proverbs 20:27) This is precisely what God meant when He said, "The reproofs of instruction are the way of life." (Proverbs 6:23) "Whoso loveth instruction loveth knowledge, but he that hateth reproof is brutish." (Proverbs 12:1)

NOTES

3. THE BENEFIT OF NEW INSIGHT IN SCRIPTURE

Vast areas of Scripture will never be meaningful to us unless we go through the experiences for which they give insight. It was for this reason that God allowed all of his servants in Scripture to experience conflicts, and it is for this very reason that we go through them as well.

Notice the basis of this in Proverbs 1:23, "Turn ye at my reproof: behold, I will pour out my Spirit unto you. I will make known my words unto you." Even though David knew his conflicts were a result of his own sin, he was able to say, "It is good for me that I have been afflicted that I might learn thy statutes." (Psalm 119:71)

The best and first response we should have to our conflicts is to read through Psalms and underline every verse which has new meaning to us. Then begin memorizing and meditating on these verses. "Man shall not live by bread alone." (Matthew 4:4)

Our next best step would be to read the chapter of Proverbs each day that corresponds to the day of the month, and ask God to reveal new principles that we can apply to our particular problem.

A third step would be the reading of biographies in Scripture and visualizing their circumstances in the light of what we are now experiencing. "There hath no temptation taken you but such as is common to man." (I Corinthians 10:13) "Wherefore, seeing we also are compassed about with so great a cloud of witnesses, let us lay aside every weight and the sin which so easily besets us, and let us run with patience the race that is set before us." (Hebrews 12:1)

4. THE BENEFIT OF UNIFYING THE FAMILY

The very foundation of the church as well as the nation is the family. When the family begins pulling apart, God often allows a member of the family to have a problem which he cannot resolve. It is God's intention to use this problem as a motivating factor to bring the entire family together.

The purpose of meeting together is for each member to clear his own life of that which would hinder his prayers, and then unitedly to commit this problem to the Lord to ask for God's blessing not only on the person with the problem, but on the entire family. Such a gathering will be a turning point for the family. Months or years later they will be able to look back and see that the hand of God's blessing began to open to them at the point of that meeting.

The senior head of the family — grandfather or father — should be the one to call this meeting together even though he may ask his pastor or a godly layman to lead the family in seeking the Lord.

5. THE BENEFIT OF UNITING THE FAMILIES OF A CHURCH

When a problem is bigger than one family can solve, it is God's intention that it be shared with the leaders of the church and then the members. As the church becomes concerned about a problem which threatens one of its families, the other families will be drawn together.

It would be important for the pastor to call a special day of prayer and fasting and give instruction to each family on how to rid their lives of anything that would hinder God from hearing their prayers. In this way one family's problems can be used as a means of purifying the church and raising the level of spiritual maturity in every other family.

NOTES

PREREQUISITES FOR EFFECTIVE COMMUNICATION

DISCERN ATTITUDES	CLARIFY BASIC PROBLEMS	AREAS	IDENTIFY NECESSARY DECISIONS	GIVING DIRECTION TO YOUTH	ILLUSTRATE BASIC IDEAS FROM . . . SCRIPTURE	PERSONAL	OTHERS
Those who work with youth must be alert to attitudes reflected in facial expressions and features, style and manner of dress, type of friends, basic interests, family relationships, conversations, etc.	In addition to stated problems and questions, they can identify many other conflicts as the teen-ager discusses or mentions personal feelings, anxieties, conflicts, habits, personal deficiencies, etc.	SELF SALVATION FAMILY PURPOSE FRIENDS DATING	Once the counselor determines the levels of conflict involved in a basic area, he is then able to guide the teen-ager in applying clear, Scriptural steps in solving them beginning with the root causes, then the root problem, then the surface cause, and finally the surface problem.	1. Communication begins by discerning attitudes which are reflected by the teen-ager. 2. Communication becomes meaningful when his questions and problems are traced back to breakdowns in basic areas of relationships. 3. Communication becomes effective when clear steps of responsible action can be given to him for reestablishing broken relationships. 4. Effective communication demands illustrations of basic principles from Scripture, personal experience, and the experiences of others.	Key sections of Scripture can be related to each of the conflict areas.	An ideal preparation to helping others is writing out personal victories in each of the 6 basic conflict areas.	Many individual facts, as well as the personal experiences of others can be used to further clarify the decisions required in each conflict level.

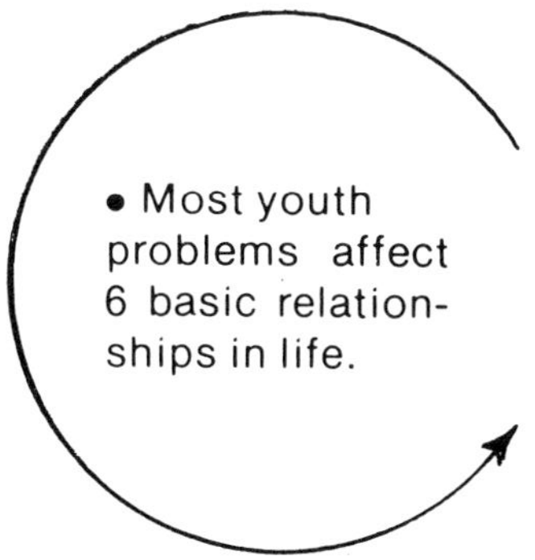

• Most youth problems affect 6 basic relationships in life.

NOTES

STEPS FOR FURTHER ASSISTANCE

In view of the principle of responsibility explained in the Seminar, we feel the following procedures are most effective in assisting those who desire direction for major conflicts:

A. ATTEND A FULL SEMINAR

A basic frame of reference is essential before further instruction is given. The session a person misses is often the session that gives the direction he is looking for. Many have found that attending a second time has provided answers which they missed the first time.

B. ASK GOD FOR WISDOM

Often God brings problems to direct our attention to Him. He delights in giving wisdom as we ask for it (James 1:6).

C. REVIEW THE PRINCIPLES

Provide at least four or five days after the seminar to re-think and re-study the principles presented.

D. ASK YOUR AUTHORITY FOR DIRECTION

Often a father or husband is grieved when one under his authority goes to another for counsel before coming to him. God may use your need to motivate him to seek the Lord in a deeper way.

E. SEEK COUNSEL FROM YOUR PASTOR

The Seminar is designed to assist the local pastor. As you share the problem with him, he may then request further assistance from us to clarify what you heard at the Seminar. By working with him, we are also assisting him to help others who may have a similar problem.

F. FOLLOW THE LIGHT YOU HAVE

Often a person has enough direction for the "next step" and finds when taking it that God then reveals enough light for further steps. "Light received brings more light. Light rejected brings darkness."

NOTES

BUILDING TRUST IN OUR DESIGNER

ACCEPTANCE OF SELF

- FORMING ATTITUDES ABOUT OURSELVES
- RESPONDING CORRECTLY TO "DEFECTS"

• A person's attitude toward himself has a profound influence on his attitudes toward God, his family, his friends, his future, and many other significant areas of his life.

NOTES

FORMING ATTITUDES ABOUT OURSELVES

• One of the major areas of conflict in both youth and adults is that of having wrong attitudes about ourselves. These attitudes affect every other relationship in our life.

- **When the most attractive and popular students on a certain campus were asked if they were satisfied with their basic appearance, over 95 percent replied that they were not!**
- **These students were aware of their basic sin nature and their need for salvation. They had placed their faith in Jesus Christ and had been reborn by the Spirit of God.**
- **But many were having continued struggles in the matter of dedicating their lives to the will of God. In further discussions with them, it was discovered that they had inwardly reasoned that if what they saw in the mirror was an example of God's love and creativity for them, they couldn't really trust Him with their future.**

HOW ATTITUDES ARE FORMED:

• RIGHT DEVELOPMENT:

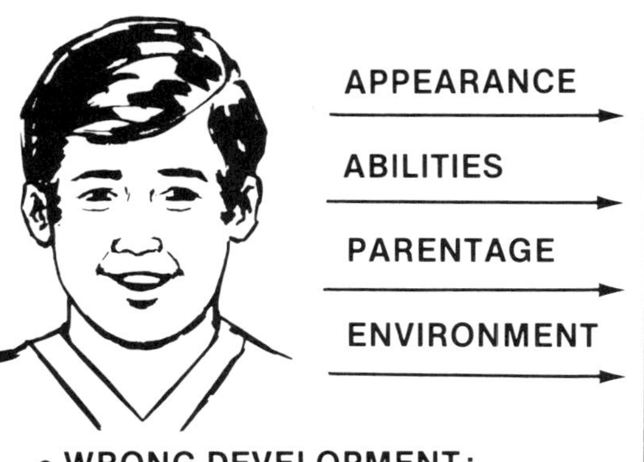

APPEARANCE →
ABILITIES →
PARENTAGE →
ENVIRONMENT →

COMPARING OURSELVES WITH THE INWARD CHARACTER OF JESUS CHRIST IN ORDER TO RECEIVE GOD'S APPROVAL

"How can ye believe, which receive honor one of another, and seek not the honor that cometh from God only?" John 5:44

"But he that glorieth, let him glory in the Lord. For not he that commendeth himself is approved, but whom the Lord commendeth." II Corinthians 10:17, 18

• WRONG DEVELOPMENT:

APPEARANCE →
ABILITIES →
PARENTAGE →
ENVIRONMENT →

MEASURING OURSELVES WITH THE OUTWARD STANDARDS OF THOSE AROUND US IN ORDER TO GAIN THEIR APPROVAL

"For we dare not make ourselves of the number, or compare ourselves with some that commend themselves; but they measuring themselves by themselves, and comparing themselves among themselves, are not wise." II Corinthians 10:12

NOTES

EVIDENCES OF SELF-REJECTION

• As we grow up, most of us have physical, mental or parental characteristics which are different from those around us.

Very often during early school years, classmates point out these differences in jest. The resulting concerns on outward appearance may cause varying degrees of self-rejection.

EVIDENCES OF SELF-REJECTION	AMPLIFICATION AND RELATED SCRIPTURE
A. OVER-ATTENTION ON CLOTHES	• Undue concern for clothes may be an attempt to cover up or compensate for unchangeable physical features which are rejected. Jesus linked these two thoughts in Matthew 6:27, 28 "Which of you by taking thought can add one cubit unto his stature? And why take ye thought for raiment?"
B. INABILITY TO TRUST GOD	• If we reject God's basic design in making us, it may then also be difficult to put confidence in the Designer for other areas of our life. "For we are His workmanship. . ." Ephesians 2:10 "I will praise thee for I am fearfully and wonderfully made: marvellous are thy works; and that my soul knoweth right well." Psalm 139:14
C. EXCESSIVE SHYNESS	• Fear of what others will think of us may then cause others to reflect our attitudes of fear back to us. This is illustrated in the life of King Saul. See I Samuel 9 and 10.
D. DIFFICULTY IN LOVING OTHERS	• We are to love our neighbor as we do ourselves. Thus, if we cannot "love ourselves" in the right way, we will also find it difficult to love others in the right way. "Thou shalt love thy neighbor as thyself." Matthew 19:19
E. SELF-CRITICISM	• Complaints about unchangeable physical features, abilities, parentage and social heritage are significant indications of self-rejection. "Woe unto him that striveth with his Maker! Let the potsherd strive with the potsherds of the earth. Shall the clay say to him that fashioneth it, What makest thou? or thy work, He hath no hands?" Isaiah 45:9

NOTES

F. WISHFUL COMPARISON WITH OTHERS	• Desiring to be different in areas that cannot be changed is a clear evidence of self-rejection. On the other hand, we should desire to be different in attitudes and character which do not conform to the image of Jesus Christ. ". . . Shall the thing formed say to him that formed it, Why hast thou made me thus?" Romans 9:20
G. FLOATING BITTERNESS	• Many have said, "I hate myself." They may be referring to things which they have said or done, or they may be referring to their whole being. In the latter case, their final hatred will be directed toward the one who made them. "For no man ever yet hated his own flesh; but nourisheth and cherisheth it, even as the Lord the church:" Ephesians 5:29
H. PERFECTIONISM	• It is healthy to a certain degree to keep improving on what we have done. But when the time expended outweighs the value of the accomplishment, then it is an unhealthy evidence of self-rejection.
I. ATTITUDES OF SUPERIORITY	• If we would boast of our achievements or use words outside our vocabulary, or if we would refuse to associate with certain classes of people, we would be exhibiting outward indications of both pride and inferiority. Whatever we have is from God. Therefore, ". . . why dost thou glory, as if thou hadst not received it?" I Corinthians 4:6,7 A person who appears superior is actually a person who inwardly feels inferior but is trying to narrow his field of comparison.
J. AWKWARD ATTEMPTS TO HIDE UNCHANGEABLE DEFECTS	• Self-conscious actions or statements to cover up unchangeable "defects" may indicate self-rejection. If we have a "defect" which we cannot change and which God through prayer has not changed, then we are able to claim II Corinthians 12:9 ". . .My grace is sufficient for thee: for my strength is made perfect in weakness. Most gladly therefore will I rather glory in my infirmities, that the power of Christ may rest upon me."
K. EXTRAVAGANCE	• An evidence of self-rejection may be in the form of lavish spending on expensive items in the hopes that they will bring new admiration and acceptance to the owner. But "a man's life consisteth not in the abundance of the things which he possesseth." Luke 12:15
L. WRONG PRIORITIES	• When we neglect God-given responsibilities in order to spend great amounts of time in pursuits which will bring acclaim from others, we may be revealing evidences of self-rejection. Rather, "let every man prove his own work, and then shall he have rejoicing in himself alone, and not in another." Galatians 6:4

NOTES

BASIC INSIGHTS ON SELF-ACCEPTANCE

• In order to accept the unchangeable features in ourselves which God has made, we must see the insights of a much bigger picture.

A. GOD'S BASIC PURPOSE IN CREATING US IS THAT WE HAVE FELLOWSHIP WITH HIM THROUGH JESUS CHRIST, AND THAT WE EXPERIENCE THE FULL POTENTIAL OF CHRIST WORKING IN AND THROUGH THESE BODIES OF OURS.

"And this is life eternal, that they might know thee the only true God, and Jesus Christ, whom thou hast sent." John 17:3

". . . I am come that they might have life, and that they might have it more abundantly." John 10:10

". . . I count all things but loss for the excellency of the knowledge of Christ Jesus my Lord:" Philippians 3:8

SUCCESS IN LIFE

Is not measured by what we are or what we have done, but rather by what we are and have done compared to what we could have been and could have done.

B. SATAN IS AWARE OF THE POTENTIAL WHICH GOD HAS PUT WITHIN OUR LIVES, AND HE DESIRES TO TOTALLY DESTROY IT OR AT LEAST PARTIALLY DIMINISH ITS POTENTIAL.

"But in a great house there are not only vessels of gold and of silver, but also of wood and of earth . . .

"If a man therefore purge himself from these, he shall be a vessel unto honor, sanctified, and ready for the master's use . . ."

"Flee also youthful lusts." II Timothy 2:20-22

C. SATAN'S INITIAL METHOD OF OPERATION IS TO GET US TO BELIEVE THAT GOD HAS CHEATED OR WILL CHEAT US OUT OF THAT WHICH WE SHOULD RIGHTFULLY HAVE.

"And the serpent said . . . God doth know that in the day you eat thereof, then your eyes shall be opened, and you shall be as gods, knowing good and evil." Genesis 3:4,5

"Beware lest any man spoil you . . . for in Him dwelleth all the fullness of the Godhead bodily. And you are complete in Him . . ." Colossians 2:8-10

NOTES

D. BEFORE WE WERE BORN, GOD PRESCRIBED OUR UNCHANGEABLE FEATURES IN ACCORDANCE WITH HIS PLANS FOR OUR LIVES.	"Thine hands have made me and fashioned me together round about . . . thou hast made me as the clay . . ." Job 10:8, 9 (also repeated in Psalm 119:73) "Thine eyes did see my substance, yet being unperfect; and in thy book all my members were written, which in continuance were fashioned, when as yet there was none of them." Psalm 139:16 "I will praise thee; for I am fearfully and wonderfully made." Psalm 139:14 "Woe unto him that striveth with his Maker!. . . Shall the clay say to him that fashioneth it, What makest thou?" Isaiah 45:9
E. GOD IS NOT FINISHED MAKING US YET.	"We are (present continuous action) His workmanship . . ." Ephesians 2:10 "The Lord will perfect that which concerneth me: thy mercy, O Lord, endureth for ever: forsake not the works of thine own hands." Psalm 138:8
F. THERE IS NO SUCH THING AS A "UNIVERSAL IDEAL" IN THE OUTWARD APPEARANCE.	". . . man looketh on the outward appearance, but the Lord looketh on the heart." I Samuel 16:7 ". . . he (Jesus) hath no form nor comeliness (attractiveness); and when we shall see him, there is no beauty that we should desire him." Isaiah 53:2
G. THERE IS A UNIVERSAL IDEAL ON INWARD CHARACTER QUALITIES. REPRODUCING THE CHARACTER OF JESUS CHRIST IN US BY THE POWER OF GOD'S SPIRIT AND GOD'S GRACE.	". . . to be conformed to the image of His Son (Jesus Christ)." Romans 8:29 "My little children, of whom I travail in birth again until Christ be formed in you." Galatians 4:19 "For it pleased the Father that in Him (Christ) should all fullness dwell." Colossians 2:9 "The fruit of the Spirit is love, joy peace, longsuffering, gentleness, goodness, faith, meekness, self-control." Galatians 5:22,23
H. OUR HAPPINESS IS NOT DEPENDENT ON OUR OUTWARD BEAUTY BUT ON OUR ABILITY TO EXPERIENCE THE CHARACTER OF THE LORD JESUS CHRIST.	"Seek ye first the kingdom of God and His righteousness; and all these things shall be added unto you." Matthew 6:33 "As for me, I will behold thy face in righteousness: I shall be satisfied when I awake, with thy likeness." Psalm 17:15

NOTES

		"Blessed (how happy) are the poor in spirit . . . they that mourn . . . the meek . . . they which hunger and thirst after righteousness . . . the merciful . . . the pure in heart . . .the peacemakers. . . the persecuted." Matthew 5:3-12
I.	**IF NECESSARY, GOD SACRIFICES OUTWARD BEAUTY TO DEVELOP INWARD QUALITIES, SINCE OUR HAPPINESS IS BASED ON HAVING THESE QUALITIES**	"Always bearing about in the body the dying of the Lord Jesus Christ, that the life also of Jesus might be made manifest in our body." II Corinthians 4:10 "Though our outward man perish, yet the inward man is renewed day by day." II Corinthians 4:16,17 ". . . Shall the thing formed say to him that formed it, Why hast thou made me thus? Hath not the potter power over the clay of the same lump to make one vessel unto honor and another unto dishonor." Romans 9:20,21
J.	**OUR FULFILLMENT IN LIFE COMES BY BEING A UNIQUE MESSAGE ON HOW TO DEVELOP THE INWARD QUALITIES OF THE LORD JESUS CHRIST.**	"But ye are a chosen generation . . . that ye should show forth the praises of him who hath called you out of darkness into his marvelous light." I Peter 2:9 "Ye are our epistle . . . known and read of all men:" II Corinthians 3:2 "A man hath joy by the answer of his mouth." Proverbs 15:23
K.	**DIFFERENCES IN APPEARANCE, ABILITIES, PARENTAGE AND SOCIAL HERITAGE ARE GOD'S SPECIAL FRAMES TO HIGHLIGHT AND AMPLIFY HIS UNIQUE MESSAGE THROUGH US.**	". . . My grace is sufficient for thee: for my strength is made perfect in weakness. Most gladly, therefore, will I rather glory in my infirmities, that the power of Christ may rest upon me . . . for when I am weak, then am I strong." II Corinthians 12:9,10 "But God hath chosen the foolish things of the world to confound the wise; and God hath chosen the weak things of the world to confound the things which are mighty . . . That no flesh should glory in his presence. . . That, according as it is written, He that glorieth, let him glory in the Lord." I Corinthians 1:27,29,31
L.	**GOD'S REPUTATION IS AT STAKE IN WHAT WE DO WITH OUR APPEARANCE, ABILITIES, PARENTAGE, AND SOCIAL HERITAGE.**	"And the Lord said unto him, Who hath made man's mouth? or who maketh the dumb, or deaf, or the seeing, or the blind? have not I the Lord? Now therefore go, and I will be with thy mouth, and teach thee what thou shalt say." Exodus 4:11,12

NOTES

RESPONDING CORRECTLY TO "DEFECTS"

A. <u>CORRECT THEM, IF POSSIBLE,</u> when the defects distract from effectively communicating God's message. For example, if my sloppy appearance detracts I should buy a new suit.

B. <u>EXERCISE THE "PRAYER OF FAITH."</u> Faith discerns and visualizes what God intends to do, and then prayer is made in harmony with that discernment. Faith is not "twisting God's arm" to do what we think is best. Faith discerns three types of sickness:

1. Sickness unto death	Psalm 90:10
2. Sickness unto chastisement	I Corinthians 11:28-33
3. Sickness to manifest the work of God and to glorify Him.	II Corinthians 12:6 John 9:2,3

C. <u>GLORY IN UNCHANGEABLE "DEFECTS."</u> Attach new meanings to old "defects:"

1. Make them <u>marks of ownership</u> to constantly remind us to whom we belong. I Corinthians 6:20

2. Make them <u>motivations to develop inward qualities.</u> The frame is not conspicuous when it surrounds the finished picture. Psalm 139:14

3. Make them the <u>means to be a better servant.</u> Outward beauty is often used to get others to serve us, but true happiness only comes by serving others. Mark 10:44

BASIC STEPS TO SELF-ACCEPTANCE

COMMITMENTS	PROJECTS
• DETECT UNGRATEFULNESS TOWARD GOD	Make a list of all the changes you would like to make in your appearance, abilities, family or social heritage. Correct what you can and list benefits for what you cannot change.
• THANK GOD FOR THE WAY HE HAS MADE YOU THUS FAR — ESPECIALLY FOR THAT WHICH YOU WANTED TO CHANGE BUT CANNOT.	See how those features you are unable to change are actually building the message God wants in your life.
• PUT YOURSELF BACK ON "GOD'S EASEL" AND PURPOSE TO COOPERATE WITH HIM IN DEVELOPING INWARD QUALITIES.	Memorize the qualities God wants to develop in you. Make a word study of each quality in Matthew 5:1-12, Galatians 5:22-24. Write out all the synonyms and antonyms possible. (List the circumstances that God may use to develop Christ-like character.)
• DEDICATE YOURSELF TO SERVING THE LORD BY REPRODUCING HIS CHARACTER IN THE LIVES OF OTHERS.	Begin a life notebook with a section on creative projects which motivate the development of Christ-like character. That which works for you may help someone else.

NOTES

BASIC QUESTIONS ON SELF-ACCEPTANCE

QUESTIONS ABOUT SELF-ACCEPTANCE	INCOMPLETE FRAME OF REFERENCE WHICH PROMPTED THE QUESTIONS	UNDERLYING PRINCIPLES REQUIRED TO SEE GOD'S PERSPECTIVE
QUESTIONS	**OUR NATURAL THINKING**	**GOD'S PERSPECTIVE**
• Why does God allow physical or mental deformities to mar the life and happiness of certain people?	• That beauty and talent are essential for happiness. (Often the most beautiful and talented people are the most unhappy.) • That there is an "international ideal" against which physical, mental, parental and social variations can be measured.	• Happiness is a by-product of responding to life from God's perspective. It is not determined by our circumstances but by our responses to them. • God is fashioning an "inward ideal" composed of eight specific qualities. (Summarized in Matthew 5)
• If God "prescribes" us before we are born, what about man's intervention which actually affects the child's appearance or abilities?	• That any "scar" or deformity is evil and unjust on God's part for His allowing it to happen. (See John 9:2)	**HUMILITY** - Chain of Command **MEEKNESS** - Yielding Rights **MOURNING** - Grieving with God **MERCY** - Forgiving all Offenders **PURITY** - Meditation **SPIRITUAL HUNGER** - Prayer and Fasting **PEACEMAKING** - Clear Conscience **SUFFERING** - Sources of Irritation (See Philippians 2:5)
• To what degree should we cover up our scars and defects?	• That God owes every person a full, happy, healthy life, and that if He does anything to shorten it, then He is being unfair and is to be blamed. (See Luke 13:1-5 and Matthew 20:1-16) • That scars or defects will repel people from us and detract from our happiness in life.	• God uses outward "scars" and "defects" to develop inward qualities, regardless of whether the "scars" were directly caused by God, or others, or us. (See Isaiah 61:2,3 on giving beauty for ashes.) • Before covering up any "defects" we must attach significant meaning to them. (Make them reminders of God's ownership and motivations to finish inward qualities.) • Any concealment of scars or defects must be done on the basis that it detracts attention from communication of inward qualities. • Self-worth increases as we make significant contributions to the body of Christ. (Romans 12, I Corinthians 12, Ephesians 4:25; 5:30)

NOTES

• THE BASIS OF ACHIEVING GREAT FAITH

AUTHORITY AND RESPONSIBILITY

• THE PURPOSES AND STRUCTURES OF AUTHORITY

• THE CONSEQUENCES OF REJECTING AUTHORITY

• STEPS TO TRANSLATE GOD'S DIRECTION THROUGH AUTHORITY

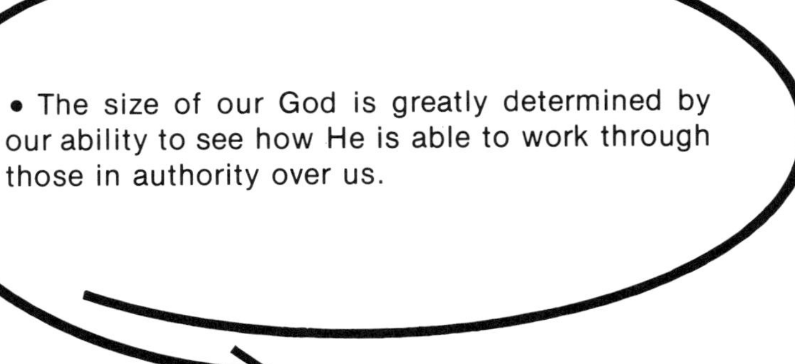

NOTES

3 BASIC PURPOSES FOR AUTHORITY

RESPONSIBILITY

• When Paul warned that "Whosoever therefore resisteth the power, resisteth the ordinance of God: and they that resist shall receive to themselves damnation" (Romans 13:2), he was referring to many more factors than we realize.

1. TO GROW IN WISDOM AND CHARACTER

The only recorded incident in the life of Christ between the ages of two and thirty was a discussion with His parents which involved authority. This occurred when He was twelve. Should He follow His spiritual calling and be about His Father's business (Luke 2:49), or should He become subject to His parents and leave His ministry at the temple? He did the latter, and the following verse reports, "And Jesus increased in wisdom and stature, and in favour with God and man." (Luke 2:52)

2. TO GAIN PROTECTION FROM DESTRUCTIVE TEMPTATIONS

The essence of submission is not "getting under the domination of authority but rather getting under the protection of authority". Authority is like an "umbrella of protection", and when we get out from under it, we expose ourselves to unnecessary temptations which are too strong for us to overcome. This is why Scripture compares rebellion and witchcraft - "Rebellion is like the sin of witchcraft." (I Samuel 15:23) Both terms have the same basic definition - subjecting ourselves to the realm and power of Satan.

3. TO RECEIVE CLEAR DIRECTION FOR LIFE DECISIONS

Correct decisions are based on faith; that is, visualizing what God intends to do. "Whatsoever is not of faith is sin." (Romans 14:23) One of the most basic aspects of faith is to realize how God gets His directions to us through those He has placed over us.

After the centurion asked Jesus to come and heal his servant, it occurred to him that just as his life was structured around a "chain of responsibility," so the kingdom in which God operates must have a similar structure of authority. When Jesus realized that he understood this, Jesus "marvelled and said to them that followed, Verily I say unto you, I have not found so great faith, no, not in Israel." (Matthew 8:10)

Our faith multiplies as we see how God speaks to us through those He has placed over us.

• Lucifer rebelled because his heart was lifted up in pride. Adam and Eve disobeyed because they believed God was withholding something good from them. But a third cause of rebellion is illustrated on the following pages— **A WOUNDED SPIRIT.**

NOTES

HOW A WOUNDED SPIRIT CAUSES

COMMUNICATION BREAKDOWN

• The following illustration is being repeated in tens of thousands of families throughout the nation. The circumstances may differ, but the results are the same.

• One summer day, a father said to his twelve-year-old boy, "A week from this Saturday, I'll take you on a fishing trip."

Excitedly the boy began to plan for that day. He gathered all the fishing gear and made a list of all the other things he would need. He mowed a neighbor's lawn, and with the money, he bought equipment for the trip.

He could hardly wait for the day to arrive. By Friday night, he had everything packed, ready to go the first thing in the morning.

Early the next morning the phone rang. It was the director of one of the organizations to which his father belonged. The director reported that the man who was to assume certain responsibilities that day was sick, and he asked if the father could take his place.

After a few moments of silence, the boy heard his father answer, "I think I can. I'll be right there."

In the rush of his regular work and all the other responsibilities, the father had forgotten about the fishing trip he had promised to his son. This was just another Saturday to him in which he could catch up on odds and ends around the house. When the call came, he decided that the need of the organization was more important than the things at home. He quickly got dressed, skipped breakfast and drove off.

As his son began to realize that the things he had anticipated would not come true, he found it hard to keep back the tears. He could have reminded his father about the day, but he decided instead that his father was too busy for him.

With a broken heart, he unpacked all the equipment he was to use that day. That night when his father returned home, and in the days following, the boy found that he could not respond to his father the way he used to.

• The inner conflicts and visible symptoms which the boy developed in the following years took the pattern outlined in "Abnormal Social Developments."

NOTES

ABNORMAL SOCIAL DEVELOPMENT

VISIBLE SYMPTOMS OF A WOUNDED SPIRIT	INNER CONFLICTS OF AN OFFENDED TEEN-AGER	ADDITIONAL INSIGHTS
1. COMMUNICATION BREAKDOWN (Silent at the dinner table, etc.)	WOUNDED SPIRIT ↓	"Looking diligently lest any man fail of the grace of God; lest any root of bitterness springing up trouble you, and thereby many be defiled." Hebrews 12:15
2. UNGRATEFULNESS (Weighs the benefits his parents provide against their offenses)	ALIENATION OF AFFECTION ↓	J. Edgar Hoover observed that one of the chief characteristics of a juvenile delinquent is the attitude that society owes him a living.
3. STUBBORNNESS (Doesn't follow through on orders.)	REJECTION OF AUTHORITY ↓	"For rebellion is as the sin of witchcraft and stubbornness is as iniquity and idolatry. . ." I Samuel 15:23
4. OPEN REBELLION (Desires equal voice with parents)	ESTABLISHMENT OF SELF-AUTHORITY ↓	The basis of Satan's rebellion and downfall was his desire to be on an equal level with God.
5. WRONG FRIENDS (Rebels are drawn to those of like spirit)	COMPATIBILITY OF REBELLION ↓	Characteristics of wrong friends: 1. Serve fleshly appetities 2. Find humor in their shame 3. Have no concern for eternity. (Philippians 3:19)
6. DEFENSE OF SENSUALITY (Self-authority produces relative standard)	FULFILLMENT OF SENSUAL DESIRES ↓	"Now the works of the flesh are manifest, which are these; Adultery, fornication, uncleanness, lasciviousness, idolatry. . ." Galatians 5:19-21
7. CONDEMNATION OF OTHERS (Focuses on the hypocrites)	DEEP SENSE OF GUILT ↓	". . .for wherein thou judgest another thou condemnest thyself; for thou that judgest doest the same things." Romans 2:1
8. FRIVOLITY AND DEPRESSION	THOUGHTS OF SUICIDE FOUR TYPES OF SUICIDE 1. MENTAL 2. MORAL 3. SPIRITUAL 4. PHYSICAL	"Even in laughter the heart is sorrowful; and the end of that mirth is heaviness." (Proverbs 14:13) See also Job 10:1.

NOTES

PARENTS' RESPONSES

ABNORMAL SOCIAL DEVELOPMENTS

VISIBLE SYMPTOMS OF A WOUNDED SPIRIT	PARENTS' RESPONSES TO OFFENDED TEEN-AGER	SCRIPTURAL CAUTIONS TO PARENTS
1. COMMUNICATION BREAKDOWN	**OVERLOOK SYMPTOMS AS TEMPORARY** (Expect son to soon forget event)	On keeping promises—"He that sweareth to his own hurt, and changeth not. . . shall never be moved." Psalm 15:4,5
2. UNGRATEFULNESS	**COMPARE TEEN'S BENEFITS WITH THEIR PAST HARDSHIPS** ("When we were your age...")	"Only by pride (evidenced by refusing to ask forgiveness) cometh contention: but with the well advised is wisdom." Proverbs 13:10
3. STUBBORNNESS	**COAX TEEN TO OBEY** ("We have to keep after him so much.")	"A brother offended is harder to be won than a strong city; and their contentions are like the bars of a castle." (Proverbs 18:19)
4. OPEN REBELLION	**INCREASED DEMANDS AND TIGHTER REGULATIONS** (More freedom requires more responsibility)	"He that soweth iniquity shall reap vanity: and the rod of his anger shall fail." (Proverbs 22:8)
5. WRONG FRIENDS	**BEGIN "FAMILY BUREAU OF INVESTIGATION"** ("We need to know more about these friends of yours.)	"Fathers, provoke not your children to anger, lest they be discouraged." (Colossians 3:21)
6. DEFENSE OF SENSUALITY	**COMPARE PRESENT MORALITY WITH THEIR PAST** (Condemn or condone activities)	". . .for I the Lord thy God am a jealous God, visiting the iniquity of the father upon the children unto the third and fourth generation of them that hate me." Exodus 20:5
7. CONDEMNATION OF OTHERS	**JUSTIFY THEIR ACTIONS AND ATTITUDES** ("We did the best we knew how.")	"He that covereth his sins shall not prosper: but whoso confesseth and forsaketh them shall have mercy." (Proverbs 28:13)
8. SEARCH FOR EXCITEMENT SUICIDAL DEPRESSION	**SHOCKED—DESPERATE GRIEVED—FRUSTRATED**	"And ye shall seek me, and find me, when ye shall search for me with all your heart." Jeremiah 29:13

NOTES

HOW FAMILY CONFLICTS AFFECT OUR FUTURE

• The leaders of a certain missionary organization became very concerned because 50 percent of their missionaries were dropping out even before the first term was over. One major problem caused this.

• As the leaders investigated the causes, they discovered that 80 percent of those who left did so for only one reason - they could not get along with their fellow missionaries.

• This was an amazing situation: Missionaries trained to share God's love with other nations were unable to love each other!

• One investigator went a step further in his questioning and discovered the reason for this. The missionary couldn't get along with his colleagues because they reminded him of members of his family with whom he never learned to get along.

• **WE PROJECT OUR FAMILY CONFLICTS TO THE PEOPLE WE WORK WITH IN THE FUTURE:**

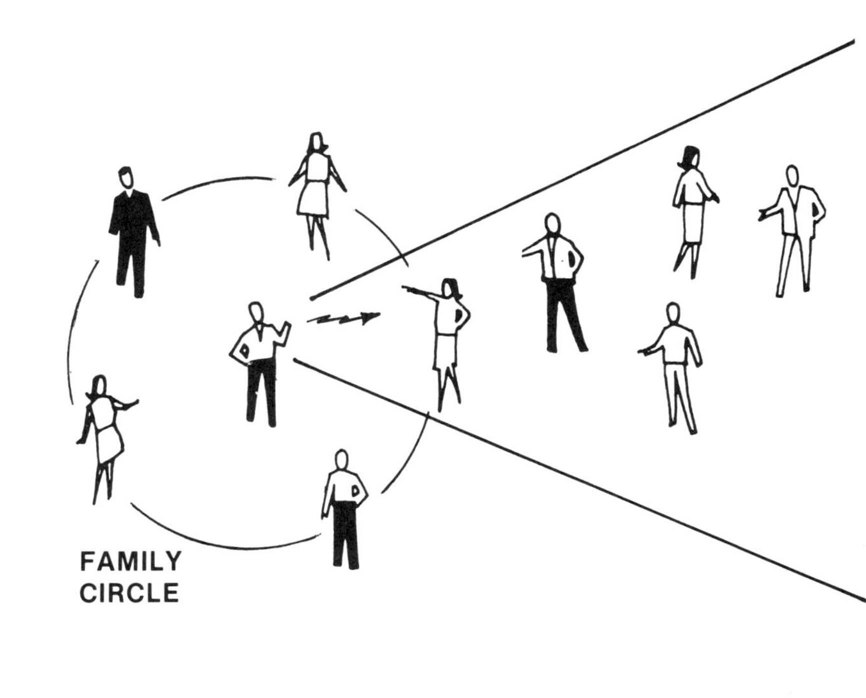

• This very same situation occurs when a fellow or girl who didn't get along with parents marries.

• The way a girl responded to the authority of her father tends to be the way she will respond to the authority of her husband.

• The way a fellow treated his mother tends to be the way he will treat his wife. A mother is very aware of a son's shortcomings and will call them to his attention. When he gets married and his wife tries to tactfully do the same, his response to her is sure to be, "You're just like my mother! She nagged at me; but I don't want you doing it to me!"

NOTES

4 BASIC STRUCTURES OF AUTHORITY

FAMILY	GOVERNMENT	CHURCH	BUSINESS
FATHER ↓ MOTHER ↓ CHILDREN	NATIONAL LEADERS ↓ LOCAL OFFICIALS ↓ CITIZENS	CHURCH LEADERS ↓ CHURCH MEMBERS	EMPLOYER ↓ EMPLOYEES

FAMILY

- "Children, obey your parents in all things: for this is well pleasing unto the Lord." Colossians 3:20
- "Children, obey your parents in the Lord: (as those whom God has set over you) for this is right. Honor thy father and mother; which is the first commandment with promise; that it may be well with thee, and thou mayest live long on the earth." Ephesians 6:1-3
- "My son, keep thy father's commandment, and forsake not the law of thy mother: Bind them continually upon thine heart, and tie them about thy neck." Proverbs 6:20,21
- "The eye that mocketh at his father, and despiseth to obey his mother, the ravens of the valley shall pick it out, and the young eagles shall eat it." Proverbs 30:17
- "A fool despiseth his father's instruction: but he that regardeth reproof is prudent." Proverbs 15:5

GOVERNMENT

- "Submit yourselves to every ordinance of man for the Lord's sake; whether it be the king, as supreme, or unto governors, as unto them that are sent by him for the punishment of evildoers, and for the praise of them that do well." I Peter 2:13,14
- "Let every soul be subject unto the higher powers. For there is no power but of God: the powers that be are ordained of God." Romans 13:1
- "For rulers are not a terror to good works, but to the evil...for he is the minister of God to thee for good." Romans 13:3,4
- "Wherefore ye must needs be subject, not only for wrath, but also for conscience sake." Romans 13:5
- "For for this cause pay ye tribute also: for they are God's ministers, attending continually upon this very thing. Render therefore to all their dues..." Romans 13:6,7

CHURCH

- "And we beseech you, brethren, to know them which labor among you, and are over you in the Lord, and admonish you: and to esteem them very highly in love for their works sake." I Thessalonians 5:12,13
- "Obey them that have rule (guide) over you, and submit yourselves: for they watch for your souls, as them that must give account, that they may do it with joy and not with grief: for that is unprofitable for you." Hebrews 13:17
- "Let the elders that rule well be counted worthy of double honor, especially them who labor in the word and doctrine... and, the laborer is worthy of his reward." I Timothy 5:17,18
- "The elders which are among you I exhort...Feed the flock of God which is among you, taking the oversight thereof, not by constraint, but willingly; not for filthy lucre, but of a ready mind; neither as being lords over God's heritage, but being ensamples to the flock." I Peter 5:1-3

BUSINESS

- "Servants, obey in all things your masters according to the flesh; not with eyeservice, as menpleasers, but in singleness of heart, fearing God." Colossians 3:22
- "And whatsoever ye do, do it heartily, as unto the Lord, and not unto men; knowing that of the Lord ye shall receive the reward of the inheritance: for ye serve the Lord Christ." Colossians 3:23,24
- "Servants, be subject to your masters with all fear; not only to the good and gentle, but also to the froward." I Peter 2:18
- "Let as many servants as are under the yoke count their own masters worthy of all honor, that the name of God and His doctrine be not blasphemed." I Timothy 6:1
- "And they that have believing masters, let them not despise them...but rather do them service." I Timothy 6:2

> "These things teach and exhort. If any man teach otherwise...he is proud, knowing nothing." I Timothy 6:2-4

NOTES

HOW TO MAKE WISE DECISIONS

RESPONSIBILITY

• One day a group of Christian students was given the following situation:

• A certain fellow met a girl whom he loved very much. They decided to get married and set the wedding date. As the time approached, he began to have various doubts about this being God's will.

• How could he be certain that it was God's will?

• The key to practical faith and direction is the ability to interpret what God is saying to us through the attitudes, reactions, and directions of those who are responsible for various areas of our life.

• Those students quickly named six of the following eight means which God uses to reveal His will to us. Not one guessed the other two.

• Their response was a significant indication why so many youth today are drifting without clear direction and are continually making wrong decisions.

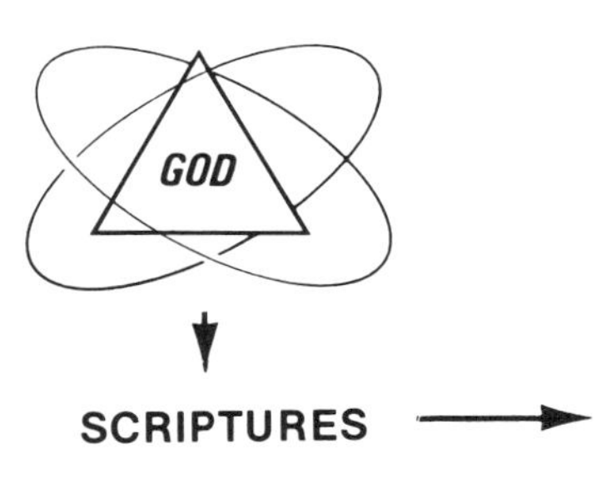

SCRIPTURES → A person may be able to read the Bible, but may miss or not understand the principles that apply directly to his situation.

GOVERNMENT → A person may fulfill the regulations of age and citizenship which government requires and still have doubts about the marriage.

MINISTERS → A minister may give encouragement on the basis that each person is a fine Christian, but the doubts may still remain.

CIRCUMSTANCES → A person, in trying to reassure himself, may try to translate circumstances as God's approval.

FRIENDS → A person's friends may give encouragement because they think that will make him happy, and they wouldn't want him to miss out on marriage.

PRAYER → A person's prayers must be based on discerning what God intends to do — not on "twisting God's arm" to do what he wants to do.

(FATHER)
(MOTHER) → **ESSENTIAL MEANS OF FINDING GOD'S WILL**

"Is this the right life partner?"

• "My son, keep thy Father's commandment, and forsake not the law of thy mother: when thou goest, it shall lead thee; when thou sleepest, it shall keep thee; and when thou awakest, it shall talk with thee." Proverbs 6:20,22

NOTES

HUMAN AUTHORITY IN THE HANDS OF A SKILLFUL GOD

• Each of us has a multitude of character deficiencies that need to be perfected. God uses those in authority to do this. "Foolishness is bound in the heart of a child: but the rod of correction shall drive it far from him." Proverbs 22:15

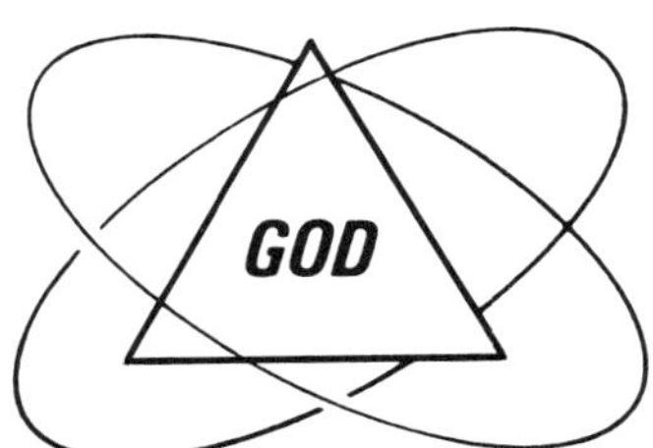

• God assures us that the heart of one who is in authority is in His hand, and that He turns it in the same way He does a meandering river by using the pressure of the current and time.

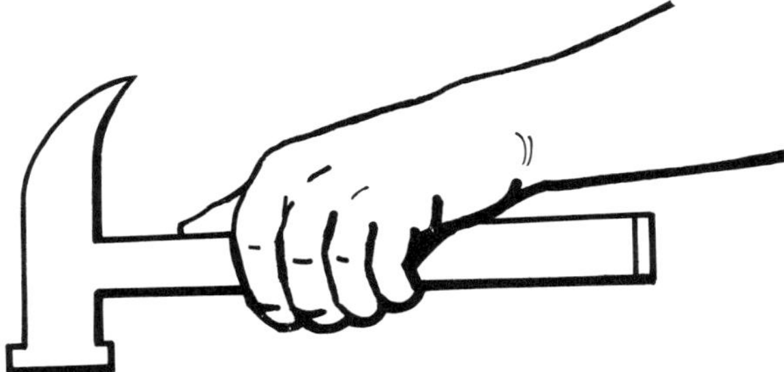

• "The king's heart is in the hand of the Lord, as the rivers of water: He turneth it whithersoever He will." Proverbs 21:1

• **GOD'S PERSISTENCE IN CHARACTER DEVELOPMENT:**

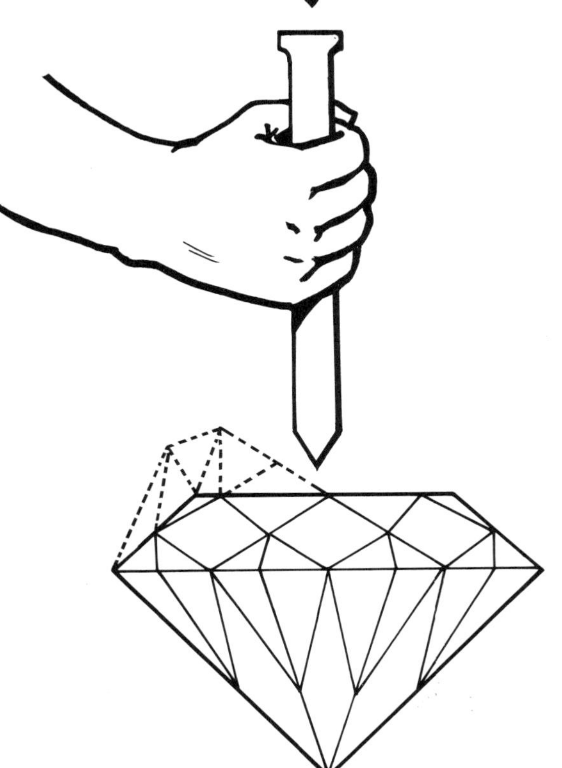

• God is even more concerned that our character become like that of Jesus Christ than He is in which "instruments" He uses to accomplish this. Therefore, if we push away or get out from under the reproofs and authority of our parents, God only has to raise up new "tools" to chip away at the rough edges of our character.

• While working with inner-city gangs, I was constantly amazed at a certain sequence of events:

• A teen-ager would say in disgust, "I'm sick and tired of taking orders from my parents!" I would inquire, "What do you plan to do about it?" He would reply, "I'm going to go and join the service!" They usually chose the Marines!

• A girl would often use marriage as a way to escape the pressure of parents'—only to have God begin to use her husband to carry on His work of character development.

NOTES

3 CONSEQUENCES OF REJECTING AUTHORITY

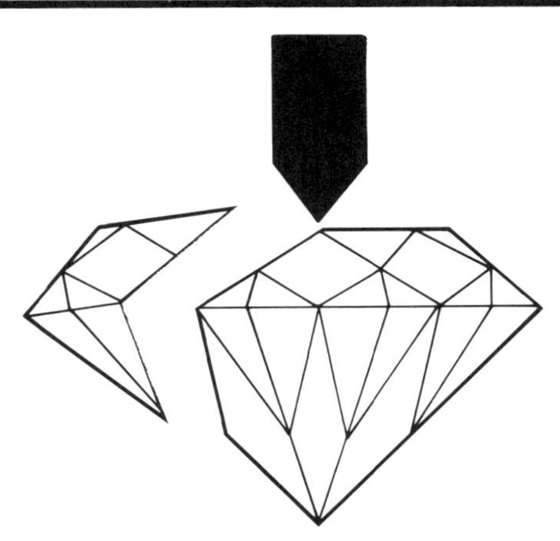

• "He, that being often reproved hardeneth his neck, shall suddenly be destroyed and that without remedy." Proverbs 29:1

GOD'S CHAIN OF RESPONSIBILITY

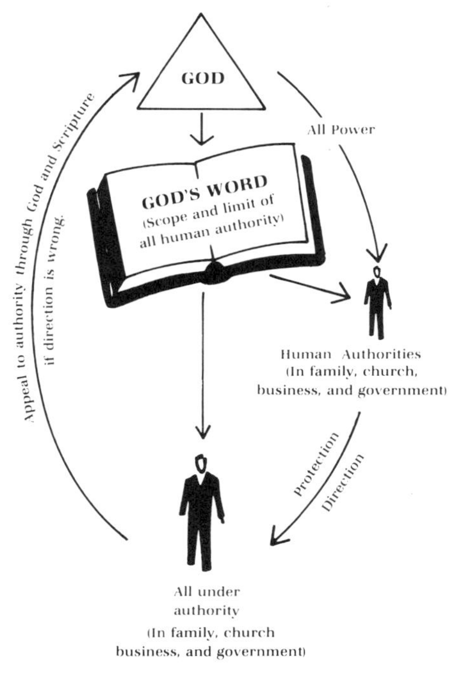

• If we continue to reject the reproofs of authority, God warns that there will be irreparable damage to the potential of our lives.

3 PHASES OF LOSS IN REBELLION

• Scripture records that on three major occasions King Saul rebelled against the word of the Lord, and on each occasion there was a specific consequence.

1. HIS CHILDREN WOULD LOSE THE HERITAGE THEY COULD HAVE HAD
[I Samuel 13:13-15]

When we rebel against the disciplines of the Lord, we fail to learn the spiritual insights and character which God intended. Thus, we are not able to pass these on to our children.

2. HIS OWN MINISTRY WOULD SUFFER
[I Samuel 15:28]

The very lack of character and wisdom which we have due to rejecting authority will greatly diminish the potential which our own ministry could have had.

3. HIS PHYSICAL LIFE WOULD BE SHORTENED
[I Samuel 28:19]

Scripture teaches a direct correlation between obedience to God and a long and healthy life:

"Honor thy father and thy mother . . . that thou mayest live long on the earth." Ephesians 6:1-3

"Be not wise in thine own eyes: fear the Lord, and depart from evil. It shall be health to thy navel, and marrow to thy bones." Proverbs 3:7,8 See also I Corinthians 11:27-32.

• The way a teen-ager responds to his parents' authority will soon be the way he responds to God's authority.

NOTES

HOW WOULD YOU ADVISE...?

ILLUSTRATION 1

A twenty-one-year-old girl who is supporting herself and living away from home firmly believes that it is God's will to marry a certain young man. This girl's parents don't attend church. Both the girl and the one she wants to marry have trusted Christ for salvation. The girl's parents strongly oppose this marriage stating only that they don't think he is the right one for their daughter, and, therefore, that the marriage won't work out. Both the girl and her boyfriend feel that the marriage will work out.

WOULD YOU ADVISE THIS GIRL TO:

☐ **A. Follow what she believes to be God's will**

☐ **B. Break up with the fellow**

ILLUSTRATION 2

An eighteen-year-old boy plans to go into the ministry. He prays about what college to attend and finally chooses a top-ranking Bible college. His parents fail to comprehend the importance of either the ministry or the Bible education, and they threaten to withhold all college funds unless he attends a near-by university. Their counsel to him is that if he learns another profession first, he can always have something to fall back on if he fails in the ministry. The son's points are that he doesn't plan to fail in the ministry, and that he needs the Bible training.

WOULD YOU ADVISE THIS BOY TO:

☐ **A. Pay his own way through Bible college**

☐ **B. Attend the university**

ILLUSTRATION 3

A teen-ager has been slipping out of her house every Sunday evening to attend a nearby church youth meeting. She knows her mother would be angry if she found out that her daughter was going to this church, so she has had to do it secretly. The services at this church are a great help to this teen-ager.

WOULD YOU ADVISE THIS TEEN-AGER TO:

☐ **A. Continue secretly attending the church**

☐ **B. Stop attending if her mother objects**

4 ESSENTIAL QUESTIONS TO ASK →

NOTES

1. DID THEY HAVE

MATURE ATTITUDES?

RESPONSIBILITY

• No matter how inconsistent or unfair those in authority may be, we are responsible for our responses to them. God can use those who are hardest to get along with to motivate us to develop mature attitudes.

ILLUSTRATION 1

• The parents of the twenty-one-year-old girl who disapproved of their daughter's marriage did so, among other reasons, because they detected underlying attitudes in both her and her boyfriend which would have been incompatible in marriage. One of those negative attitudes was a stubborn self-will. The parents sensed that each expected to be "the center of the stage." Neither had learned to submit to authority. They had no conception of "deference", which is regard for the wishes of another. A big step of correction could be taken by following her parents' wishes and waiting for marriage, so that proper attitudes could be learned by both the girl and the fellow. If, after a period of time, they still felt it was God's will to marry, it would then be a lot easier for God to change the parents' minds.

ILLUSTRATION 2

• The father of the eighteen-year-old boy who planned to go into the ministry detected in his son attitudes of ungratefulness, stubbornness and insensitivity to the feelings of others. Even though the father wasn't a Christian, he realized that these attitudes would cause his son to fail in the ministry. The very fact that his father had apprehensions of his failure in the ministry should have been a significant indication to the son. A proper response to his father's counsel would have been an essential step in developing these qualities.

ILLUSTRATION 3

• The teen-ager who began to secretly attend a near-by church had previously developed the attitudes of rebellion and self-will toward her mother. By responding properly to her mother, she would allow her mother to see that her old attitudes had changed as a result of attending the church, and she would be advancing the most powerful encouragement as to why her mother should allow her to continue attending the church.

• God is not nearly as concerned with what we go through as He is with our response to what we go through. In all that He designs or allows us to experience, His chief concern is that our attitudes become consistent with those of His Son, Jesus Christ. He was subject to the authority of His parents as He was growing up. "Though he were a Son (the Son of God), yet learned he obedience by the things which he suffered." Hebrews 5:8

NOTES

2. DID THEY DISCERN

BASIC INTENTIONS ?

• Learning to understand what those in authority are really trying to achieve is essential, especially when we are commanded to do something which violates Scripture or moral convictions.

RESPONSIBILITY

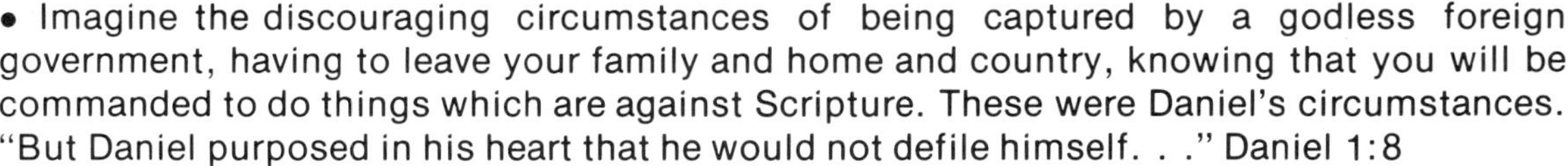

• Imagine the discouraging circumstances of being captured by a godless foreign government, having to leave your family and home and country, knowing that you will be commanded to do things which are against Scripture. These were Daniel's circumstances. "But Daniel purposed in his heart that he would not defile himself. . ." Daniel 1:8

• Having done this, however, he displayed mature attitudes to those in authority over him. These attitudes brought him into "loving favor" with the prince of the eunuchs. Later the prince commanded Daniel and those with him to eat and drink that which violated Scripture. Daniel discerned that the basic intention of the prince was not to violate his convictions but to make him healthy and wise.

ILLUSTRATION 1

• The basic intentions of the parents who disapproved of their daughter's marriage were not to restrict her happiness but rather to help her achieve a lasting happiness. They intended to pass on to her the insights and lessons which they had learned, perhaps the hard way. They wanted her to avoid unnecessary problems. They knew they themselves would be involved in her problems if she made the wrong choice in marriage. They intended to derive pleasure and joy from their daughter's happy marriage and looked forward to the possibility of a happy relationship with grandchildren.

ILLUSTRATION 2

• The basic intentions of the father who wanted his son to go to the university were not to "talk him out of the ministry" but to provide him with the tools for being successful in life. He intended to use the boy's college education to build mature attitudes in his son. He wanted to be proud of his son's achievements. He intended to rest in the fact that his son was building security in his vocation. He intended that his son be grateful and appreciative for what he had done for him. He intended to keep a channel of communication open so that his son would be responsive to future advice.

ILLUSTRATION 3

• The basic intentions of the teen-ager's mother were not to stop the girl from going to church but to develop obedience toward her parents. This obedience involved assuming responsibilities around the home rather than "running off all the time." The mother observed that some of the friends her daughter had met at this church were not obeying their parents and also condemned their parents for not being as "spiritual" as they were. She did not want her daughter to develop these attitudes.

NOTES

3. DID THEY DESIGN CREATIVE ALTERNATIVES?

RESPONSIBILITY

• A spirit of obedience increases our ability to design creative alternatives. But a spirit of resistance stifles our ability to do this.

• When Daniel discerned the ruler's intentions, he worked out an alternative which would not violate his moral convictions and would also allow those in authority to achieve their objectives. Notice the respect and creativity and careful choice of wording in his request, "Prove thy servants, I beseech thee, ten days; and let them give us pulse to eat, and water to drink. Then let our countenances be looked upon before thee, and the countenance of the children that eat of the portion of the king's meat: and as thou seest, deal with thy servants." (Daniel 1:12,13)

ILLUSTRATION 1

ALTERNATIVES FOR THE GIRL WHO WANTED TO GET MARRIED WERE:

- ☐ Discuss with her parents the qualities she should look for in a husband.
- ☐ Give her parents ample opportunity to become acquainted with the boyfriend before there was any discussion of marriage.
- ☐ Ask her parents to point out areas where both she and her boyfriend could improve.
- ☐ Request that her parents set up guidelines to help her discern whether she has met the right life partner.
- ☐ Be willing to show deference to her parents on the timing of the engagement.

ILLUSTRATION 2

ALTERNATIVES FOR THE FELLOW WHO WANTED TO GO INTO THE MINISTRY WERE:

- ☐ Accept the challenge of motivating new spiritual interest within his father. This is the best preparation he could have for the ministry since this is one of the most important functions of the ministry.
- ☐ Work out with his father and his minister areas of training at the university which would be useful both in the ministry and in another vocation.
- ☐ Develop a personal program of study in the Scriptures and contacts with students at the university which would provide further training for the ministry.

ILLUSTRATION 3

ALTERNATIVES FOR THE TEEN-AGE GIRL WERE:

- ☐ Ask forgiveness of her mother for past attitudes and actions which were wrong.
- ☐ Commit her mother to the Lord prior to asking if she could attend the youth group, with the understanding that the Lord is able to speak to her through her mother.
- ☐ Determine ahead of time that she would silently thank the Lord for whatever decision her mother gave and continue to develop right attitudes in the home.

NOTES

4. DID THEY GIVE GOD TIME TO WORK IN

CHANGING DECISIONS?

•"When a man's ways please the Lord, He maketh even his enemies to be at peace with him." (Proverbs 16:7)

• "The king's heart is in the hand of the Lord, as the rivers of water: he turneth it withersoever he will." Proverbs 21:1

• One of the most significant illustrations of God's ability to "change the heart of the king" is contained in the account of Pharoah freeing the nation of Israel. As Pharoah hardened his heart, God increased the pressure until he agreed to let the Israelites go. Meanwhile, the nation of Israel became strong as they obeyed those who were ruling them. . ."there was not one feeble person among their tribes." (Psalm 105:37)

ILLUSTRATION 1

• When the twenty-one-year-old girl followed the creative alternatives, her parents asked that the fellow finish his education and then get financially prepared for marriage. They felt that if he wasn't the right one, the interest would diminish. During this time, however, both developed inward qualities which increased the respect of her parents for the boy. This resulted in the parents' full approval of the marriage. On their wedding day, her father said with tears in his eyes, "This is the happiest day in my life!"

ILLUSTRATION 2

• When the eighteen-year-old boy followed the directives of his father and attended the university, he not only developed training which was extremely helpful in later years of ministry but also found his father taking an active part in spiritual pursuits as well as encouraging him to go into the ministry.

ILLUSTRATION 3

• The teen-age girl agreed in prayer that she would willingly accept and thank the Lord for whatever answer her mother gave her. When she asked her mother if she could go to the youth group, her mother became extremely angry and said, "No. You can't go to that youth meeting! I want you to stay home tonight!" The girl's gracious response was, "Is there something you would like me to do around the house tonight?" This response shocked her mother. In unbelief she commented, "Yes. Get out in the kitchen and do the dishes.!"

The girl cheerfully began the project. Before she had finished, her mother came into the kitchen and gruffly asked, "Do you have your homework done for tomorrow?" The daughter replied that it was completed. Minutes later, the mother returned to the kitchen and said, "Since you've done the dishes and your homework, I guess you can go to that meeting tonight; but make sure you're home by nine o'clock!"

NOTES

7 STEPS OF ACTION

WHEN ASKED TO DO SOMETHING YOU THINK IS WRONG

• It is easy for us to think that we are following Christ and are even suffering for Him when we disobey commands that violate His Word. But unless we have carefully applied each of the following steps, we are only deceiving ourselves.

1. CHECK OUR ATTITUDES

- ☐ An independent spirit is the basis of disloyalty
- ☐ A condemning spirit is the basis of self-righteousness
- ☐ An ungrateful spirit is the basis of pride
- ☐ A lazy spirit is the basis of dishonesty and poverty
- ☐ A bitter spirit is the basis of selfishness
- ☐ An impure spirit is the basis of self-indulgence

2. CLEAR OUR CONSCIENCE

- ☐ Correct those attitudes which have offended
- ☐ Fulfill the wishes and unfinished directions of those in authority
- ☐ Acknowledge to the person that we were wrong and ask forgiveness
- ☐ Make any restitution which is necessary
- ☐ Learn "deference"—limiting freedom to avoid offending another's taste

3. DISCERN BASIC INTENTIONS

- ☐ Ask them what their goals and wishes are
- ☐ Find out what their frame of reference is regarding the command
- ☐ Ask them to point out any of your blindspots
- ☐ Discern bigger goals which God may have designed to be accomplished through the situation

NOTES

4. DESIGN CREATIVE ALTERNATIVES

- ☐ Remove any resistant spirit in order to be creative
- ☐ Use difficult situations to expand your frame of reference
- ☐ Gain insights for difficult situations from Proverbs
- ☐ Design an alternative which he will see can reach his goal

RESPONSIBILITY

5. APPEAL TO OUR AUTHORITY

- ☐ Have the spirit of a learner and a servant
- ☐ Explain personal convictions without a spirit of condemnation
- ☐ Present the creative alternative
- ☐ Explain how it will reach his goal
- ☐ Leave the final decision up to him

6. GIVE GOD TIME TO CHANGE OUR AUTHORITY'S MIND

- ☐ Expect God to bring outside pressure on the authority
- ☐ Expect him to respond with extra pressure on you
- ☐ Realize that God will use his pressure for our ultimate benefit
- ☐ Build right responses which will be a basis for his changed decision

> • Only when the above six steps have been fully applied, are we scripturally ready for step number seven. In my experience, I have met very few who have actually been called upon to take it.

7. SUFFER FOR NOT DOING WHAT IS WRONG

- ☐ Disciples were to be willing to be rejected by family rather than to deny Christ (Matthew 10:32-39)
- ☐ Disciples were to proclaim the Gospel even when forbidden by government officials and religious leaders (Acts 4:19)
- ☐ Daniel was willing to be killed rather than cease his worship of God to worship the king (Daniel 6:12-16)

NOTES

PRINCIPLE OF AUTHORITY IN EMPLOYMENT

• One afternoon, a teen-ager in desperation said, "What should I do—quit my job now or go in tonight and get fired?!"

The teen-ager went on to explain the problem. "I've worked at this store since the beginning of this school year, and nothing I do seems to please my boss. I was fired from the last job I had, and if I get fired from this one, it'll look terrible on my record. So I guess I'd better quit."

I told the teen-ager that I would call his boss and see what I could work out. When I called the manager of the store and explained to him that one of his employees had come for counsel on how he could do a better job at the store, he was quite willing and pleased to cooperate in any way he could.

He explained that when this teen-ager first began working at the store, he was not very good with the customers, but after a while this began to improve. In fact, it improved too much. Now the teen-ager would spend half an hour at a time talking with his friends. The manager explained that he didn't mind a conversation of five minutes or so, but he didn't feel such long conversations were right since they hindered the boy from putting the stock on the shelves.

I assured him that he was right, and that I would do my best to convey these ideas to the teen-ager. Later that day, the teen-ager wanted to know how my conversation turned out with his boss. The following conversation took place:

"Suppose Jesus Christ Himself was the manager of that store. Would that make a difference in the quality of your work?"

• He replied, "It sure would! I'd do my best all the time." I then explained, "Do you realize that God expects you to consider that you are actually working for Jesus Christ on your job?" We then looked at Colossians 3:22-24:

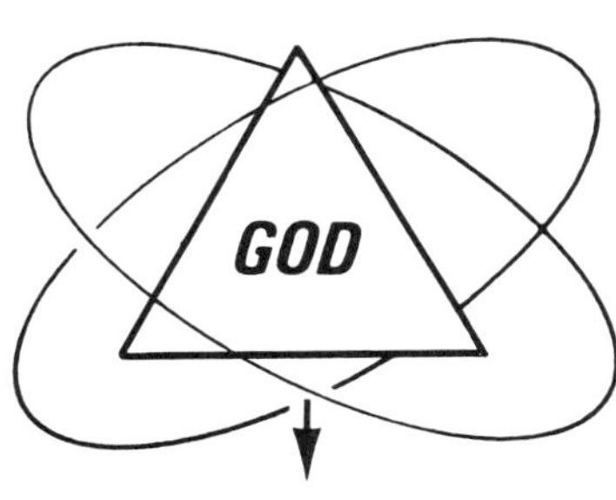

EMPLOYER

EMPLOYEE

- Servants, obey in all things those who are your masters.
- Not with eyeservice as menpleasers; but in singleness of heart, fearing God. (As a sincere expression of your devotion to the Lord.)
- Whatsoever you do, do your work heartily. (Put your whole heart and soul into whatever you do.)
- Work as for the Lord rather than for men: knowing that from the Lord you will receive the reward of the inheritance.
- For you serve the Lord Christ. (You are actually employed by the Lord Christ and not just by your earthly employer.)

NOTES

SPECIFIC QUESTIONS ON AUTHORITY

1. HOW OLD DO I HAVE TO BE BEFORE I'M OUT FROM UNDER AUTHORITY?

We never outgrow the need to be under authority, and, in fact, we are all commanded to be under authority at all times. "Likewise, ye younger, submit yourselves unto the elder. Yea, all of you be subject one to another, and be clothed with humility: for God resisteth the proud, and giveth grace to the humble." I Peter 5:5

2. WHEN DOES THE PARENTAL "CHAIN OF RESPONSIBILITY" END?

The parental "chain of responsibility" ends when they delegate that authority to someone else — as in marriage or the ministry. However, even before this, a certain measure of independence should be earned by learning to discern and obey the wishes of parents. When they are confident that we will do what they would do in a given situation, they will give more freedom to make decisions.

3. WHAT IF I'M AN ADULT AND STILL SINGLE?

By this time, we should have earned the position of being in a "chain of counsel." If we haven't, there must be some serious deficiencies in our attitudes or understanding.

Whatever our age, however, we are instructed in Scripture to always be responsive to our parents' counsel: "Hearken unto thy father that begat thee, and despise not thy mother when she is old." Proverbs 23:22

4. UNDER WHOSE AUTHORITY AM I IF MY PARENTS ARE DIVORCED?

The parent who is legally responsible for you becomes your direct chain of responsibility. The separated parent may be a part of your chain of counsel. If the parent with whom you are living remarries, he or she automatically delegates part of his or her authority to your step-parent.

5. WHAT IF MY PARENTS DON'T CARE WHAT I DO?

There are reasons why a parent has ceased caring what his teen-ager does. The main reason is usually that in the past the teen-ager has had a strong will and has done what he wanted to anyway. The parents then just stop competing with him.

When a teen-ager dedicates his life to the Lord and clears his conscience with his parents and places himself under their authority, he will usually see a gradual or a dramatic change in their concern for what he does.

NOTES

RESPONSIBILITY

6. WHAT IF I'M SINGLE AND LIVING IN AN APARTMENT?

First, be very sure that God has led you to move away from your parents, and that they were fully in harmony with the move. When God designed the family structure, He purposed that each one in the family meet basic needs for the others—especially social needs. When a single person leaves his family apart from God's direction, he exposes himself to many unnecessary temptations to wrongly fulfill these social needs. If your parents are in full harmony with your move to another location, it is important to maintain good lines of communication with them in order to receive counsel from them.

7. WHAT IF I'M A WIDOW OR DIVORCED?

Your direct line of authority would be to God. However, it would be very essential to build around your life as many godly counselors as you can, especially parents and parents-in-law. God takes special care of the widow. He is their protector: "A father of the fatherless, and a judge of the widows, is God in His holy habitation." (Psalm 68:5) The book of Ruth gives significant guidance to the young widow.

If you are divorced and your former husband is not remarried, take whatever steps you can to be reunited. By so doing, you will be able to get back under his "umbrella of protection," and allow God to work through the marriage to achieve Christ's character.

8. WHAT IF I MARRIED THE WRONG PERSON?

Your marriage may not have been one that God would have arranged; however, since He has established the authority of the marriage relationship, He will use whatever marriage you enter into to perfect His character in you. When your ways please the Lord, He will even make your enemies to be at peace with you. (Proverbs 16:7) This will happen to an even greater degree with your life partner.

9. WHAT IF I DON'T RESPECT THE AUTHORITY OVER ME?

It is important that we learn how to distinguish between an authority's position under God and his human personality. We are to reverence his position, although at the same time we may be very aware of personality deficiencies.

To say that we reject an authority because we don't respect him would be as much in error as tearing up a speeding ticket because we didn't like the attitude of the arresting officer.

NOTES

ANSWERING QUESTIONS ON AUTHORITY

RESPONSIBILITY

QUESTIONS ABOUT CHAIN OF RESPONSIBILITY	INCOMPLETE FRAME OF REFERENCE WHICH PROMPTED THE QUESTIONS	UNDERLYING PRINCIPLES REQUIRED TO ANSWER QUESTIONS FROM GOD'S PERSPECTIVE
IF SOMEONE ASKS . . .	**HE MAY THINK . . .**	**BUT HE MUST LEARN THAT . . .**
What if my parents don't really care what decisions I make?	That if his parents don't openly oppose him he has their consent to make his own decisions ?	When parents sense an inward spirit of resistance, they may feel that to oppose their son's or daughter's plans will only cause more argument so they might as well let him do what he wants. If the parents really don't care, then God will raise up other "tools" of authority to develop Christ-like qualities.
How does the chain of responsibility work when parents are divided in their counsel?	That parents who disagree in their counsel only illustrate that God is not speaking through them? That one parent is against him and therefore not co-operating with him.	When both parents disagree in their counsel, God is communicating important information through both of them. It is the son's or daughter's responsibility to interpret what God is saying and work out a creative alternative. If parents are antagonistic to each other, either one may grant unwise privileges to the children in order to gain their favor. In such cases the children must show deference and appreciation to each parent.
What if parents are divorced and there is a step-father in the family?	That God was not aware of this circumstance when He allowed him to be born in that particular family?	This principle follows the legal chain of responsibility. The step father would be in the new chain of responsibility and the real father would be in the chain of counsel.
What if my parents tell me to do something that I know is wrong ?	That he must either be blindly obedient or exhibit a spirit of disobedience.	If the basic intention of the parents is actually to get him to violate God's moral laws, and he has tactfully presented a creative alternative and given God time to change their minds, and has had the right attitudes, then he must appeal to their understanding that he cannot do what they ask.

NOTES

QUESTIONS ABOUT CHAIN OF RESPONSIBILITY	INCOMPLETE FRAME OF REFERENCE WHICH PROMPTED THE QUESTIONS	UNDERLYING PRINCIPLES REQUIRED TO ANSWER QUESTIONS FROM GOD'S PERSPECTIVE
IF SOMEONE ASKS . . .	**HE MAY THINK . . .**	**BUT HE MUST LEARN THAT . . .**
When does the chain of responsibility end for a single person who does not get married?	That there will come a time when he can throw off the restraints which his parents have placed on him?	Every person must be under authority throughout his lifetime; if not to parent, to employers, government, etc. (I Peter 5:5) Younger to elder, one to another, in humility.
What if I'm single but living in an apartment and supporting myself?	That he has no responsibility to be loyal to the standards of the parent by following their wishes no matter where he may be. That there is value in making independent decisions even if they prove to be wrong.	When a teen-ager becomes obedient to the wishes of his parents he earns the position of being under chain of counsel rather that chain of responsibility. (Parents grant more freedom for decision making because they know it will be in harmony with their basic intentions.) When a son or daughter inwardly or outwardly resists the parents' wishes, this destroys the process of earning independence.
What if the parents are so domineering they just won't let go even if the son or daughter is old enough to make decisions?	That if the parents' motives are selfish or unjust, God is not able to work through their counsel.	God even works through the wrath of parents to reveal character deficiences in the son or daughter, to develop additional character strengths or to reflect "healing" attitudes back to the parents. (Psalm 76:10, Romans 13:1-6, Proverbs 13:1)

NOTES

GAINING THE INNER RADIANCE OF A TRANSPARENT LIFE

A CLEAR CONSCIENCE

- IMPERATIVES OF A CLEAR CONSCIENCE
- RATIONALIZATIONS HINDERING A CLEAR CONSCIENCE
- BASIC STEPS IN GAINING A CLEAR CONSCIENCE
- CAUTIONS IN GAINING A CLEAR CONSCIENCE

- A clear conscience is listed in Scripture as one of our most essential weapons for successful spiritual achievement.
(I Timothy 1:18, 19)

NOTES

DEFINITION OF A CLEAR CONSCIENCE

• A clear conscience involves that inner freedom of spirit toward God and others that comes by knowing that God's Holiness is not offended by one's thought or action, and that no one can point a finger at you and say, "You've offended me, and you've never asked for my forgiveness."

SCOPE OF A CLEAR CONSCIENCE

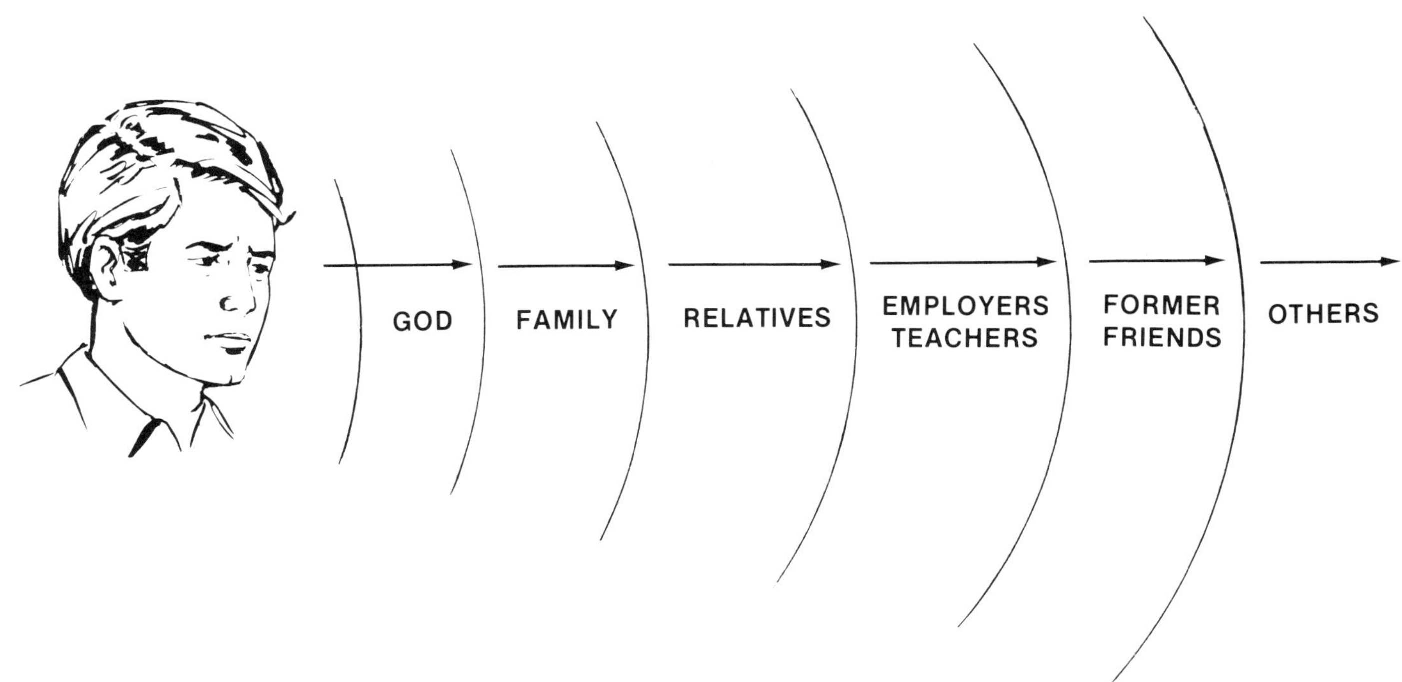

NOTES

IDENTIFYING THE PROBLEM

• The greatest single hindrance to gaining a clear conscience is the feeling that the ones we offended were wrong too! In fact, we often feel that they were mostly wrong. Our focus on blaming them balances our own guilt and forces us to live with both guilt and blame.

THE BALANCE OF GUILT

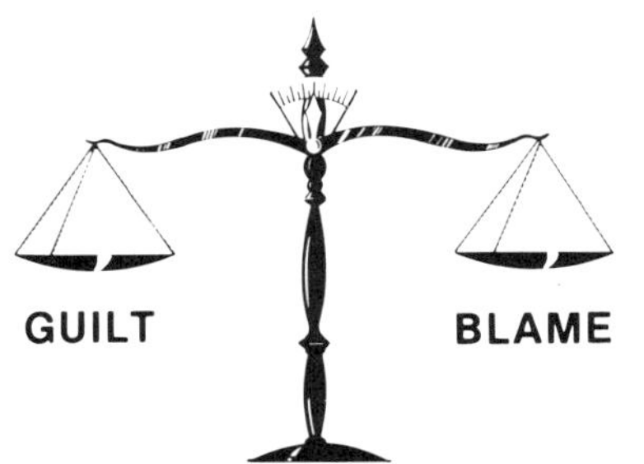

• It is our natural inclination to find other people or circumstances which are to blame for what we have done in order to justify or excuse our offenses.

The greater our guilt, the more we must blame. The resulting bitterness and guilt are devastating to our mental and emotional balance.

THE SPLINTER AND THE BEAM

• A "splinter" and a "beam" are actually the same size when viewed from reverse perspective.

When we sense that our brother is offended because of "some little thing we did to him," we must remember that in his eye this "little thing" is a beam!

We may think we were only 10 percent wrong, but in his eye we were 90 percent wrong.

THE DESTRUCTIVE POWER OF WRONG ATTITUDES

• It is essential that we recognize and confess wrong actions against those whom we have offended. But it is even more important to discern, confess and change wrong attitudes which were either caused by or resulted from our wrong actions.

This is usually more difficult than we realize. We are so involved with our own thoughts and emotions that we fail to realize the attitudes which we are actually reflecting to the people around us.

More than we realize, people are reacting to our attitudes. It is, therefore, essential that we learn how to "judge ourselves" in wrong attitudes in order that we are not judged by others.

The following illustrations are used by permission of teen-agers who wrote them out for this purpose.

NOTES

CONFLICTS CAUSED BY WRONG ATTITUDES

- **FAMILY CONFLICT #1**

• "Friday I came home for lunch and both of my brothers were there. When I came in the door, the first thing my younger brother said was, 'What are you doing here?' I said that I came home for lunch. Then he said, 'Well, you can just go back to school where you belong.' Since they were there before me, they should have had my lunch ready. But they hadn't done a thing. I said, 'Why didn't you fix me something?' My brother said, 'We didn't feel like it!'

"When I asked why they were acting that way, they said that it was none of my business. We had a few wrong words. After this, I ended up going back to school without eating lunch and by being very disappointed with my brother. I want very much to get along with him. I hope the Lord will show me how this is possible."

CONSCIENCE

- **FAMILY CONFLICT #2**

• "While I was washing the floor, my little sister came in. (She had been out playing.) I asked her to get upstairs and help my other sister clean her room. She just gave me one of those looks as if to say, 'Just who do you think you are—giving me orders?'

"Then she bluntly said, 'No!' Mom was on the phone, so I took matters into my own hands and began to help her walk up the stairs. I ended up dragging her by her arms. It didn't hurt her, but to make trouble, she began to scream and cry as if I were trying to kill her."

- **FAMILY CONFLICT #3**

• "Well, I was sitting in front of the television—naturally. My dad came in and told me to go and do something besides watch television. So I went over and got one of my friends. We were playing in the garage and were hitting the door with a basketball when my dad came out swearing at us as he always does.

"I said, 'Well, you don't have to swear about it.' He said, 'I'll swear if I want to.' I told him, 'Not around me. Swear some other place.' Well, this set off the fuse. He grabbed a stick from the garage and came at me, swinging. I told my friend to scatter. He ran one way, and I ran the other.

"We went over to his house and my friend told his mother what had happened. She said he can't come over anymore. At this rate I'll lose all my friends. When I came home, my dad said, 'If you don't stop causing trouble, I'm going to stick you in a home.' He always threatens to stick me in a home."

- **FAMILY CONFLICT #4**

• "Dad, Mom and I were at the breakfast table when we started discussing my future occupation. Somehow I said the wrong thing! I said that my life as a married woman would have little outside activity, etc. I gave Mom's as an example of such a life. I didn't mean for it to cause friction, but it sure did! She told me I was ungrateful, unwilling to help around the house, etc., etc. I said many things I shouldn't have. It's so-o-o hard. I love her very much, but we always have a tense feeling between us."

NOTES

STEP 1: LIST THEIR OFFENSES

• The first step in solving conflicts with a particular person is to privately list all the offenses which he has committed against you. (This is in preparation to follow Matthew 18.)

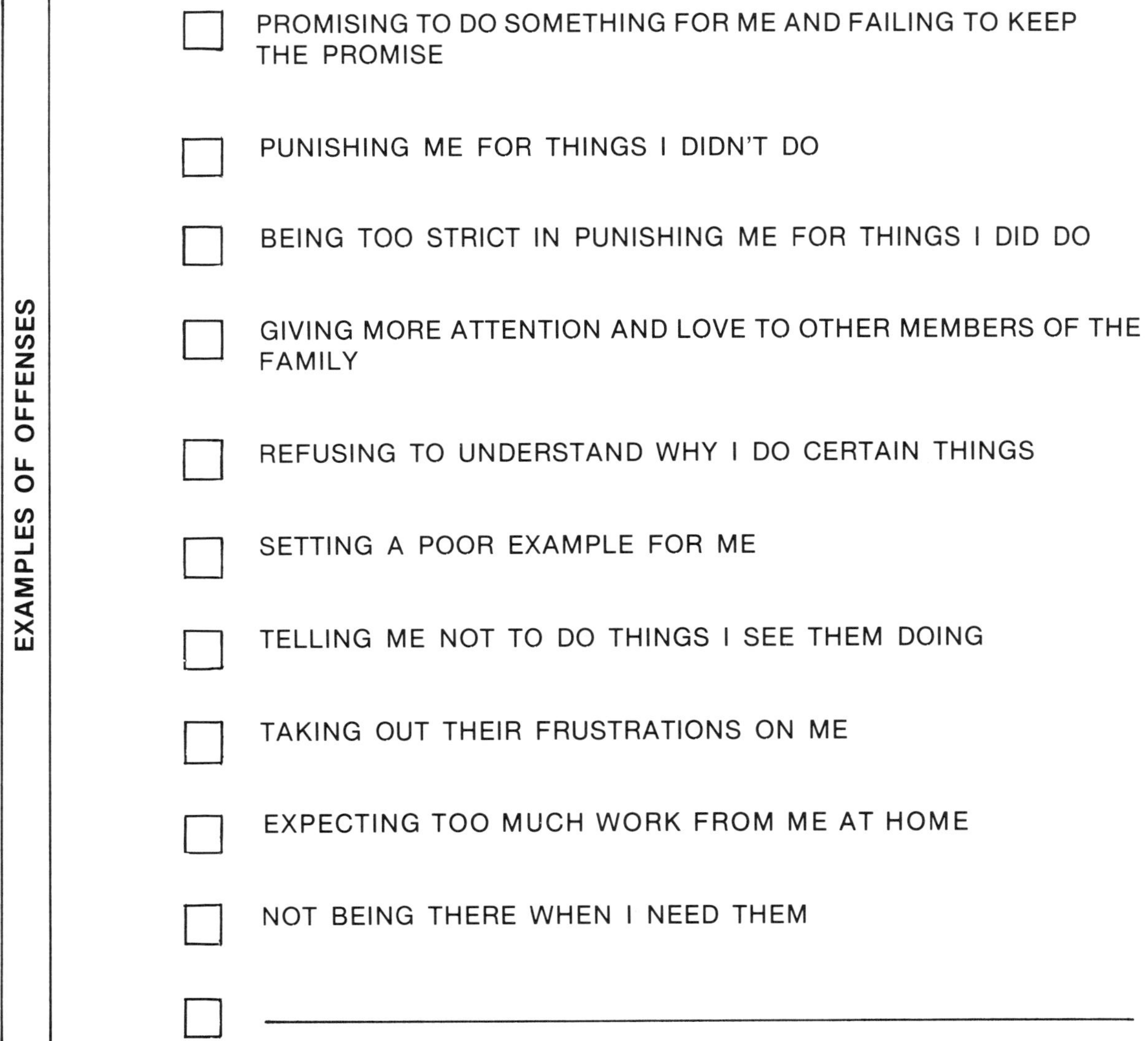

EXAMPLES OF OFFENSES

- ☐ PROMISING TO DO SOMETHING FOR ME AND FAILING TO KEEP THE PROMISE
- ☐ PUNISHING ME FOR THINGS I DIDN'T DO
- ☐ BEING TOO STRICT IN PUNISHING ME FOR THINGS I DID DO
- ☐ GIVING MORE ATTENTION AND LOVE TO OTHER MEMBERS OF THE FAMILY
- ☐ REFUSING TO UNDERSTAND WHY I DO CERTAIN THINGS
- ☐ SETTING A POOR EXAMPLE FOR ME
- ☐ TELLING ME NOT TO DO THINGS I SEE THEM DOING
- ☐ TAKING OUT THEIR FRUSTRATIONS ON ME
- ☐ EXPECTING TOO MUCH WORK FROM ME AT HOME
- ☐ NOT BEING THERE WHEN I NEED THEM
- ☐ ______________________________

NOTES

STEP 2: LIST YOUR OFFENSES

• It is relatively easy to remember the faults of others, but when it comes to listing our own faults, we may discover a lapse of memory. To compensate for this difficulty, the following questions are suggested:

☐ **POOR ATTITUDE**

If your parents were to rate your attitude around the house, would they say it was above average, average or below average?

☐ **UNGRATEFULNESS**

When is the last time you thanked your parents for the ordinary things they do for you, such as providing meals, working to maintain a home, car and other benefits?

☐ **STUBBORNNESS**

What is your immediate response when asked to do something around the house?

- ☐ I do it immediately
- ☐ I tell them I'll do it later
- ☐ I ask them why someone else can't do it
- ☐ I ask them why it needs to be done
- ☐ I tell them I can't do it

☐ **UNTRUTHFULNESS**

Have you done anything to cause your parents to lose confidence in you?

Have you told them only part of the truth at times so that they would agree with you?

Have you made decisions on your own which your parents should have made with you?

☐ **BITTERNESS**

Have you been harboring resentment and bitterness for things your parents have done toward you?

☐ **LAZINESS**

How neatly have you kept your room? How often have you spent time watching television when you knew you should be doing other things?

NOTES

STEP 3: PURPOSE TO ASK FORGIVENESS

- This is by far the most difficult step. It must be done in an attitude of complete sincerity and genuine repentance.

CONSCIENCE

A. IDENTIFY THE BASIC OFFENSES

It is important to distinguish between immediate offenses and basic offenses. They are not always the same. It does little good to ask forgiveness for a small offense when in reality that offense is only a fractional part of a much greater offense.

- In the family conflicts described on page forty-four, the statements by the offending party reveal previous offenses which were brought into the present conflict.

ILLUSTRATIONS (From page 3)	STATEMENT BY OFFENDING PARTY	IMMEDIATE REACTION	BASIC OFFENSE
CONFLICT #1	"Well, you can just go back to school where you belong!"	"A few wrong words."	Wounded pride. Expecting to be served. Failure to "Serve one another in love."
CONFLICT #2	"Just who do you think you are, giving me orders?"	"Taking matters into my own hands."	Harboring resentment since she had to wash floors while her sister was out playing.
CONFLICT #3	"Telling me to go do something besides watching T.V."	Hitting the garage door with the basketball.	Laziness, disrespect, ungratefulness, stubbornness and self-righteousness.
CONFLICT #4	"You're ungrateful, unwilling to help around the house, etc., etc.!"	"Saying many things I shouldn't have."	Ungratefulness and laziness in duties at home.

B. ASK FORGIVENESS FOR BASIC OFFENSES

There are several ways to ask forgiveness which are guaranteed not to work - such as, "I was wrong, but you were too;" "If I was wrong, please forgive me;" "I'm sorry;" etc. There is one genuine statement which reflects true sincerity and humility —

- "God has convicted me of how wrong I have been in (my attitude and actions). I know I have wronged you in this, and I've come to ask, will you forgive me?"

NOTES

THE POWER OF A CLEAR CONSCIENCE

- The following verses are only a few of those which refer to the imperative of a clear conscience.

A SENSITIVE CONSCIENCE IS THE MARK OF A MATURE CHRISTIAN	"For everyone that useth milk is unskillful in the word of righteousness: for he is a babe. But strong meat belongeth to them that are of full age, even those who by reason of use have their senses exercised to discern both good and evil." Hebrews 5:13, 14 (See also I Timothy 1:5)
PAUL TESTIFIES TO THE IMPORTANCE OF A CLEAR CONSCIENCE	"And herein do I exercise myself, to have always a conscience void of offense toward God, and toward man." Acts 24:16 "For our rejoicing is this, the testimony of our conscience, that in simplicity and godly sincerity, not with fleshly wisdom, but by the grace of God, we have had our conversation in the world, and more abundantly to you-ward." II Corinthians 1:12
PAUL WARNED TIMOTHY THAT NEXT TO HIS FAITH, A CLEAR CONSCIENCE WAS HIS MOST ESSENTIAL WEAPON	"This charge I commit unto thee, son Timothy. . . that thou by them mightest war a good warfare; holding faith, and a good conscience; which some having put away concerning faith have made shipwreck." I Timothy 1:18,19
PETER EXPLAINS WHY A CLEAR CONSCIENCE IS ESSENTIAL IN ORDER TO WITNESS	"Having a good conscience; that, whereas they speak evil of you, as of evildoers, they may be ashamed that falsely accuse your good conversation in Christ." I Peter 3:16
EVEN HEALTH AND PHYSICAL APPEARANCE ARE AFFECTED BY THE LACK OF A CLEAR CONSCIENCE	"Happy is he whose transgression is forgiven, whose sin is covered. When I kept silence (in confessing my sin), my bones waxed old through my roaring all the day long (the weight of guilt). For day and night thy hand was heavy upon me: my moisture is turned into the drought of summer." Psalm 32:1, 3, 4

NOTES

REINFORCING THE CONSCIENCE

• Since it is possible to diminish the effectiveness of the conscience by disregarding or rationalizing conviction, it is important to identify the forces producing conviction in the conscience.

REPROOFS FROM SCRIPTURE	GOD'S CHARACTER QUALITIES		OUR CHARACTER QUALITIES	REPROOFS OF LIFE
				PARENTS
	LOVE →	CONVICTION	← HATE	← RELATIVES
	TRUTH →		← DECEIT	← HEALTH
WORD OF GOD →	JUSTICE →		← UNFAIRNESS	← CHILDREN
	PURITY →		← IMPURITY	← GOVERNMENT
	MERCY →		← BITTERNESS	← CIRCUMSTANCES
				← LIFE PARTNER
				← ENEMIES
				← FINANCES

CONSCIENCE

- LIGHT OF CHRIST - The Light of Christ is an awareness of the basic qualities which God wants to develop within each life. These correspond to the essential qualities of His nature. "This is the light that lighteth every man that cometh into the world." John 1:9

- THE WORD OF GOD - The Word of God more clearly defines the basic qualities to be developed. As we see the standards in Scripture, we become more sensitive to our need to develop them.

- ALERTNESS TO THE LIGHT - When any one of these qualities is deficient or violated, we are sensitive to this condition. The sensitivity itself is the conviction of our conscience. ". . . Which show the work of the law written in their hearts, their conscience also bearing witness, and their thoughts the meanwhie accusing or else excusing one another." Romans 2:14, 15, and 1:18-21

- REPROOFS OF LIFE - God has ordained that the individuals and circumstances surrounding our lives will reinforce our sensitivity to the qualities which should be developed within us. Their reproofs are used by God to reinforce conviction. "A fool despiseth his father's instruction: but he that regardeth reproof is prudent." Proverbs 15:5

NOTES

THE PURPOSE OF A CLEAR CONSCIENCE

A. BOLDNESS TO WITNESS

• At a summer camp, Don, a high school sophomore, was deeply concerned over his inability to tell others of his faith in Christ. Our conversation went as follows:

"How long has it been since you've been able to witness?"

Don: "For about a year."

"Can you think of anything that happened a year ago that might have caused your present inability to witness?"

Don: "Well, last year I was on the high school basketball team, and once I let out a string of swear words in the locker room. The fellows were really shocked since I was supposed to be a Christian. Ever since then, I've been ashamed to talk to others about the Lord."

Don had good reason not to witness! He knew his friends would call him a hypocrite. Notice how God relates a clear conscience to effective witnessing:

> • "But sanctify the Lord God in your hearts: and be ready always to give an answer to every man that asketh you a reason of the hope that is in you with meekness and fear: Having a good conscience; that, whereas they speak evil of you, as of evildoers, they may be ashamed that falsely accuse your good conversation in Christ." (I Peter 3:15, 16)

• At that same summer camp, a senior girl revealed the same problem regarding her fear and inability to tell others of Christ at school. When she was asked if she could pinpoint a cause for this, she reported the following situation:

Jan: "Things were going along just fine until one day in math class. We had a test that day, and my girlfriend let me see some of her answers. I've really felt horrible since, and I know what my girlfriend would say if she heard me telling others I was a Christian. She'd say, 'You big hypocrite!'"

NOTES

B. FREEDOM TO RESOLVE CONFLICTS

• Often the lack of a clear conscience may be the one stumblingblock to the salvation of others in the family. Such was the case with Tom.

Tom: "My parents aren't Christians, and they seem to make things as difficult as they can for me. They want nothing to do with church or the Bible."

"Tom, how important is it to you that your parents become Christians?"

Tom: "It's very important to me! I really want to see them accept Christ."

"Then there's something very important you must do."

Tom: "But there's really not too much I can do. We just don't seem to get along no matter how hard I try."

"Tom, here's what you can do. Get alone somewhere and carefully write down all the things you have done which cause your parents to get angry with you. Put these under general topics such as laziness, ungratefulness, poor attitudes. Then go to each of them and ask for their forgiveness for these things."

Tom went home determined to carry this out. Two weeks later I received a note from him. Here is what he wrote:

"I did what you suggested and went to each member of my family and made amends with them. Each one was deeply touched by this - even my younger brother. I've been trying to live up to Christian standards here at home, but I've slipped a couple of times. I have also taken your advice and am memorizing a verse of Scripture each day. My mother is coming to church with me regularly now. Thank God!"

Tom wrote again

"I just thought I would write and tell you of the latest developments in our family. My mother recently went to talk with our pastor, and she rededicated her life to Christ. Now there are two of us in our family. I'm very thankful to the Lord for answering prayer."

C. ALERTNESS TO MAKE WISE DECISIONS

• One rainy night, the president of a lumber company was driving home on a winding forest road. As he rounded one curve, he was startled to see a boy on a bicycle right in his path. He slammed on his brakes to avoid hitting the boy, but on the slippery pavement, he could not stop in time. He heard the quick crunch and thud against the front of his car.

In that split second, he had to make a decision - a decision which was to influence the rest of his life.

NOTES

• He backed up the car, drove around the boy lying on the road, and in a cold sweat stepped on the gas and drove home.

The next morning as he was eating breakfast, his wife turned on the radio. At that very moment they were reporting the hit-and-run accident which occurred the night before. In addition to the first car hitting the boy, another car had come and not being able to avoid him, ran over the boy. He was in critical condition in the hospital.

The man's wife made a comment about how terrible it was that the first driver had not stopped. Her husband nervously agreed.

A few moments later, his son came running into the kitchen to report, "Hey, Dad, your front headlight is broken!" The father quickly explained, "Yes, I broke it going into the garage last night. I'll have to get it fixed."

That day at the office he could not concentrate. Finally, at noon, he drove to the police station and explained that he was the one who had run into the boy. He was put into jail.

It seemed that the entire town was incensed at this accident. The judge found it necessary to make a public example of the seriousness of this crime. The hit-and-run driver was sentenced to twenty years in prison!

After the trial, he asked the judge, "What would have been the penalty if I had taken the boy to the hospital?"

The judge assured him, "I don't think there would have been any. It was an accident. You would have done what you could."

THE HIDDEN CAUSE OF A WRONG DECISION

• A reporter became interested in finding out why a responsible businessman and father would make the wrong decision at the scene of an accident. Upon further inquiry, he learned about the following incident from the man.

"When I was a boy, my father came home one day with a beautiful pocket watch. I saw him put it in the top drawer of his dresser. One day I wanted to show the watch to the fellows at school. I thought of how important it would make me feel.

"I didn't think my father would like the idea, so without telling him, I carefully unwrapped it from the napkin around it and slid it into my pocket. I decided I would put it back that night, and he would never know the difference.

"That day in school I was showing it to the fellows, and one of them wanted to hold it. As he was giving it back, he dropped it. It seemed to break into a thousand tiny pieces. My heart sank. I picked up as many pieces as I could find. That night I wrapped all the pieces in the napkin and put it back into my father's top dresser drawer.

"A week or so later, my father discovered the broken watch. In a rage, he asked who had done it. I was really afraid, so I told him I didn't know anything about it. He didn't say anything more to me. As I look back, I can see that ever since then, I've run from an accident rather than face the consequences."

• Many, many decisions in life are influenced by the state of our conscience!

NOTES

D. POWER TO OVERCOME TEMPTATION

• A six-year-old girl came to her mother one day and solemnly asked, "If I do something wrong, isn't it enough to ask God to forgive me?" Her mother carefully explained that if she had offended someone else, she should also ask that person to forgive her.

The little girl turned around and slowly went to her room. A short while later she returned, deep in thought, and asked, "Mommy, what if the person won't forgive me?" Her mother reassured her that if she were truly sorry for what she had done, she would certainly be forgiven.

Again the little girl turned and walked to her room. About ten minutes later, she returned and slowly explained: "I didn't lie to my grandma, and I didn't lie to my brother, but I lied to you." Her mother asked, "How did you lie to me?" "Three nights ago when I came into your room, you asked me if I had had a nightmare because you said I could only sleep with you and Daddy if I had a nightmare. I told you that I did—but I didn't.

"The next morning when everyone asked me what the nightmare was, I had to make one up." By this time she was in tears, and her eleven-year-old brother walked into the room, wondering what she was crying about.

After the mother explained, the little girl asked her brother, "Don't you ever lie?" He replied, "Yes. When I was your age, I did." In surprise she asked, "Haven't you lied since?" His emphatic answer becomes extremely significant in the light of our need to build responses to overcome temptation.

"No. It's just not worth it! If you lie, you have to go back and tell the truth anyway, and then ask forgiveness, and it's just not worth it!"

THE SECRETS OF A SWINDLER

• One of the shrewdest "con artists" of our day revealed some of his trade secrets in a book he wrote. In the book he explained how he was able to sell such items as the Brooklyn Bridge, Miami Beach and the Empire State Building to intelligent businessmen. Here is his basic method of operation.

He would first approach a successful businessman on a small "investment opportunity." This "opportunity" would not take much capital but in a very short time it would pay tremendous returns. For example, the businessman would be invited to invest one-hundred dollars in some product which would be sold for one-thousand dollars in a few weeks.

As the businessman looked over all the details, it appeared to be a real opportunity—all except for a little "quick dealing" which the con artist was going to do behind the scenes so that they would both "come out ahead." This behind-the-scenes activity was minimized as "only normal in business" and "what everyone else is doing." On the other hand, the nine-hundred dollar profit was emphasized and kept in front of the businessman.

NOTES

• When the businessman invested his hundred dollars on the small venture, the con artist knew by experience that he was also hooked for the big venture.

True to his word, the con artist returned in a few weeks with nine-hundred dollars and triumphantly laid it on the businessman's desk as he told him what a wise investor he was. Then he left.

A few weeks later, he returned with new enthusiasm. He just found out from reliable sources that a large part of Miami Beach (or something else) was going to be sold at a bargain price. If the businessman would invest one-hundred thousand dollars, he would multiply it to a million in no time!

The con artist explained that if any of his "customers" balked at this point, he had only to remind them that they were partners and had engaged in a "little infraction of the law" which no one else knew about.

CONSCIENCE

• In precisely the same way, Satan uses a defiled conscience to defeat a Christian in ever-larger temptations. Rarely is the Christian aware of the final "price tag" on temporary "pleasures" of sin. The guilt of his transgression becomes Satan's method of blackmail to go deeper and deeper into sin.

• The Indians applied the principle mentioned in Psalm 32:1-4 of "moisture turning into the drought of summer" in detecting a guilty person among their tribesmen.

When a crime was committed, they would line up all the suspects. They would then heat a knife. Each suspect was told to stick out his tongue. The flat side of the knife was put against the tongue for an instant, then taken away. If the Indian were innocent, it would not burn him; but if he were guilty, the knife would burn his tongue.

The principle was that a guilty person's mouth becomes dry and, therefore, the heat against a dry tongue would burn it. On the other hand, the innocent person's mouth and tongue would be moist and the hot knife would only turn the moisture into steam. The same result occurs when testing a hot iron by first licking one's finger. The heat only singes the water—not the finger.

E. ABILITY TO BUILD GENUINE FRIENDSHIPS

• The most basic quality needed for friendships is sincere humility. This is the one quality which is sure to result from gaining a clear conscience.

At one major point in my life, I made a list of all those who weren't as friendly toward me as they could be. In each case, I recalled that there was something I had done or neglected to do which accounted for their lack of friendliness.

NOTES

• I had not gone back to any of them sooner because in almost every case, I felt they had wronged me in more serious ways than I had wronged them. In most cases, I had decided that they were at least 90 per cent wrong.

When God made it clear to me through His Word and the conviction of His Holy Spirit that I should forgive them, forget about their 90 per cent, and take care of my 10 per cent, I went back to each one and asked for his forgiveness.

I can honestly say that these are now among my best friends. In fact, several of them are among the greatest supporters of the work in which I am now involved.

When I purposed to make things right with those seventeen whom I had wronged, there was one I almost did not get on the list. I did not plan to ever see him again; and besides, I did not think I was more than maybe 2 per cent wrong. But I knew he had ill feelings toward me, and I remembered the Scripture,

> "If thou bring thy gift to the altar and there rememberest that thy brother hath ought against thee, leave there thy gift by the altar and go thy way. First be reconciled to thy brother, then come again and offer thy gift." (Matthew 5:23,24)

One day he stopped at my home to borrow something. Before he left, I had the opportunity to talk with him alone and ask his forgiveness. He not only forgave me but thanked me for asking his forgiveness.

This man became one of my most enthusiastic supporters and through his reports to others, a chain of events occurred which later resulted in gifts of over $30,000 being given to the youth work in which I was involved.

AN UNEXPECTED BONUS OF A CLEAR CONSCIENCE

• Another illustration of this vital point comes from a high school sophomore named Cal. He asked me if he should go back to the owner of a store where he had once worked. While he was working there, he had taken some money out of the cash register. His question in going back came because he did not have any money to pay back the owner.

I assured him that God was deeply concerned that he go back as soon as possible and confess what he had done. He could pay part of it now and assure the owner that the total amount would be returned soon.

One week later, I saw Cal. He was beaming with joy as he exclaimed:

"I went back to the owner of the store. He was really surprised to see me and especially amazed that I would confess what I had done and offer to pay it back. Not only did he forgive me, he gave me a good-paying job! He said that the courage and honesty I had in coming back to him are the qualities he's looking for in his employees."

• How true God is on this point:

"He that covereth his sins shall not prosper, but whoso confesseth and forsaketh them shall have mercy." (Proverbs 28:13)

NOTES

COMMON RATIONALIZATIONS

- One of the hardest deaths to die is the death to pride. The mind is ingenious at devising reasons which will circumvent or postpone death to pride.

- Anyone who has ever experienced making things right will clearly remember the many reasons or excuses he had for not really having to go back to ask forgiveness. Here are a few common rationalizations.

1. "IT HAPPENED A LONG TIME AGO."

If it happened so long ago, why do you still remember it? Since you have remembered it for such a long time this is all the more reason to make it right.

2. "THE ONE I WRONGED HAS MOVED AWAY."

With all the friends he left behind it surely would not be too difficult to find out where he moved. If he moved to another state, the telephone operator may be able to contact him so you can talk with him.

3. "IT WAS SUCH A SMALL OFFENSE."

At this point the question must be repeated, "Has it been eating away at your conscience?" If so, it is big enough to be taken care of.

4. "THINGS HAVE GOTTEN BETTER."

With uncanny regularity, those who purpose to go back and make things right with one with whom they're not getting along will find the situation improving before they ask forgiveness.

So often this improvement is God's way of preparing the other person to forgive us, but we mistakenly use it as a reason for not asking for forgiveness.

5. "I'M JUST BEING TOO SENSITIVE."

So is the person you've wronged! A sensitive nature is not something to shy away from but rather to develop. Strong spiritual meat belongs to those who are mature Christians; in other words, those who by use have their senses exercised to discern between good and evil. (Hebrews 5:14)

NOTES

6. "NO ONE'S PERFECT."

That's true. But apparently the standard of perfection you have set is too low. Your own conscience confirms the fact that it is too low, and your conflicts with others stand as another witness to this fact.

7. "THEY WON'T UNDERSTAND."

You'll be amazed how clearly they will understand. Our job is to obey; God will take care of their understanding. If they appear not to understand, it may be that your asking forgiveness has caused them to be convicted about their own need to ask forgiveness.

8. "MAKING IT RIGHT WILL INVOLVE MONEY WHICH I DON'T HAVE."

Better to have an honest debt than a dishonest weight of conscience. Borrow the money if need be, or make arrangements with the one from whom you stole it to pay it back by installments. However, I have not yet known a case which involved money in which God did not clearly show His hand of power to provide. Here are the details of one unusual example:

- A Christian businessman hired a Christian contractor to build a house for him. The businessman specifically instructed the contractor not to hire a certain mason, because he felt he would do inferior work.

Several weeks later, the businessman came to inspect the progress of his house. To his amazement and anger, he found that the mason contractor whom he did not want had been hired. In a heated discussion with the Christian contractor, he expressed his displeasure at what had been done.

Other sub-contract work was, in the opinion of the businessman, quite unsatisfactory and had to be corrected at extra expense. This led to further heated disagreement so that when a final bill was presented, it was refused.

For seven years, the businessman ignored the $1,300.00 statement which he had received from the contractor.

Both men became active in youth work and one day they both discovered each other at an area youth conference. They avoided one another as much as possible for several meetings. Finally the conviction became so great on both sides that they met together after a meeting.

The businessman acknowledged that he was wrong in his anger and lack of Christian testimony and that his asking forgiveness was to be "backed up by his pocketbook." He asked the contractor to send him a new bill, and he would pay it.

Later he assured me that he did not have the money to pay the account in full at that time.

NOTES

Within a week, the contractor, who assured me he had never expected to receive the money, sent a new statement: "In rechecking my bills for the job on your house, I believe that if you would discount my original bill by one-half, it would cover my expenses."

This meant that the businessman had to raise $650.00 in order to clear his conscience. He gathered together $100.00 for the first installment and sent it to the contractor.

Three days later he received a letter from his employer. The letter began with the statement, "We are happy to inform you that because of your record, the enclosed bonus check is being sent to you."

In the letter was a bonus check for $1,310.00! Not only did the Lord pay the $650.00 to the contractor, He gave an equal amount to the businessman—plus an extra $10.00.

When I heard this, I could hardly contain myself for joy. I was, therefore, rather surprised that the businessman was not as enthusiastic as I was. He did not associate the check as God's provision for the debt but instead thought, "Well, I expected a bonus, although I didn't know how much it would be."

One year later, he was also expecting a bonus check. He figured it would be about $1,000.00. Just before the close of the year, it seemed that God wanted to clarify that the $1,310.00 really had come from Him. He sent an electrical storm which struck the steeple and roof of a church insured by the businessman; and in that one claim, his bonus check for the entire year was practically wiped out!

9. "I'LL DO IT LATER."

Procrastination is one of the worst enemies to a clear conscience. You can be sure that "later" if it ever comes, will never be as good a time as now! "Later" there will probably be other things to make right. Perhaps even because of death there will be no opportunity to gain forgiveness from those you wronged.

10. "I'LL ONLY DO IT OVER AGAIN."

This is truly a statement from one who has never asked forgiveness in the right way! If you offend again, you must ask forgiveness again. You will discover that the pain of truly humbling yourself and asking forgiveness will be much greater than the pain of self-control.

11. "THE OTHER PERSON WAS MOSTLY WRONG."

You don't have to live with his conscience. You do have to live with yours. No doubt he is also using this excuse for not making things right with you! When you make your 30 per cent or 20 per cent or 10 per cent right and forget the 70 per cent or 80 per cent or 90 per cent fault on his part, you will probably be surprised to hear him ask you to forgive him for his wrong. Someone has to begin the humbling process. Let it be you, and you will receive the greater blessing.

NOTES

CONSCIENCE

12. "MY PARENTS WON'T UNDERSTAND."

I'm sure that Abraham's wife would not have understood if he had told her that he was going to sacrifice their son in accordance with God's command. Instead, he got up early in the morning and immediately obeyed God's Word. It is significant that there is no mention that he told his wife what he was about to do. Discussing God's clear commands with others is usually a method of procrastination.

However, if a parent stops you in your attempt to make something right, then you must follow his direction.

13. "I'LL LEAVE THE WORST OFFENSE UNTIL LAST."

In asking forgiveness, always make the worst offense right first. If you don't, you will find that abnormal guilt will center around little inconsequential wrongs which really don't need a special forgiveness.

14. "IF I PURPOSE NOT TO DO IT AGAIN, WON'T THAT BE ENOUGH?"

Not doing it in the future will not erase the wrongs of the past. The one you've wronged will not know about your purposing, and he will think your good behavior is a sly way to get something you want. This or a similar false accusation will be so discouraging to you that you might become bitter.

For example, if someone lied to you, they could tell the truth for months, but you would always remember the lie and wonder if they were telling the truth.

15. "THEY'RE NOT CHRISTIANS—WHAT WILL THEY THINK?"

They will think that they have finally discovered a true example of a Christian. Here is an example of this:

A high school junior explained that she had cheated on an exam. However, she was not sure she should confess it to the teacher since he was not a Christian and probably would not understand. She was encouraged to go and make it right regardless of what he would think.

The next day after school she got up the courage and walked into his room. After telling him what she had done and asking him to forgive her (and to make her grade lower because of it), she heard him make this statement,

"Well, you're the first student who's ever come back to ask forgiveness for cheating. I'd say that you are the first example of a real Christian I've ever seen!"

The reward of those who gain and who help others gain a conscience void of offense toward God and man:
"Blessed are the peacemakers: for they shall be called the children of God." Matthew 5:9

NOTES

16. "IF I GO BACK IT WILL GET MY FRIEND IN TROUBLE."

It needn't—if you go back in the right way. The basic requirement for asking forgiveness in the right way is to concentrate on only that which you have done. To involve someone else is to shift part of the blame. This is not complete death to pride.

• One or more of these rationalizations is all too likely to cause you to not follow through on even the first one on your list. I'll never forget the inner conflict I had the very first time I went back to ask someone to forgive me.

From the beginning I began to rationalize. My first excuse was that it was such a small thing. (I had stolen some toy soldiers from a neighbor's yard.)

"If it's too small," the thought came in surprising clarity, "why do you remember it after this long a time, and why is it on your conscience?"

My next excuse was, "But they've moved away." Just then I remembered what their new location was.

Following this excuse, I reasoned that they were not Christians and probably would not understand. But I knew God would answer by saying, "You obey Me, and let Me take care of their understanding."

As I wondered just how important it was to go back and ask forgiveness, I was impressed with the idea that my growth and effectiveness as a Christian would be greatly diminished if I were not obedient at this point. How true that was!

I went to the phone book and looked up their new address. Later, as I walked up their front walk, I must honestly confess that I was secretly hoping they weren't home. But then I realized that if they weren't, I'd only have to come back some other time. I knocked on the door and waited—half holding my breath and rehearsing what I was going to say.

The door swung open, and the father, with a pleased and surprised voice, invited me in. The whole family "just happened" to be in that living room when I walked in. First they asked a few questions about my family and the neighborhood. Then they asked, "Well, what brings you over here today?"

I explained that recently God had convicted me of an offense I had committed against them and that I really wanted to make it right. I told them I was wrong for stealing the soldiers from them and wanted to pay for them and would like to ask them to forgive me for taking them.

Not only did they thoroughly and quickly forgive me, but our friendship was deepened in that visit. Later they told some friends that that visit was the greatest testimony of Christianity they had ever received.

As I walked from that home several minutes later, I was filled with an inexpressible joy and freedom. I shall never forget this triumphant feeling. It has helped me to make other things right since.

NOTES

AN ILLUSTRATION OF APPLICATION

• After studying the preceding material, a minister diligently applied it to his own life and wrote the following account:

• "I thought that the need to gain a clear conscience would be the least of all my worries until I was involved in a course on Basic Youth Conflicts. I have never cheated on a test or a reading assignment—not since high school anyway. I lived a clean life, even through the teen years. Since age twelve, I have visualized myself in the ministry and have eagerly and conscientiously tried to know God's perfect will for my life. God has given me a perfectly wonderful wife, and we have made a happy adjustment in our married life.

• I WASN'T AWARE OF CONFLICTS WITH ANYONE . . .

". . . anyone, that is, except my mother. For ten years I have struggled to resolve my conflicts with her. I had come to the place where I had resigned myself to these conflicts and was trying to make the most of a bad situation. I told myself, 'This is just my 'thorn in the flesh,' I guess. Nothing I do will please my mother. I cannot do anything right. She doesn't seem to appreciate the fact that I am in the ministry. In fact, she has been very critical and cutting in some of her remarks.'

• MY LETTER OF APOLOGY DIDN'T WORK

"One time in Bible School I felt very convicted about the unhappiness that existed. I wrote a letter of apology, but it was mailed to my brothers and sisters to try to shame them into doing the same. This upset me very much. I felt that I had been wronged, that my apology had not been accepted.

"Mother came to all of my graduations and to my wedding. Each time, there was an unhappy scene, a furious verbal battle, and icy tension. Efforts to please her were misunderstood. All of these events had this dark cloud hovering somewhere on the horizon. I tried very hard to do the right thing—the Christ-like thing. Somehow I just couldn't avoid getting involved in an argument and saying things for which I was sorry. I kept asking myself why this was happening. How did I get involved? Why did I say what I did? When will I ever learn to keep quiet? Why do I always feel I have to justify myself?

• I HAD RESENTED MY MOTHER'S ADVICE

"My years in Bible School did not help to improve the situation. Mother had resisted my going to Bible School in the first place. She argued that I should get an education that would give me a job if I failed in the ministry. I resented her advice. I had received my call from God, and if I remained in God's will, there could be no such thing as failure.

NOTES

"All the circumstances that led in the direction of Bible School were clearly the leading of God. I announced that I would leave home immediately if she so desired. I was determined to go to Bible School, even if it meant that she would disown me. I remembered a missionary speaker who visited our church who said that she had to leave her home for the cause of Christ, never to return again. I could do it too! I was willing to pay any price to be in God's 'perfect will.'

"The Bible School counseling routine revolved around the usual concerns: the academic, the social, the spiritual and the financial. In my senior year I felt greatly depressed about my family relationship and about my failure in the letter of apology. One counseling dean advised me against going home that summer if I expected to continue my schooling.

• MY NERVOUS CONDITION WAS AT AN ALL-TIME LOW

"I could hardly drink a glass of water without spilling it. My shaking hands were a real embarrassment to me. A second dean advised me to get a job working with my hands for a year or so before continuing my schooling.

"However, a college did seem to be 'God's best' for me that fall. I spent the next three years in a small liberal arts college in a quiet midwestern town where my nervous condition improved greatly. I got involved in the program and activities of a local church and in the accepting atmosphere of that community of believers, I found myself in many ways.

"I dated occasionally but I was more concerned to get the most out of my studies. 'You come this way only once,' I reasoned.

"After completing my college work, I felt led to continue my education in seminary. A counseling course there did help me to increase my self-awareness. The concept of God's unconditional acceptance struck a responsive cord in my hungry heart.

"Following graduation from seminary, I felt led of God to accept the pastorate of a small city church. I joined a group of the local ministers in a weekly fellowship. In our first year together, we took a personality analysis test.

• I HAD REPRESSED MY RESENTMENT

"My first test revealed the following: 'You appear to nave repressed some of your deeper feelings and are thus consciously unaware of some of them. Your early environment undoubtedly contributed to this, and you need feel no sense of guilt or inadequacy. However, you should try to discover your deep inner feelings, for they are a most important part of you.'

"Subsequent tests also pointed to this problem of the 'deeper feelings.' The group discussion did help me to become aware and give voice to my frustration, but somehow the insight I needed to give me victory eluded my grasp.

NOTES

• MY SPIRITUAL AND EMOTIONAL STRENGTH WAS BEING DRAINED

"Throughout my ministerial preparation and in the ministers' fellowship, I tried to find a solution to the thing that was draining my spiritual and emotional strength. My tests told me, 'Your feelings and thinking are not working harmoniously.' My devotional and prayer life were at a stand-still. Through the years, I made a nuisance of myself with my friends by giving my detailed descriptions of my frustrations and unhappiness toward my family difficulties. They listened politely and felt sorry for me.

"Our ministers' fellowship elected to take a counseling research course led by the Rev. Bill Gothard. In the course, we discussed the way to resolve conflicts with members of our families. Several new concepts were presented.

CONSCIENCE

• I BEGAN TO SEE MY MOTHER AS A TOOL IN GOD'S HAND

"It was most helpful to picture each Christian as an uncut jewel and our parents as God's tools to chip off the rough edges so that the finest facets of the jewel may become visible. God knew I needed my family to chip off the rough edges of my personality.

"The idea that I needed to acknowledge to my mother that I had had the wrong attitude toward her and that I needed to ask her forgiveness for this was not an easy pill to swallow. My pride had blinded me to my own wrong. I had justified myself by feeling that my mother was 'mostly wrong.' The concept of God's 'chain-of-command' made sense, and it made me uncomfortable too!

• COULD I HONESTLY THANK GOD FOR MY MOTHER?

"I reflected on my bitterness and unforgiving attitude toward my mother. Could I honestly thank God for all that I resented in my mother? After all, I am not the only one who has trouble getting along with her. Desperately I tried to salvage some justification for my behavior toward my mother. Finally I surrendered and said, 'I thank Thee, Lord, please forgive my ingratitude.'

"Next came the bitterest pill of all. I must seek the forgiveness of my mother. How should I do it? What would I say? I had apologized before and it had failed. She was two thousand miles away. Should I make a phone call? That would be very expensive. One rationalization after another still left me without an honest answer. She would not accept my apology, I was sure of that.

• I BEGAN THE PAINFUL PROCESS OF ASKING FORGIVENESS

"That afternoon I shared some of my mother's recent letters with Bill in an attempt to identify the basic wrongs which I had committed against her. He could see in them some of the unhappiness she felt toward me and other members of my family. Very carefully we examined and identified the basic wrongs together. There was ingratitude, rejection of parental authority (violation of the chain of command), pride, disrespect and a failure to love as I ought. Here in a matter of two or three hours, my entire lifetime was opened up before me.

NOTES

"I could see that my first apology attempt did not hit the basic wrong. Then, too, my approach must reflect complete humility, free from any hint that 'I was wrong but you were too!' My heart was heavy for several days as I prayed and thought through the entire matter.

• I WORKED OUT WHAT I WAS GOING TO SAY . . .

". . . on paper (complete with pauses). Then I called my mother long distance. After itemizing each basic offense to Mother, I said, 'Mother, I was wrong, will you forgive me?' My mother was so surprised she hardly knew what to say. I was not sure that she understood, so I repeated the question, 'Will you forgive me?'

"To this day I can remember her saying, 'Yes.' However, after the phone call, I was still not completely at peace. What if she wrote to my brothers and sisters and told them? What would they think? Would they understand?

• ONE CALL LED TO SEVERAL MORE

"At our next ministers' meeting I shared my experience and my dilemma with Bill. We discussed the possible feelings of my brothers and sisters toward me. I could see now how my attitude toward my mother had hurt my testimony as a minister of Jesus Christ. I did not deserve their respect. All day long I wrestled with Bill's prescription—a series of phone calls!

"Wherein had I wronged them? Had I identified the basic wrong? Was my attitude right? Was the time right?

"I made the series of calls. When I talked to the brother who lived nearest my mother, I inquired about her welfare. His answer came as a thrilling report—

"'I don't know what you did; I have never seen her happier in her life. Usually I hear a constant flow of complaints about her health. All day Saturday while I was there, she never offered one complaint. She said you had asked her forgiveness. This was an answer to my prayer. You don't know what this means to me.'

"What a relief! I fully expected to receive a letter from Mother which reflected all the former unhappiness she felt for me. It was not unusual to receive ten and twelve-page letters within a couple of days after she had received a letter from me or talked to me. The ten-page letter did not come. In fact, it was two weeks before I heard from her at all. When she finally did write, her two-page letter was completely free from bitterness and unhappiness!

• THIS EXPERIENCE BECAME A NEW BEGINNING FOR ME

"All my brothers and sisters assured me of their forgiveness. My heart was and is overflowing with the joy akin to that of the new birth. I enjoy a new sense of God's presence, a new awareness of a clear conscience, a new capacity to love, and a new sense of purpose. I thank God for this new light that I have received."

NOTES

HOW TO GAIN A CLEAR CONSCIENCE

• There are several basic steps which must be followed in order to receive the forgiveness of the one who has been wronged. Here is a suggested check list:

1. LIST THOSE WHOM YOU HAVE OFFENDED

In making such a list, it is very helpful to use the assistance of two "mirrors"—the mirror of memory and the mirror of others' attitudes towards you. Behind each of these mirrors must be the mirror of God's Word. We are instructed not only to look into the mirror of the Word but to correct what we see is wrong. (James 1:23-25)

• LOOK INTO THE MIRROR OF MEMORY

Our memory is constructed in such a way that we tend to forget unpleasant events. Therefore, it is quite significant that we are not able to forget certain events involving wrongs which we have committed against others.

☐ **Have you stolen money or other items from stores, family members, neighbors, employers or others?**

☐ **Have you lied to anyone?** One lie which is not confessed can cause a person to mistrust you for the rest of your life.

☐ **Have you lost your temper with anyone?** Having anger can cause a deep wound in a friendship. You may have been justified in what you said but not in the way you said it.

☐ **Have you damaged the reputation of anyone? Have you engaged in gossip, back-biting, slander or other activities which have hurt another's reputation?** Slander is telling the truth with the intent of hurting another.

NOTES

- [ ] **Have you been ungrateful for what others have done for you?** Failing to show proper appreciation to those who have gone out of their way or made personal sacrifice to help you is certain to offend them.

- [ ] **Have you held a bitter spirit toward anyone? Has someone offended you, and instead of forgiving them, have you maintained a bitter spirit toward them?** When you pray the Lord's prayer, you are asking God to forgive you in the same way you have forgiven those who have wronged you.

- [ ] **Have you rebelled against or resisted the authority of those who are over you? Has your attitude or have your actions reflected a disrespect for the proper authority of parents, teachers, employers, law officials or others in authority?**

- [ ] **Have you had a prideful spirit? Have you conveyed the idea that you or your work is more important than that of those around you? Have you illustrated this with an argumentative spirit or a disinterest in ordinary people?**

- [ ] **Have you failed to give genuine love when others reacted to you? Did you respond back to them with a genuine desire to learn and meet their real needs, or did you react to them because they reacted to you?**

CONSCIENCE

• LOOK INTO THE MIRROR OF OTHERS' ATTITUDES TOWARD YOU

Whether we realize it or not, we are projecting attitudes to the people around us. These attitudes cause them to form an image of us. When people react to us or build walls against us, it is important for us to look at their reaction and see if they are mirroring back to us the wrong attitudes which we have had toward them.

- [ ] **Do my parents have the attitude that since I am my own boss, they will let me do what I want?**

- [ ] **Do they observe a lack of gratefulness for all they have done for me?**

- [ ] **Do my brothers and sisters avoid me because they feel I don't need them, and that they are only a bother to my life? Do they feel I am sincerely interested in making them successful?**

- [ ] **Do my neighbors have the feeling that I am too busy for them and am not interested in the problems they are facing?**

- [ ] **Does my employer feel that my heart is not really in the work I am doing, and that I am really there for my benefit rather than helping him reach his goals?**

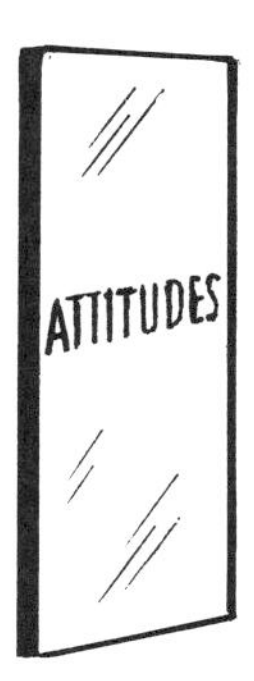

NOTES

2. LIST YOUR OFFENSES IN ORDER OF IMPORTANCE

• It is very important to ask forgiveness first of those who have been offended most. If this is not done, it is possible to attach an exaggerated sense of guilt to trivial offenses.

• This problem of exaggerated guilt was illustrated to me one day when two eighth graders came running up to tell me something. One proudly announced, "I have 78 people I have to go back to and ask forgiveness." The second then spoke up, "I have 65 to go back to!"

Both their carefree attitudes and the large number of people they felt they had offended sounded warning notes to me. I happened to know that the first eighth grader had an intense hatred toward her mother, so I inquired, "Did you list your mother among the 78 from whom you plan to ask forgiveness?"

She quickly and firmly responded, "I sure didn't! I'll never forgive her!"

The guilt she had for her mother was transferred to the many other trivial offenses and resulted in a sense of exaggerated guilt for these.

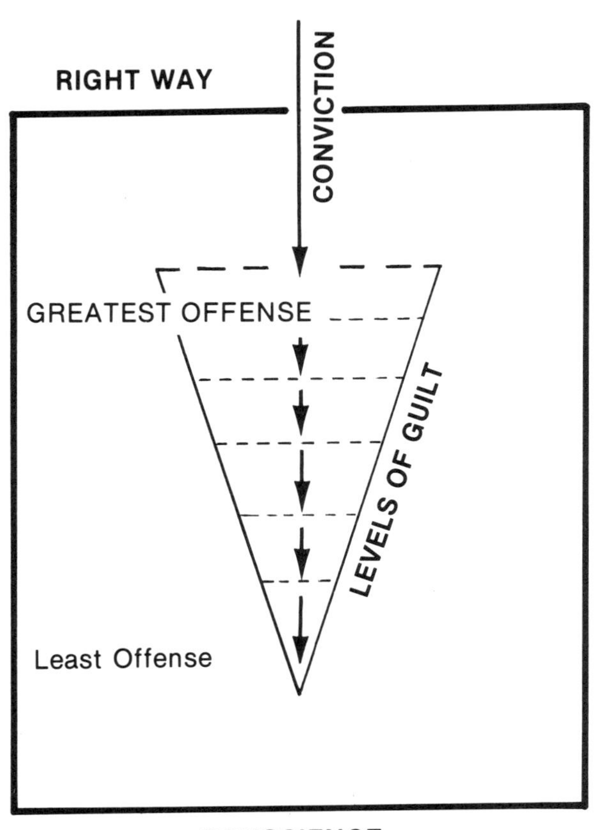

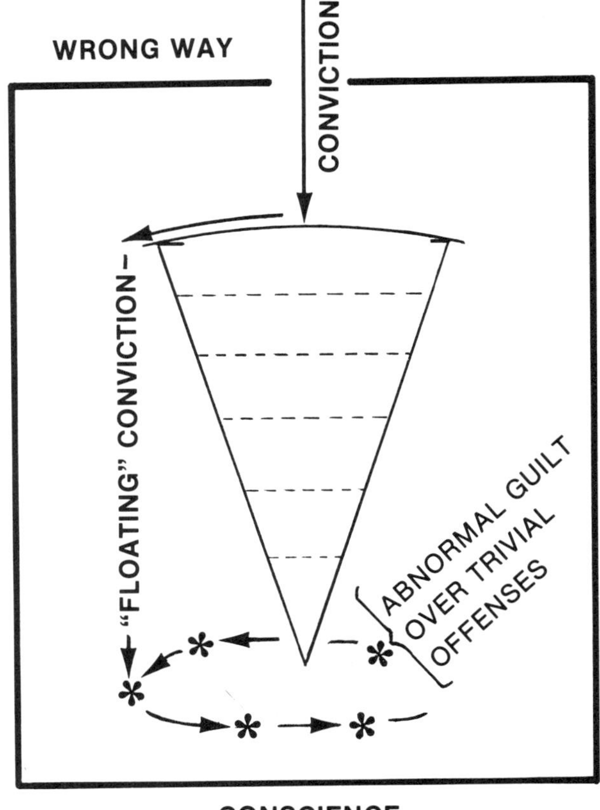

NOTES

3. CAREFULLY CHOOSE THE RIGHT WORDING

• When the prodigal son purposed to return home and ask for his father's forgiveness, he carefully worked out what he was going to say, and when he met his father, he repeated what he had planned to say, word for word. (Luke 15:17-19 and 21)

We must think through the words we are going to use in asking for forgiveness, and we must be sure they reflect the following insights and attitudes:

A. YOUR WORDS MUST IDENTIFY THE BASIC OFFENSE

Many people ask for forgiveness and never receive it because they do not see how they have deeply hurt the one from whom they are asking forgiveness. To help you identify the basic offense, put yourself in the other person's place and relive the offense—through his eyes and feelings. Think of all the harm and hurt and disappointment your offense has caused him. Let your offenses break your heart. Neither God nor men despise a broken heart. (Psalm 51:17. See also James 4:8,10)

The basic offense usually involves an underlying attitude such as ungratefulness, disrespect, dishonesty, self-centeredness, pride, laziness, etc. Specific actions will result from these basic attitudes.

For example, a son may be habitually lazy and ungrateful. One day his mother or father may "erupt" over a certain chore which he neglected to finish. It will do little good for him to only ask forgiveness for not finishing the chore. In fact, if he does ask for their forgiveness regarding only this, they probably won't be inclined to forgive him since his wrong attitudes of laziness and ingratitude must first be confessed and corrected.

B. YOUR WORDS MUST REFLECT FULL REPENTANCE AND SINCERE HUMILITY

Just as soon as you purpose to acknowledge where you have been wrong and to ask forgiveness, you can be sure that pride will attempt to come to your "rescue." Pride tries to assure you that you weren't really so bad and that they were wrong too.

• These prideful attitudes will manifest themselves in statements such as the following:

NOTES

EXAMPLES OF WRONG WORDING

- **"I WAS WRONG, BUT YOU WERE TOO."**

I list this because, strange to say, it is actually used by many people. One teen-ager used it when trying to gain forgiveness from his parents. The statement not only reflected pride but also a basic bitterness toward his parents. This was actually the basic offense. Rather than receiving forgiveness, he was "grounded" for two weeks!

- **"I'M SORRY ABOUT IT, BUT IT WASN'T ALL MY FAULT."**

This statement is only one step better than the preceding one. It does not blame the person, but neither does it accept much responsibility for what happened. The person who makes this statement has failed to cover the step of looking into the two mirrors.

- **"I'M SORRY."**

Several teen-agers have told me they used this to try to gain forgiveness, and the response of the other person was an angry, "Well, I'm sorry too!"

The person asking forgiveness does not specify in this statement what his offense is, which is an essential part of gaining a clear conscience. A variation of this unsuccessful approach is, "I APOLOGIZE."

- **"IF I'VE BEEN WRONG, PLEASE FORGIVE ME."**

This is most people's favorite! It is really saying,

"If my personality (for which I'm not responsible) has offended you, there must be something wrong with your ability to get along with others. But I'll be big-hearted about this and assume that maybe it's my fault (which I'm not fully convinced it is) and ask you to forgive me—if you still think I'm wrong, that is."

One teen-ager tried this approach after an argument with several friends. His friends sensed the pride in this approach and responded by saying, "You tell us where you were wrong, and we'll forgive you."

He then said, "I'm not sure where I was wrong, but if I was, will you forgive me?"

Their answer was the same, "You tell us where you were wrong, and we'll forgive you."

NOTES

• **"I'M SORRY ABOUT THE WAY I LIED TO YOU, PLEASE FORGIVE ME."**

This approach still reflects areas of pride. One of the hardest statements for any person to make is, "I was wrong." It is a lot easier to say, "I'm sorry about . . " It is also much easier to say, "Please forgive me" than it is to ask, "Will you forgive me?" and wait for the answer.

CONSCIENCE

EXAMPLES OF RIGHT WORDING

"GOD HAS CONVICTED ME OF HOW WRONG I'VE BEEN IN ________ (BASIC OFFENSE). I'VE CALLED TO ASK WILL YOU FORGIVE ME?"

This request, spoken in the right attitude, is certain to be well-accepted by the one to whom it is directed. This approach must include correction of any attitudes or actions which caused the offense and also restitution for any personal loss which was suffered by the one offended.

4. DETERMINE THE PROPER TIME AND METHOD TO ASK FORGIVENESS

• The importance of actually going to the offended person to ask for his forgiveness is emphasized in Matthew 5:23 and 24, "Therefore, if thou bring thy gift to the altar, and there rememberest that thy brother hath ought against thee; leave there thy gift before the altar, and go thy way; first be reconciled to thy brother, and then come and offer thy gift."

Jesus Christ trained his disciples to go back to the ones they offended to ask for forgiveness and also to forgive those who offended them. When Peter thought that some were taking advantage of this arrangement, Jesus emphasized, "And if he trespass against thee seven times in a day, and seven times in a day turn again to thee, saying, I repent; thou shalt forgive him." (Luke 17:4)

Notice that each time the offender must return to the one he offended and ask for forgiveness. In going back, it is important to consider the following:

NOTES

A. WHAT IS THE BEST METHOD OF APPROACH?

☐ A PHONE CALL is usually the best method of asking a person to forgive you—especially when asking forgiveness for past moral offenses or trying to contact someone who is no longer near you. The phone provides privacy and allows you to get right to the point.

☐ A PERSONAL VISIT is another acceptable method of asking for forgiveness. In some cases it may be even more appropriate than making a phone call.

[No] A LETTER—Please don't write a letter. Most people are tempted to use this method because it is so easy and the least painful to their pride. But it is not effective for many reasons. First, it documents your past offenses and your purpose is to erase them. Second, a letter can be misused by the one receiving it. This only complicates the problem. Third, it often embarrasses the one receiving it, and they may never reply to it. Fourth, a letter doesn't allow you to gain their verbal assurance of forgiveness. That is a very important factor for you and for the one you have offended. A verbal forgiveness allows him to become free of his bitterness.

CONSCIENCE

B. IS THIS A CONVENIENT TIME FOR THE OTHER PERSON?

If you wanted to ask forgiveness of a neighbor woman, you probably should not go during the dinner hour when she is busy preparing the meal for her family. Go at a time when you are relatively sure the person is able to see you. If you are not sure of such a time, make a phone call to arrange an appointment.

C. IS IT A TIME WHEN YOU WOULD BE UNINTERRUPTED?

In most cases, it is best to be alone with the person when you are asking for forgiveness, otherwise, you may cause him embarrassment. If there are others around at the time, just ask if you could see the person alone for a minute. If you are at his home, you could step into another room or outside to the porch.

D. WOULD HE BE IN THE PROPER MOOD TO GRANT FORGIVENESS?

If something has just happened through your fault and as a result the tempers of the ones you wronged are out of control, this would be a poor time to ask forgiveness.

In such a situation, show a silent sorrow and repentance. When tempers are back to normal, ask forgiveness.

Make a determined effort to go to a person when he is in the best possible mood to forgive you. This may include an evaluation of the best time of day or the best day of the week. For example, a call after the dinner hour would be better than a call before or during the dinner hour.

NOTES

SPECIAL CAUTIONS IN ASKING FORGIVENESS

CONSCIENCE

1. CONFESS ONLY TO THOSE OFFENDED

• If a sin is committed against God, then confession should be made to God alone.

If a sin is committed against God and also involves another person, then confession should be made to God and to the other person.

If a sin is committed against God and also involves a group, then confession should be made to both God and to the group.

It is both inappropriate and potentially harmful to extend the confession to persons outside the "circle of offense."

2. CLEAR GREATEST OFFENSES FIRST

• We have a dangerous tendency to take care of minor offenses before we take care of major offenses. Invariably this produces a "floating guilt" which then becomes attached to trivial offenses and produces an abnormal sense of guilt. Guilt is a destructive force to our entire mental, emotional and spiritual being. It was designed to guide and motivate us in keeping "short accounts" with God and with others.

The longer this guilt exists, the more destructive it becomes. For this reason, a major problem is created when we have allowed guilt from a major unconfessed offense to be transferred to lesser offenses.

• When guilt from a greater offense is attached to a lesser offense, confession does not bring a sense of full forgiveness.

3. AVOID GIVING SENSUAL DETAILS

• David's prayer of confession in Psalm 51 is an excellent example of identifying the basic offense and avoiding sordid details. This principle is also illustrated in the confession of the prodigal son when he asked for forgiveness for the shameful life he had been living. (Luke 15: 17-21)

In Scripture we are warned that, "It is a shame even to speak of those things which are done of them in secret." (Ephesians 5:12) This warning definitely applies when asking for forgiveness. It is neither important nor appropriate to review impure details of an offense. This only tends to stir up the mind of the hearer to the past.

NOTES

IDENTIFYING BASIC OFFENSES

• The following examples illustrate the importance of identifying the basic offense.

CONSCIENCE

ACTUAL OFFENSE	WRONG CONFESSION	RIGHT CONFESSION
Bitter attitudes toward a person for damaging your reputation	"Please forgive me for being bitter toward you." (Implies blame for causing the bitterness)	"God has convicted me of how wrong I have been toward you in not showing you the love that I should have. Would you please forgive me?"
Refusing to obey parents or employer	"I realize I was wrong in arguing with you yesterday. Will you forgive me?"	"I realize that I have been wrong in my attitude of pride and in not responding to your authority. My arguing with you yesterday revealed these wrong attitudes to me and to you. Will you forgive me?"
Complaining about your mother's cooking	"I realize I was wrong in complaining about your cooking. Will you forgive me?"	"I realize I've been wrong in my attitude of ungratefulness for all the things you've done for me. Will you forgive me?"
Behaving improperly on a date	"I realize that I was wrong in necking with you on our date. Will you forgive me?"	"I realize that I have been wrong in my selfish actions and attitudes toward you when we were dating. It would mean a great deal to me if you would forgive me. Would you forgive me?"

NOTES

4. EXPECT POSSIBLE REJECTION OF YOUR REQUEST

The one you ask for forgiveness may have a balance of guilt and blame.

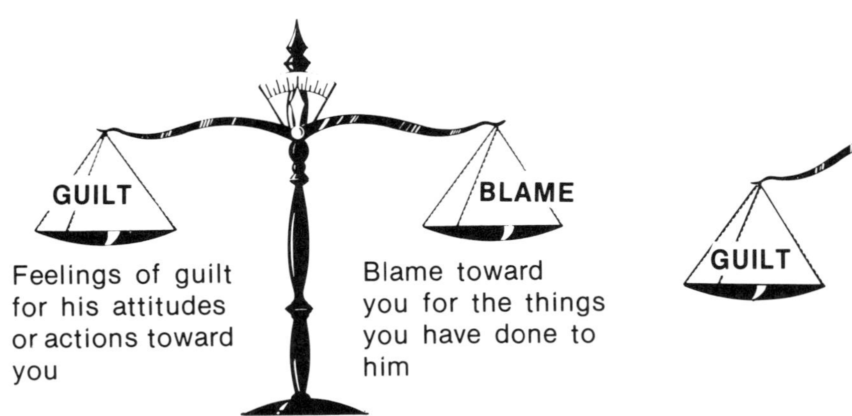

AFTER you ask for his forgiveness you upset the balance of guilt and blame within his mind and emotions.

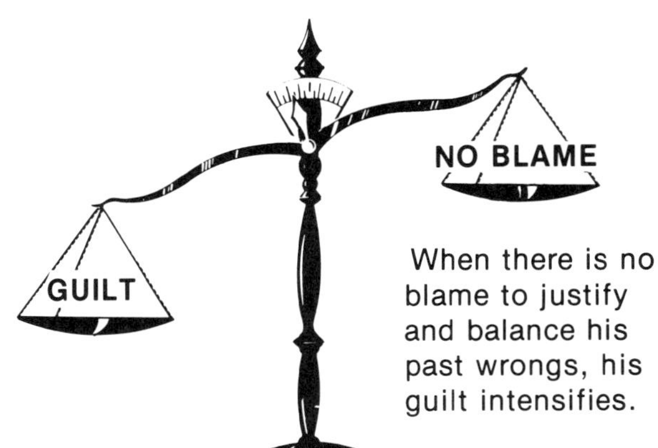

• The above situation explains why the one you ask to forgive you may instinctively tend to withhold his forgiveness until and unless he sees that you are fully repenting for what you have done to him. This also explains why the one you ask to forgive you may also at the same time ask you to forgive him for things he has done or said against you.

5. BE AS BRIEF AND CLEAR AS POSSIBLE

• There is a major danger in talking too much while trying to ask for forgiveness. Therefore, be as brief and as clear as possibie. The more you say, the greater the danger will be that you will say something wrong. It is all too easy to involve matters which are not pertinent to the main subject.

Talking too much will not only "sidetrack" the whole purpose of your coming, but may give the impression that you are trying to justify or explain your offenses in order to minimize them. Often this leads directly to arguments.

6. DON'T INVOLVE OTHERS IN YOUR CONFESSION

• Before asking for forgiveness, focus on what you are fully responsible for.

If there is an attempt to minimize your offense by making a full explanation of all the circumstances surrounding it, it will be very difficult to avoid implicating others.

NOTES

7. CLEAR YOUR CONSCIENCE QUICKLY

• There is a danger in waiting too long before asking forgiveness. During this wait, you will tend to decrease the magnitude of your offenses and the one you have offended will tend to increase their magnitude. This will make it all the more difficult to gain forgiveness.

A dangerous lapse of time in asking for forgiveness will usually come when you decide to "fit it in" to your schedule or in your next visit with the person. Gaining a clear conscience is a project in itself and demands your special time and attention. Do not wait for opportunities to come to you. Make your own opportunity at the appropriate time.

A further obvious danger in waiting too long is the tendency to decide not to ask for forgiveness after all.

8. WAIT FOR GOD'S TIMING TO WITNESS

• Unless the other person asks specific questions about your faith or salvation, don't try to combine witnessing with asking for forgiveness. Your act of confession and restitution is witness enough at this point. You can also be sure that he will be watching your life and listening to all of your words more closely in the days ahead. Further opportunities to witness will usually be provided in the future as changes are observed in your life.

SPECIAL SITUATIONS

• No doubt special situations will arise which are not discussed in the preceding material. Here are a few:

• WHAT IF I REALLY CAN'T LOCATE THE ONE I'VE OFFENDED?

A high schooler explained that about seven years previously he had stolen some tools from a neighbor. Now he wanted to make restitution so he could gain a clear conscience. The family had moved and left no forwarding address, and no one seemed to know where they were.

I suggested that he commit the problem to the Lord and reaffirm his desire to make it right if and when he ever located the family. The very next day an unexpected visitor came to his home. It was this neighbor whom he hadn't seen for over seven years!

A book could now be written of similar illustrations. The amazing stories of so many illustrate a basic principle in restitution. God is far more concerned that we gain a perfectly clear conscience than we could ever be. Thus He is able and willing to work out many unusual opportunities for us—if we are totally set upon obedience to Him.

NOTES

- **WHAT IF THE PERSON I WRONGED HAS DIED?**

Such a problem occurred in the life of David. The principle he followed was to go to the nearest relative and make restitution since his offense also affected and offended him. An offense is rarely confined to just one person.

On the other hand, there are situations in which the only ones who were involved in an offense have died. Many who have faced this problem have discovered a full freedom from guilt by confessing the offense to God in the presence of a mature Christian and claiming God's forgiveness which is assured in Scripture (I John 1:9). James advises us to "confess your faults one to another, and pray one for another, that ye may be healed." (James 5:16)

CONSCIENCE

- **WHAT IF I COMMIT THE SAME OFFENSE AGAIN?**

Then you must go back and ask forgiveness again. At this point, it is significant to re-emphasize that this practice of acknowledging guilt and of asking forgiveness was a basic principle of Christ's teaching and was constantly emphasized by Him.

No doubt some well-meaning but self-willed individual was constantly offending Peter and then asking his forgiveness. Probably about the fifth or sixth time, Peter came to Jesus and asked, "Lord, how many times must I forgive my brother; seven times?" The well-known answer of Jesus certainly validates all that has been emphasized on this subject, "Nay, but I say unto you seventy times seven."

This continual relationship among the disciples accounted for the fact that they could enjoy such a presence of the Holy Spirit and also be in one accord. Jesus in His very first message to the disciples laid down the stern proposition, "If you forgive not men their trespasses, neither will your heavenly Father forgive your trespasses." (Matthew 6:15)

- The practical value of this principle was recently illustrated in the life of a college student. For many years and on countless occasions, he had stolen. In fact, he admitted that he just couldn't stop stealing.

The importance of a clear conscience was given to him as the initial step in not only solving his problem but in becoming a successful Christian—which he wanted to be.

He made a long list of the items he had stolen and the people to whom he would have to go to make restitution. He listed them in order of importance, accepted this project, and began to make the entire slate clean, one by one.

The following week at work, he saw a pair of expensive sunglasses which were just the type he was looking for. This was his first encounter with temptation since purposing to gain a clear conscience. During the inner struggle which followed, he reasoned that if he took the glasses, he would only have to add them to his already too long list and go through the painful process of returning them to his employer and telling him what he had done.

NOTES

• WHAT IF A PERSON WON'T FORGIVE ME?

If you have been sincere in your repentance, and if you have identified the basic offense, and if your request for forgiveness has reflected genuine humility, it is indeed rare to have him not forgive you. If such a case should occur, you must then prove to him by a changed life and attitude that you really were sincere. Allow the Holy Spirit to convict him through your good works toward him. (Romans 12:20,21. See also I Peter 2:12)

• WHAT IF MY PARENTS WON'T LET ME ASK FORGIVENESS?

In such cases, it may be that the Lord is using the parents' resistance to cause the teen-ager to re-examine his motives and methods of gaining a clear conscience. If, after rethinking these, his parents still object to his asking forgiveness, the principle mentioned in Numbers 30:3 and 5 must be applied:

> "If a woman also vow a vow unto the Lord, and bind herself by a bond, being in her father's house in her youth; . . . if her father disallow her in the day that he heareth; not any of her vows . . . shall stand . . ."

The principle of God's chain-of-command is clearly emphasized in these verses and must be followed by the teen-ager. God's responsibility will be to reveal new insights to the teen-ager or to his parents in regard to his asking for forgiveness.

• WHAT IF I DON'T FEEL SORRY FOR WHAT I'VE DONE?

It is quite natural to lack repentance when we feel the other person is partly at fault. We have a tendency to magnify his fault and to minimize ours. Therefore, our first requirement is to honestly list the things he has done and to fully forgive him. If we do not feel inclined to do this, we should cover the next step first.

Review in detail the wrongs we have done. Our mind and emotions are constructed in such a way that we cannot say, "I will feel repentant" and expect feelings of repentance to arise. But if we would take the time to rethink all the details of the wrongs we have committed and their many consequences, then the emotions of repentance would be a natural by-product.

• An essential preparation to asking for forgiveness is to relive our offenses through the eyes and emotions of the person we offended.

NOTES

• THE BASIC FACTORS INVOLVED IN WORRY AND ANGER

PERSONAL RIGHTS

- TURNING BITTERNESS TO FORGIVENESS
- TRANSFORMING SOURCES OF IRRITATIONS
- YIELDING PERSONAL RIGHTS

• In order to have the mind of Christ as stated in Philippians 2:5 and enjoy the freedom and peace that results, we must learn the secret of dealing with our rights and expectations. The following pages describe what is involved.

NOTES

6 BASIC ASPECTS OF FORGIVENESS

• Forgiveness deals with our emotional response toward an offender. Pardon deals with the consequences of his offense. Unless we have the authority we may not be able to pardon an offense, but we can always forgive.
• Forgiving a person is "clearing his record" with us and transferring the responsibility for any punishment to God. Forgiveness will make it possible for us to have the same openness toward him after he offends us as we had before he offended us.
• The following insights assist us in looking at forgiveness from God's point of view:

RIGHTS

1. FORGIVENESS INVOLVES A POSITIVE ATTITUDE TOWARD THE OFFENSE RATHER THAN A NEGATIVE ATTITUDE TOWARD THE OFFENDER

If our initial focus after being offended is on the offender, it is difficult not to become bitter. But if we first focus on the offense and forget for the moment who offended us, we are much better able to look at the offense as a significant aspect of our personal character development. Our proper attitudes as a result of the offense become the important concern. By using this approach, both the offender and the offense fade into insignificance and our response to the offense becomes the major concern.

2. FORGIVENESS VIEWS THE OFFENDER AS AN "INSTRUMENT" IN GOD'S HAND

In the final analysis, it is God who uses even the "wrath of man to praise Him." Psalm 76:10 King David could have become very bitter toward the vile, hateful person who tried to humiliate him by publicly accusing him and cursing him. Instead, he viewed him simply as an agent of a higher power. He said, "The Lord hath bidden him (to curse me)." II Samuel 16:11

Jesus Christ could have become bitter toward those who beat Him and nailed Him to the cross, but He looked at them as carrying out the purpose of God for His life. Because of this, He was able to say, "Father, forgive them; for they know not what they do." Luke 23:34

3. FORGIVENESS LOOKS AT THE WOUNDS OF THE OFFENSE AS GOD'S WAY OF DRAWING ATTENTION TO THE OFFENDER'S NEEDS

When the girl possessed of the devil continually disrupted Paul's meetings, he could have become bitter at her disturbances. Her offenses toward his ministry, however, caused him to become keenly aware of her spiritual needs and as a result he healed her. Acts 16:16-18

NOTES

4. FORGIVENESS RECOGNIZES THAT BITTERNESS IS ASSUMING A RIGHT WE DON'T HAVE

Only God has the right to punish. "Vengeance is mine; I will repay, saith the Lord." Romans 12:19 A response of bitterness is an instinctive means of revenge toward the one who has offended us. Most of us are prone to use silence toward the offender as a means of punishing that person. (See also Romans 12:17-20)

5. FORGIVENESS REALIZES THAT THE OFFENDER HAS ALREADY BEGUN RECEIVING THE CONSEQUENCES OF HIS OFFENSES

A person's happiness is dependent upon his harmony with God and others. An offense toward us simply indicates that he is violating one or more principles and these violations will have a deep effect upon his own happiness and success. If he has wronged us, we can be sure that he is insensitive toward others around him and will suffer from conflicts with them as well.

The reproofs of conscience, friends, circumstances, etc. are sufficient tools of God to emphasize to him his offenses. When he recognizes the seriousness of his offenses, he will not give us the privilege of helping him if we have not reflected a loving spirit toward him through our attitudes.

RIGHTS

6. FORGIVENESS INVOLVES COOPERATING WITH GOD IN THE OFFENDER'S LIFE

When someone intentionally offends us, we can be sure that he is going to be fully aware of our responses to him. In this case, we have a significant opportunity to demonstrate the potential forgiveness of God to him. As he sees our openness and love to him, he will be able to comprehend the same openness and love that God has toward him, in spite of his offenses toward God.

When someone unintentionally offends us, it indicates that the offender has personal deficiencies which he may not be aware of. In this case, our continued openness toward him may provide the opportunity to be of personal help to him in the areas revealed by his offenses.

The reward of meeting his needs will be a spirit of joy in us as we see him sharing with others the same attitudes he saw in us when we properly responded to his offenses.

- Forgiveness is having a greater concern for a person after he offends me than I did before he offended me. It is using the hurts of others as the basis of demonstrating Christ's love back to them.

NOTES

VIEWING FORGIVENESS FROM GOD'S PERSPECTIVE

- **OUR PERSPECTIVE WHEN OFFENDED**

"Lord, how often shall my brother sin against me and I forgive him? till seven times?" Matthew 18:21

Notice that the focus of Peter's mind was retaliation. It was only a question of how long he had to wait before gaining revenge.

- **GOD'S BIGGER PERSPECTIVE**

"Jesus saith unto him, I say not unto thee, until seven times: but, until seventy times seven.

"Therefore is the kingdom of heaven likened unto a certain king, which would take account of his servants. And when he had begun to reckon, one was brought unto him, which owed him ten thousand talents. But forasmuch as he had not to pay, his lord commanded him to be sold, and his wife, and children, and all that he had, and payment to be made.

A man so hopelessly in debt would have no ability to pay this debt just as we have no ability to repay God for what it cost Him to redeem us with the blood of Jesus Christ.

"The servant therefore fell down, and worshipped him, saying,Lord, have patience with me and I will pay thee all. Then the lord of that servant was moved with compassion, and loosed him and forgave him the debt.

This man is not yet willing to admit that he can't pay back what he owes.

"But the same servant went out, and found one of his fellowservants which owed him an hundred pence: and he laid hands on him, and took him by the throat, saying, Pay me that thou owest.

"And his fellowservant fell down at his feet, and besought him, saying, Have patience with me and I will pay thee all. And he would not: but went and cast him into prison, till he should pay the debt.

It is quite possible that this fellow was motivated by the desire to get a reserve of money so he would never again have to bear the humility of poverty. Yet this is the quality of heart God wants each of us to have throughout life. "Blessed are the poor in spirit..." (Matthew 5:3)

"So when his fellowservants saw what was done they were very sorry, and came and told unto their lord all that was done. Then his lord, after that he had called him, said unto him:

> **"O thou wicked servant, I forgave thee all that debt, because thou desiredst me: shouldest not thou also have had compassion on thy fellowservant even as I had pity on thee?**

"And his lord was wroth, and delivered him to the tormentors, till he should pay all that was due unto him. So likewise shall my heavenly Father do also unto you, if ye from the hearts forgive not every one his brother their trespasses." Matthew 18:22-35

- **You must "forgive one another even as God for Christ's sake has forgiven you." Ephesians 4:32**

NOTES

THE CONSEQUENCES OF BITTERNESS

• When Jesus said, "Forgive seventy times seven," He was keenly aware of the mental, emotional, physical and spiritual consequences of brooding over resentments.

A. PHYSICAL CONSEQUENCES

• CHEMICAL BALANCE Ulcerative colitis, toxic goiters, high blood pressure are only a few of the scores of diseases caused by bitterness. Our resentments call forth certain hormones from the pituitary, adrenal, thyroid and other glands. Excesses of these hormones can cause diseases in any part of the body. (See None of These Diseases, S. I. McMillen, Spire Books, 1968, pp. 69-72.)

• FACIAL FEATURES Refusing to forgive results in physical fatigue and loss of sleep. We may try to hide our resentments, but soon they will also be etched into our eyes and facial muscles as permanent reflections of our inward feelings.

• BONE HEALTH The life of the flesh is in the blood.(Leviticus 17:11) But the "factory" for the blood is the marrow of our bones. The health of our bones, therefore, determines the health of our body. Bitterness has a direct and devastating effect upon our bones. For a study of this see: Psalm 32:3; Proverbs 15:30; Proverbs 17:22; Proverbs 14:30; Proverbs 12:4; Ezekiel 32:27.

B. SPIRITUAL CONSEQUENCES

• **An inability to love God** is the immediate result of hating another person. "If a man say, I love God, and hateth his brother, he is a liar: for he that loveth not his brother whom he hath seen, how can he love God whom he hath not seen? And this commandment have we from him, that he who loveth God love his brother also." (I John 4:20,21)

• **Doubts regarding our relationship with God** commonly accompany bitterness. This is quite natural since most of us have at some time repeated the Lord's prayer in which we pray, "Forgive us our trespasses as (in the same way) we forgive those who trespass against us." (Matthew 6:12)

Hence, if we refuse to forgive other people, we are actually asking God not to forgive us. The significance of this point is emphasized by Jesus Christ, "For if ye forgive men their trespasses, your heavenly Father will also forgive you: But if ye forgive not men their trespresses, neither will your Father forgive your trespasses." (Matthew 6:14,15)

• **Major hindrances to the spiritual development** of others may result when we refuse to forgive—especially if we claim to be in a right fellowship with God. Our attitudes of bitterness will repel them from whatever it is that we are trying to convince them of. If we are to allow Christ to live in us we must allow Him to forgive through us.

NOTES

C. EMOTIONAL CONSEQUENCES

Depression is one of the most significant consequences of refusing to forgive the people who wrong us. It requires emotional energy to maintain a grudge. Just as we become weary when our physical energy is exhausted, so we become depressed when our emotional energy is exhausted.

Bitterness and resentment create an "emotional focus" toward the person who offended us. This focus is the chief cause of becoming just like the one we resent. The more we focus on his actions toward us, the more we resemble the basic attitudes which prompted his actions.

D. MENTAL CONSEQUENCES

A medical doctor illustrates the mental consequences of holding resentments with this description:

"The moment I start hating a man, I become his slave. I can't enjoy my work any more because he controls my thoughts. My resentments produce too many stress hormones in my body, and I become fatigued after only a few hours of work. The work I formerly enjoyed is now drudgery. Even vacations cease to give me pleasure. . .I can't escape his tyrannical grasp on my mind.

"When the waiter serves me porterhouse steak, it might as well be stale bread and water. My teeth chew the food, and I swallow it, but the man I hate will not permit me to enjoy its taste." (McMillen, p. 72)

It is for this reason that Solomon wrote, "Better is a dinner of herbs where love is, than a stalled ox and hatred therewith." (Proverbs 15:17)

E. MULTIPLYING THE CONSEQUENCES OF BITTERNESS

Bitterness is all too easily passed on from one generation to another, thus affecting hundreds of descendants. The sins of the parents are visited to the third and fourth generations of those who hold hatred in their heart. (Deuteronomy 5:9) Notice how this relates to discipline in the following illustration.

FIRST GENERATION	Bitterness toward parents for their strict discipline	**PROMPTS**	Leniency and inconsistency in disciplining their children
SECOND GENERATION	Bitterness toward parents for their leniency—feeling they don't care	**PROMPTS**	Strictness and inconsistency in disciplining their children
THIRD GENERATION	Bitterness toward parents for their strict discipline	**PROMPTS**	Leniency and inconsistency in disciplining their children
FOURTH GENERATION	Bitterness toward parents for their leniency—feeling they don't care about them	**PROMPTS**	Strictness and inconsistency in disciplining their children

NOTES

• A SEQUENCE OF BITTERNESS TO THE THIRD AND FOURTH GENERATION

The mother of two teen-agers sensed that there was a wall between her and her daughters. They rarely confided in her and became quite bitter whenever she would try to discipline them, even when they were clearly in the wrong.

She knew of only one problem on her part which may have caused this - she tended to overcorrect them. One day she asked, "Why am I so strict with my daughters? I find myself constantly being too sharp with them, and I know this has been going on for quite a few years." The following two questions pinpointed part of the problem:

"Did you get married with your parents' full approval?"

"Did they predict that your marriage would not be very successful?"

She was surprised to hear these questions and even more surprised to see how her past lack of forgiveness and bitterness toward her parents affected her discipline of her children. The following sequence began with her parents:

• FIRST GENERATION (HER PARENTS)

There were conflicts, bitterness, arguments and lack of discipline in family habits. These factors had already isolated the grandparents from their parents; and when the children saw these habits and inconsistencies, their respect and desire for counsel from them was shattered.

Discipline was irregular and inconsistent. The daughter resented all that her parents stood for and refused to heed their advice in regard to her marriage. The parents not only disapproved of her marriage but repeatedly warned her that her marriage would not be successful.

She purposed that it would be, and thus a contest was established which would have devastating effects for generations to come.

• SECOND GENERATION (HERSELF)

The daughter left her parents physically but not emotionally. She was not free in her marriage because that "contest" had been declared. She was out to prove her marriage would be successful. She pictured her parents sitting back, waiting to say, "We told you so!"

As the normal adjustments in marriage occurred, she kept imagining what her mother would say and thus kept many problems to herself. When her children were born, she saw this as a new means of winning her point. "After all, it takes successful parents to raise successful children " she reasoned.

This pressure of proving her point and the fact that her reputation was involved with the behavior and performance of her children caused her to be overcritical of them. She was not free to respond objectively in discipline. Always in the back of her mind was the question, "What would my parents think if they knew this?"

Consequently, she overcorrected her children, even into their teen-age years.

NOTES

• THIRD GENERATION (HER DAUGHTERS)

The teen-age daughters felt that the rules were too strict and that there was not enough freedom. This attitude paved the way for them to develop unwise friendships outside the home and to confide less and less in their mother. At ages sixteen and eighteen, each of them was secretly engaged to fellows who were unacceptable to the mother.

They had bitterness toward their mother for overcorrection and for not understanding them and were quite willing to enter into marriages which were unacceptable to her with the confidence that they would be successful.

The mother warned them that it would not work out and tried to use her own experience as proof. This only re-established the contest more keenly in the minds of the daughters. They felt they could see why their mother's marriage didn't work out; and they were sure this would not happen to them, especially since they "really loved each other" and they could see their parents hadn't loved each other.

• FOURTH GENERATION (GRANDCHILDREN)

The attitudes of the grandchildren would become identical to those of their parents unless the chain of bitterness was broken.

Note: The mother did break this chain of bitterness by following the steps of action explained in the material - Gaining a Clear Conscience.

• THE POWER OF BITTERNESS TO CHANGE US

When a teen-ager expressed deep bitterness toward a relative; and when it was suggested that this relative be forgiven, the teen-ager exclaimed, "I'LL NEVER FORGIVE THAT RELATIVE AS LONG AS I LIVE!!"

In a casual way, I commented, "That's too bad."

"Why is that too bad?" she asked, "and why do you say it that way?"

"Because within twenty years you're going to be just like that relative."

This thought so shocked and horrified the teen-ager that the immediate response was, "Oh no! Then I'll forgive her!!!"

"On second thought, however," that teen-ager questioned, "How can you prove to me that I'll become just like her?"

THE FOLLOWING ILLUSTRATIONS WERE USED

NOTES

BEING CONFORMED TO OUR FOCUS

• **RIGHT EMOTIONAL FOCUS**

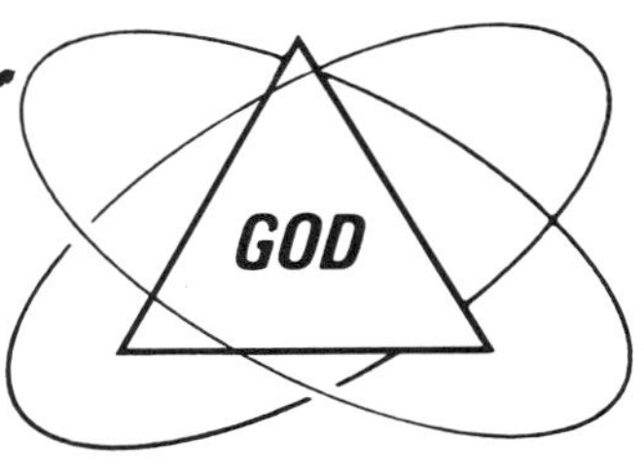

CONFORMITY

Concentrating on Christ and His Word and allowing His Spirit to produce basic change in us. (II Corinthians 3:18)

CONCENTRATION

Strengthening our emotional focus toward God by comparing His actions and attitudes with our actions and attitudes.

CONVERSION

Being born again by the Spirit of God through faith in Jesus Christ. (John 3:3)

• The ultimate purpose of "the first and greatest commandment" is to establish our full concentration and conformity to Christ. "...thou shalt love the Lord thy God with all thy heart and with all thy soul, and with all thy mind, and with all thy strength." (Mark 12:30)

• **WRONG EMOTIONAL FOCUS**

CONTEMPT

Reacting to the offenses of the person who hurts us.

CONCENTRATION

Strengthening a wrong emotional focus toward him by continually reviewing his offensive actions.

CONFORMITY

Developing similar basic attitudes as the one resented in our attempt not to reproduce his actions.

• The moment we react to a person, we begin measuring ourselves by his actions. This unwise action produces attitudes of pride, selfishness and bitterness. Other people see in us the same attitudes we condemned in the ones whose actions we resent. "...but they measuring themselves by themselves, and comparing themselves among themselves are not wise." (II Corinthians 10:12)

NOTES

HOW WE BECOME LIKE THOSE WE RESENT

• A bitter young father recalled his unhappy childhood days and renewed his vow, "I'll never be like my dad!"

His dad drank, was unfaithful to his wife, and had grossly neglected his son.

Now the son was married and had his own family. He never drank, he was very faithful to his wife, and he spent long hours with his family. Yet, those who were closest to him said, "You're just like your father!" Why was this true?

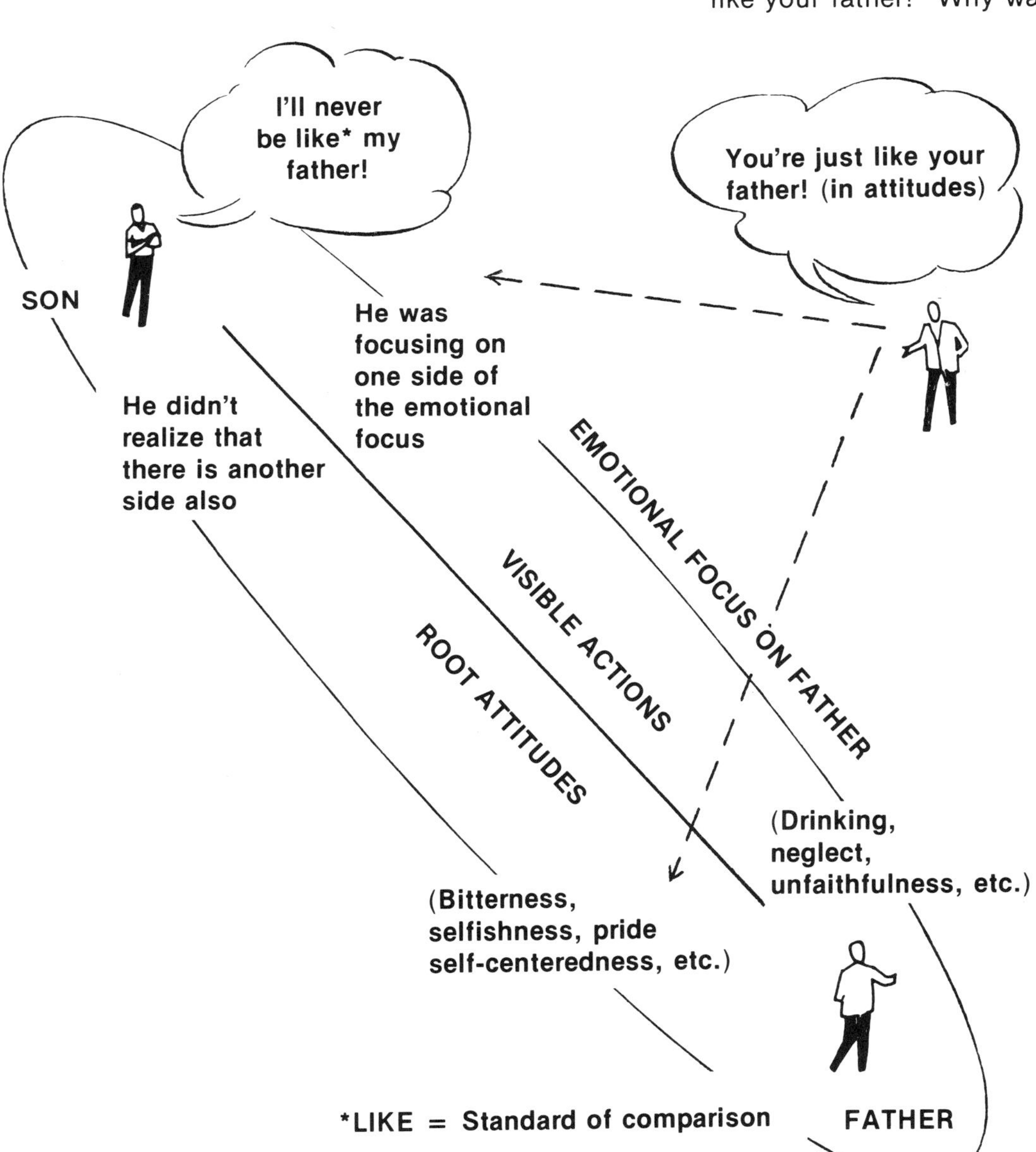

• When that son stated, "I'll never be like my father!" he established a standard of comparison with his father.

The "emotional focus" on the visible actions of his dad made it impossible for him to stop thinking about his father. These thoughts became the dominating concerns on his mind.

The more he thought about the actions of his dad, the deeper his bitterness became.

This bitterness was easily detected by all those who were close to him. Also evident were pride, selfishness, stubbornness and a host of other destructive root attitudes.

These were the same attitudes which the father had. Those who were closest to both of them were thus able to say to the son, "You're just like your father."

NOTES

BASIC STEPS TO GAIN A FORGIVING SPIRIT

• It is one thing to agree to forgive someone after he offends you. It is quite a different thing to have a spirit of forgiveness toward every offender whom God allows to come into your life. In order to gain this, we must understand the following factors.

1. REALIZE THAT GOD IS WORKING THROUGH THE ACTIONS OF YOUR OFFENDER

As long as we think that the one who hurts us is acting independently, we can hardly help growing bitter. But as soon as we realize that God "raised him up" for a specific purpose in our lives, we will be able to gain a forgiving spirit. He may think evil against us, but God means it for good. (Genesis 50:20) "Surely the wrath of man shall praise Thee: the remainder of wrath shalt Thou restrain." (Psalm 76:10)

2. THANK GOD FOR THE BENEFIT HE PLANS THROUGH EACH OFFENSE

God's command to give thanks in all things is especially essential at this point. (I Thessalonians 5:18) We don't have to be thankful in order to thank God. Thanking God is an act of the will. Being thankful is an act of the emotions.

When our lives are dedicated to God, He puts a protective wall around us so that nothing can touch us except that which God permits. He permits it for a purpose, and this purpose is for our ultimate joy and reward. It is for this reason we can thank God for each offense.

3. DISCERN WHAT CHARACTER QUALITIES GOD WANTS TO DEVELOP IN ME THROUGH THE OFFENSE

When we wrongly react to an offender, we are revealing various lacks of character which need to be developed such as, love, meekness, patience, faith, gentleness, self-control, etc. Even if we respond correctly to an offender, other qualities will have to be strengthened such as joy, peace, godliness, etc.

4. EXPECT TO SUFFER FOR DOING RIGHT AS A NORMAL PART OF CHRISTIAN LIVING

Many of us have the mistaken idea that if we are Christians we won't have to suffer, yet the Scripture clearly states, "For unto you it is given in the behalf of Christ, not only to believe on Him, but also to suffer for His sake." (Philippians 1:29) "Yea, and all that will live godly in Christ Jesus shall suffer persecution." (II Timothy 3:12) "If we suffer we shall also reign with Him." (II Timothy 2:12)

NOTES

OUR RESPONSIBILITY TO "HEAL" OFFENDERS

• When God allows someone to offend us, He is entrusting to us the responsibility of demonstrating Christ's love and presence to him. Who can stand in the presence of the Lord Jesus Christ very long and remain the same person?

- **THE PURPOSE OF OUR LIFE CALLING**

"For this is thankworthy, if a man for conscience toward God endure grief, suffering wrongfully. . . for even hereunto were ye called, because Christ also suffered for us, leaving us an example, that ye should follow in His steps:"

THE EXAMPLE: "He did no sin, neither was guile found in His mouth: who, when He was reviled, reviled not again; when He suffered, He threatened not: but committed Himself to Him that judgeth righteously: He bore our sins in His own body on the tree, that we, being dead to sins, should live unto righteousness:

THE RESULT: "By His stripes you were healed." (I Peter 2:19,21-24)

- **THE BASIS OF REMOVING UNBELIEF:**

If a Christian would respond to those whom God has brought into his life as Christ did to those who abused Him, he would see a new response on their part toward the Gospel.

One evening a woman made a hurried visit to the home of a family which I was visiting. I hadn't seen her for quite some time so I inquired, "How is everything going for you?" Her reply was, "Horrible! I'm getting a divorce. I can't stand to live with that man any longer!"

I asked her if I could give her a three minute message. She agreed. I asked her if she could visualize the abuse and beatings and rejection and agony which Jesus Christ suffered in His life. She said she could. I emphasized that His response to those who did it to Him was one of love and forgiveness, and by His stripes we were healed according to I Peter 2:19-24.

Then I asked her if she knew what the very next verse was following this section. She didn't and was startled to hear it—"Likewise, ye wives be in subjection to your own husbands; that if any obey not the word, they also may without the word, be won by the conduct of the wives." (I Peter 3:1) (Six verses later it also states, "Likewise, ye husbands. . .")

NOTES

HOW WE BENEFIT BY BEING OFFENDED

• The energizing power needed to live the entire Christian life is called in Scripture, "the grace of God." (I Corinthians 15:10; Titus 2:11,12, etc.) God gives a certain amount of this grace to every person, but the proud resist the grace they get and lose God's power. How do we get more grace? "God resisteth the proud but giveth grace unto the humble" James 4:6.

Thus, whenever we are humbled, we receive at that moment an added measure of God's grace.

OFFENSE **1.**

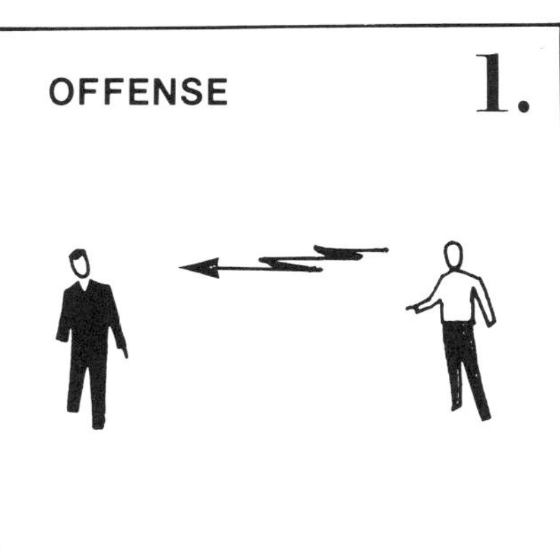

An undeserved offense toward you

LOVE **2.**

A right response while the offense continues

LOVE **3.**

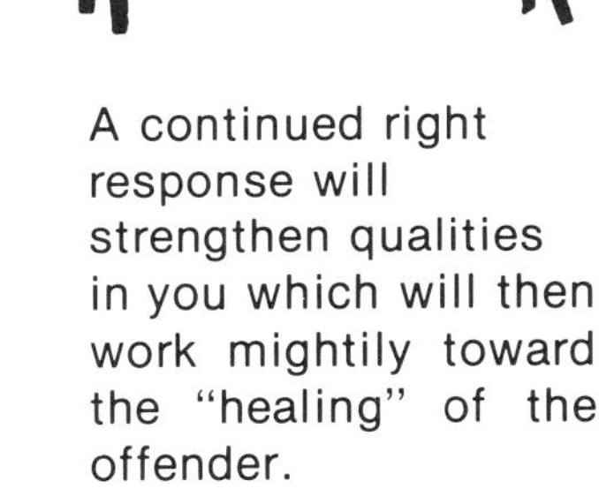

A continued right response will strengthen qualities in you which will then work mightily toward the "healing" of the offender.

REPORTS TO OTHERS **4.**

Your offender will soon tell his friends of your godly response to him.

INVOLVEMENT **5.**

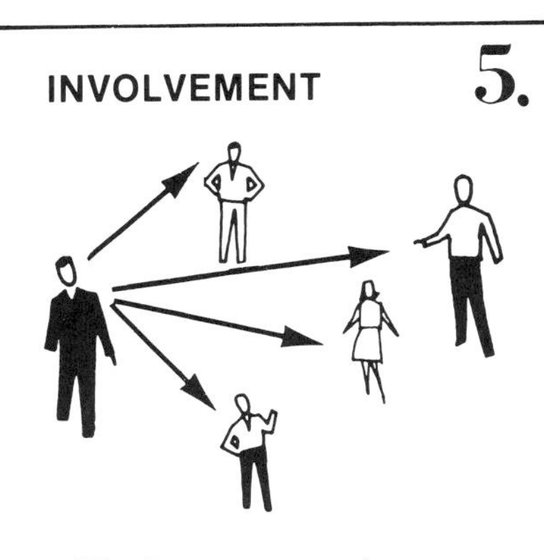

Their response to you will give you many new opportunities to share the Gospel and build new friendships.

JOY **6.**

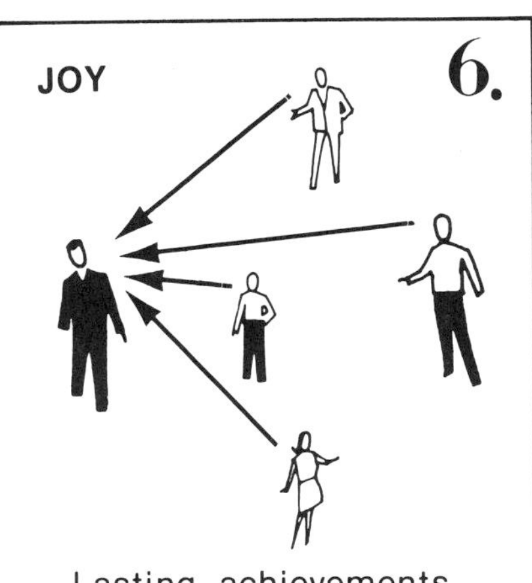

Lasting achievements in their lives will bring continuous joy and fulfillment to you.

NOTES

HOW WE LOSE BY A WRONG RESPONSE

• When we go through the humbling experience of having been offended and react to our offenders, we allow our pride to trample on the grace which God gave for the situation, and we are then left to our own ways thereafter since no new grace will be given to us until we humble ourselves again.

OFFENSE **1.**

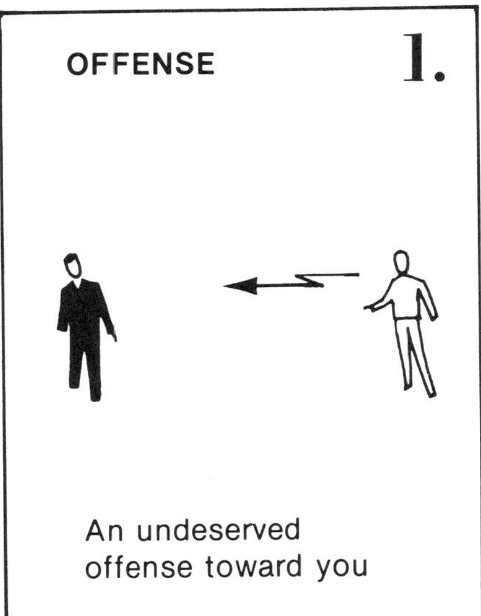

An undeserved offense toward you

RESENTMENT **2.**

A wrong reaction to the offender

BARRIER **3.**

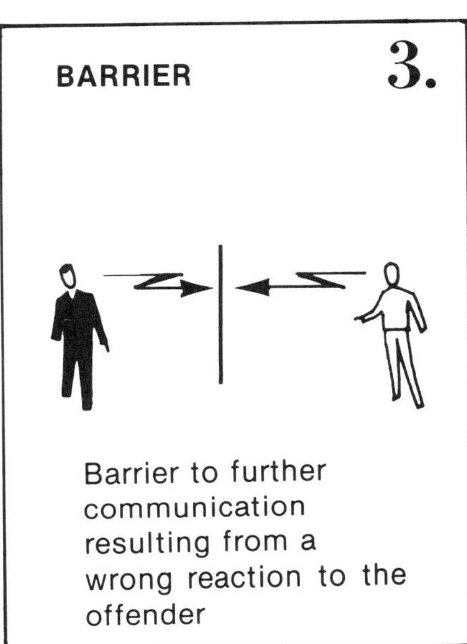

Barrier to further communication resulting from a wrong reaction to the offender

REPORTING **4.**

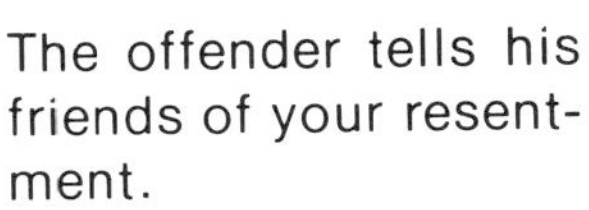

The offender tells his friends of your resentment.

REACTION **5.**

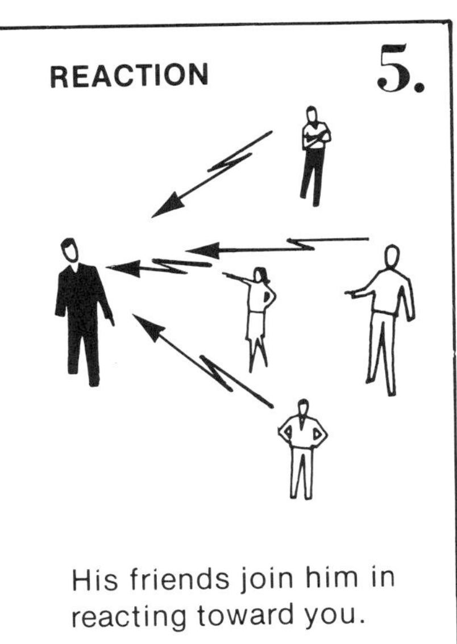

His friends join him in reacting toward you.

NEW BARRIERS **6.**

New barriers and bitterness occur as others take up the offense.

• Every person we "heal" through a right response to their offenses becomes an "open door" to the lives of others who also need to know how to apply these principles to their lives. Those we offend become closed doors to further opportunities in our lives.

NOTES

• IRRITATIONS: GOD'S INVITATIONS TO REEVALUATE OUR RIGHTS

• Both insight and discernment are needed to identify and transform sources of irritation into spiritual motivation.

TRANSFORMING SOURCES OF IRRITATION

INTO SOURCES OF SPIRITUAL MOTIVATION

• Every one of us has experienced sources of irritation. Their benefit or harm can be compared to a grain of sand.

In the eye, it will cause an irritation, infection and loss of vision. But in an oyster, it will cause an irritation, concretion and then a pearl.

NOTES

IDENTIFYING IRRITATIONS

• Many of our attitudes and actions are influenced more than we realize by that which irritates us. Therefore, it is extremely important that we identify and "transform" every source of irritation.

• IDENTIFYING THREE MAJOR SOURCES OF IRRITATION

1. PEOPLE—The personality traits, idiosyncrasies and inconsistencies of others provide an ever-present source of potential irritation.

A serious-minded student was working his way through college. He had to get up every morning at 5:00 a.m. This meant that he had to go to bed earlier than the others in his dorm. The walls between the rooms didn't keep out very much sound, and there were often loud, boisterous discussions in the surrounding rooms. These disturbances didn't decrease even after repeated requests for cooperation. The student was unable to change his working hours or his dorm room. Thus, his fellow students became a repeated source of irritation to him.

2. ENVIRONMENT—The deficiencies, inconveniences, undesirable elements and pressures of our environment constitute a second source of potential irritation.

A rather large family lived in a home which had only one bath. In the morning it seemed that everyone needed to get ready for the day at the same time. The inconvenience of this situation provided a source of irritation for everyone.

3. SELF—The defects, weaknesses, illnesses and personal deficiencies which we are not able to remove constitute a third source of potential irritation.

A teen-ager was in a hurry to drive to a friend's home and tried to take a new way which he thought might be shorter. He failed to slow down for a sharp turn and skidded off the road. The car crashed into a tree and seriously injured him. Since that time, he suffered from pains in his back and legs which the doctors could not seem to alleviate even after several operations. These pains became a constant source of irritation to him.

• TWO CLASSIFICATIONS OF IRRITATIONS

There are many irritations which we experience which we can and should remove. A squeaky door can be oiled; an angry neighbor can be appeased; and a personal habit can be changed. There are other irritations, however, which are beyond our power to correct or remove. These irresolvable irritations provide the basis for a significant process which God intends to take place within each of our lives.

NOTES

UNDERSTANDING THE PURPOSE OF

IRRESOLVABLE IRRITATIONS

• The unavoidable irritations which come from other people, from our environment or from our own selves are extremely significant. These irritations are God's way of increasing our sensitivity to the needs of other people or expanding our world of opportunity or developing the inward qualities which are so essential to successful living.

• If we react wrongly to these irritations, we destroy their potential benefits. If we respond to them with insight and proper action, we allow God to achieve His highest purpose in us—to reshape our lives as closely as possible to the ideal He has given us in the life of His Son. (Romans 8:29)

• When a specific purpose is achieved through a certain irritation, God is then free to remove that irritation from our lives. Thus we read in Scripture, "When a man's ways please the Lord, He maketh even his enemies to be at peace with him." (Proverbs 16:7)

• If we continually retreat from these irritations, we force God to choose between raising up new irritations or setting aside His highest plan for our life.

• Therefore, if some irritations seem to be rather permanent or irresolvable, we can be confident that they have a permanent benefit in our development and ministry.

• Such was the case with the "thorn in the flesh" which Paul experienced. God explains the reasons why He gave such an irritation to Paul. God was afraid Paul would be puffed up, so there was given him a "physical handicap" which was a thorn in his flesh, a messenger from Satan to hurt and bother him and prick his pride.

• "And lest I should be exalted above measure through the abundance of the revelations, there was given to me a thorn in the flesh, the messenger of Satan to buffet me, lest I should be exalted above measure. For this thing I besought the Lord thrice, that it might depart from me. And he said unto me, My grace is sufficient for thee: for my strength is made perfect in weakness. Most gladly therefore will I rather glory in my infirmities, that the power of Christ may rest upon me. . . for when I am weak, then am I strong." (II Corinthians 12:7-10)

REFLECTION OF CHRIST'S QUALITIES

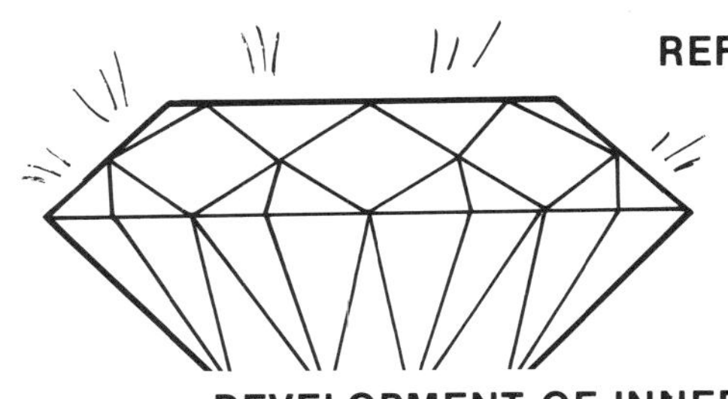

DEVELOPMENT OF INNER PERSONALITY

SOURCE OF IRRITATION

RIGHTS

NOTES

3 WRONG RESPONSES TO SOURCES OF IRRITATION

SCRIPTURAL WARNINGS AGAINST THESE RESPONSES:	
1. DEFENDING IN THE FACE OF EMOTION "There is a time to keep silence and a time to speak." (Ecclesiastes 3:7)	• **DEFENDING SELF** "Mom hollered about something I did wrong. She was very tired since she had had a bad day. I had had a bad day, too, and thought I was as tired as she. I tried to defend myself and it seemed to make her angrier. She tried to bring me down to the size I really am by comparing me to others. It ended up with my trying to explain that I'm not perfect, but I am trying to do well."
2. BLAMING SOMEONE ELSE "Accuse not a servant unto his master lest he curse thee and thou be found guilty." (Proverbs 30:10)	• **BLAMING ANOTHER** "Friday night my mother and I were at it again. What caused it? I really couldn't say. We were discussing who would do what around the house. It seemed to me that my sister never does anything, and I get stuck with the work. My mother says a lot of things to me when she gets angry. I know she doesn't mean it, but it hurts. It hurts so much I can't describe it. Sometimes I wonder why the Lord chose me for her to take out her anger on."
3. HOLDING IN ANGER ". . . anger resteth in the bosom of fools." (Ecclesiastes 7:9)	• **HOLDING IN ANGER** "Mother and I were riding home from the grocery store. I must have been following the car in front of me too closely and wasn't prepared when he stopped. I realized his car was slowing down, and I braked lightly at first, then harder to avoid hitting him. Mother stated something to the effect that I was showing off by trying to stop right on his tail. Most of the groceries on the back seat toppled to the floor (lemon pie, etc.) I felt resentful, but as usual, didn't say anything."

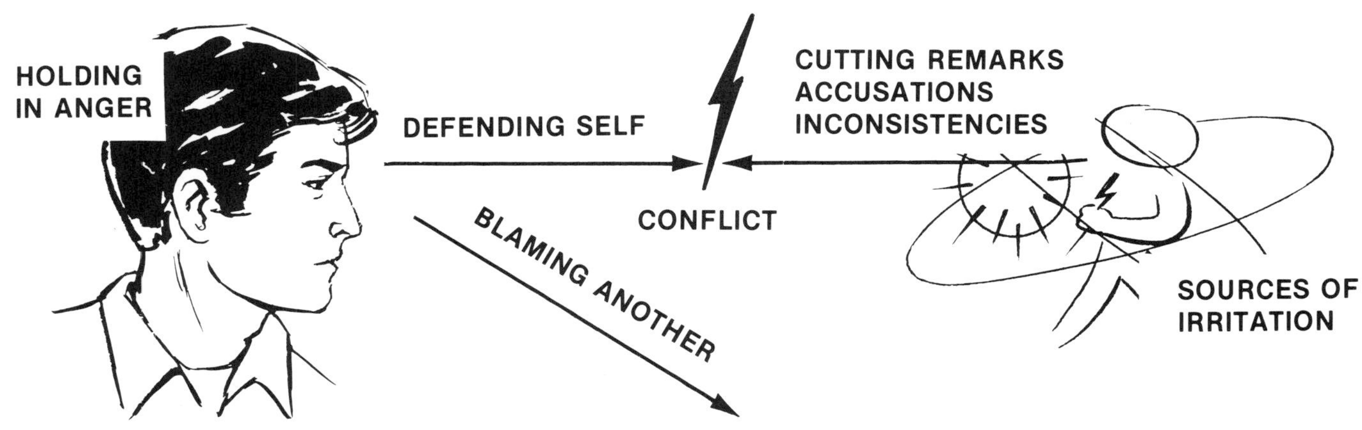

NOTES

3 RIGHT RESPONSES TO SOURCES OF IRRITATION

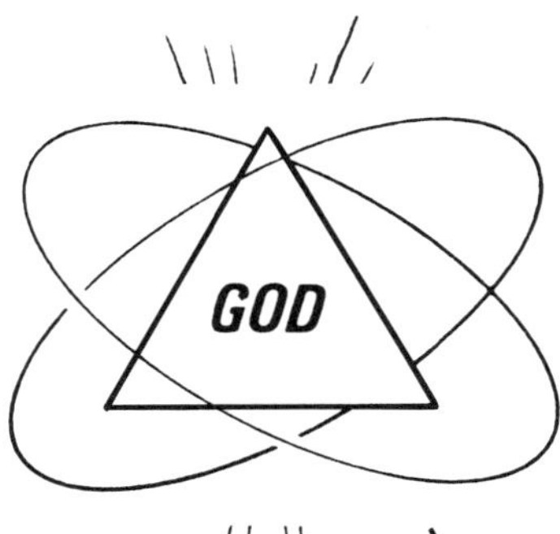

3. DETERMINE ULTIMATE OBJECTIVES—Matthew 5, Galatians 5

What qualities does God want to develop in me?
How is He using this irritation to force me to develop these qualities?

2. IDENTIFY POSSIBLE CAUSES—I Corinthians 11:31,32

Did I in any way cause this?
Have I done things in the past to cause this?
Have I neglected to do what I should have done?

1. THANK GOD FOR THE IRRITATION—I Thessalonians 5:18

Since I am dedicated to God, I belong to Him.
God is bigger than the irritation. He can stop it.
He wants the best for me; therefore, it has purpose.

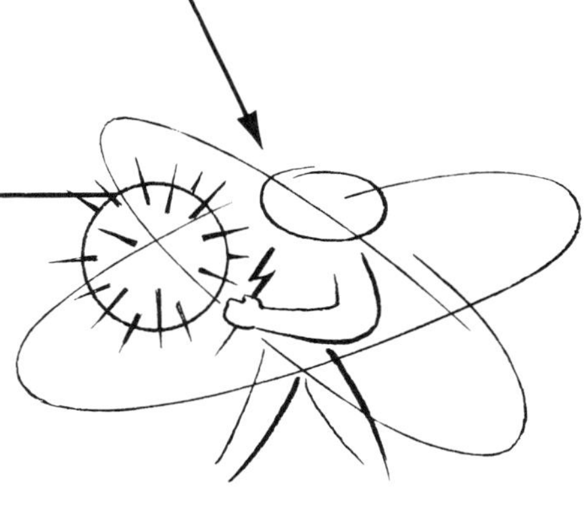

NOTES

STEP 1:
THANK GOD FOR THE IRRITATION

• **PREREQUISITES FOR STEP 1:**

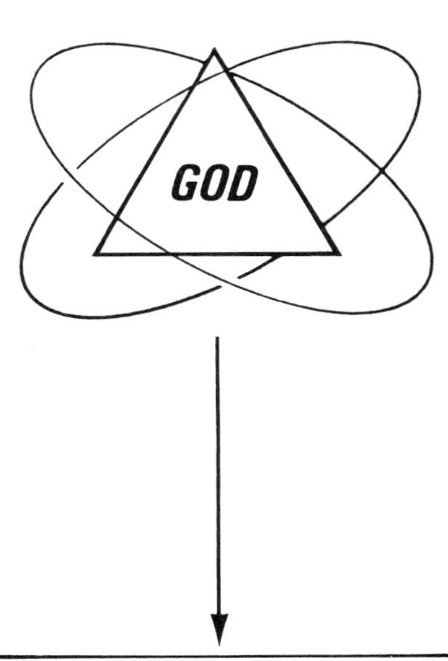

A. A TOTAL DEDICATION TO GOD

Even though God created us, we do not actually belong to His family until we receive the supreme Gift He has provided for us through believing in His Son, the Lord Jesus Christ. (John 3:16; Romans 6:23; 10:9)

B. A PERSONAL COMMITMENT TO HIS OBJECTIVES

God has a purpose for each one of our lives. He wants us to dedicate ourselves to His will and begin building all our thoughts, desires and activities around His purposes. (Romans 8:29)

C. THANK GOD FOR THE IRRITATION

- ☐ I belong to God, and, therefore, I am His responsibility
- ☐ His work and reputation are affected by my responses
- ☐ He wants the best for me.
- ☐ He is bigger than the source of irritation.
- ☐ He has allowed the irritation for my ultimate benefit.

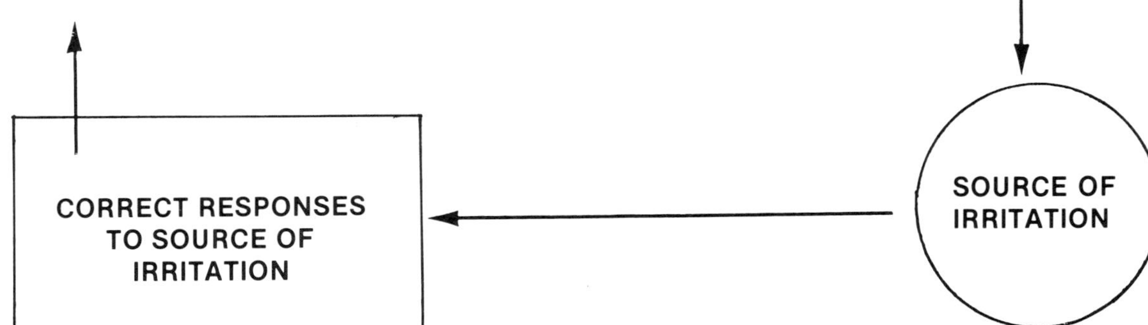

RIGHTS

NOTES

STEP 2:
IDENTIFY POSSIBLE CAUSES

• **THREE PURPOSES FOR IRRITATIONS**

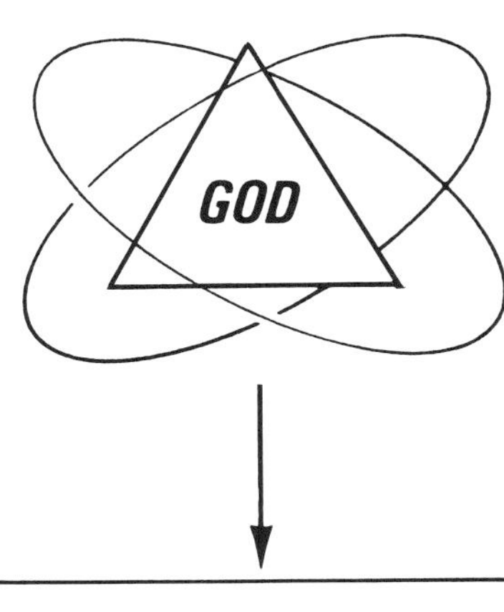

A. IRRITATIONS OF "REPROOFS"

Since we tend to forget unpleasant events, we often neglect to correct or gain forgiveness for the offenses which caused those unpleasant events.

Those we offend, however, tend to remember and review them. Then, when they have an opportunity to irritate us, they quickly do so.

B. IRRITATIONS OF "REFLECTORS"

Those around us tend to reflect the attitudes and character deficiencies which we have. Since we are already sensitive to these deficiencies, they become doubly irritating when we see them in someone else. Our tendency is to react to those who point them out in us rather than use their reactions as motivations to change or improve.

C. IRRITATIONS OF "REMINDERS"

God wants us to live in the freedom of a clear conscience. Therefore, He uses sources of irritation as painful but helpful reminders to clear up past offenses which He sees will hinder future relationships - with Him or others.

• Since we cannot sincerely thank God for something which we are not thankful for, steps 2 and 3 guide us in discovering the ultimate benefits of sources of irritation.

RIGHTS

IDENTIFY POSSIBLE CAUSES

☐ "Did I cause this irritation by something I did or failed to do?"

☐ "Does this irritation reflect a personal fault or lack of character development in me?"

"I will correct that which is wrong and ask forgiveness. Also, I will make restitution where it is necessary."

NOTES

STEP 3:
DETERMINE CHARACTER GOALS

• GOD'S ULTIMATE PURPOSES

• From the very beginning, God chose that those who believe in Him should become like His Son, Jesus Christ. (Romans 8:29)

• This process involves the development of basic inward qualities. For this objective, "All things work together for good..." (Romans 8:28)

• WHAT QUALITIES DOES GOD WANT TO DEVELOP IN ME?

Matthew 5:3-12: Humility, repentance, meekness, spiritual hunger, mercy, purity, peacemaking, endurance in persecution

Galatians 5:22: Love, joy, peace, patience, gentleness, goodness, faith, meekness, self-control

RIGHTS

IRRITATIONS	QUALITY TO BE PRODUCED
From one who is hard to love	Genuine love based on mature insight
From circumstances of sorrow	Continuous joy even in the midst of pain
From conditions of confusion	Inward peace and steady confidence
From irritating inconveniences	Sympathetic flexibility
From obvious needs of others	Wise generosity
From unwelcome responsibilities	Consistent trustworthiness
From people who intrude upon personal rights	Surrender of personal rights
From temptations of wrong desires	Self-control

• The steps of responding to sources of irritation are clearly defined in I Peter 2:18-21. "For this is thankworthy, if a man for conscience toward God endure grief, suffering wrongfully. For what glory is it, if, when ye be buffeted for your faults, ye shall take it patiently? but if, when ye do well, and suffer for it, ye take it patiently, this is acceptable with God. For even hereunto were ye called: because Christ also suffered for us, leaving us an example, that ye should follow His steps."

NOTES

YIELDING PERSONAL RIGHTS

• Anger is the opposite of meekness. We cannot have both in our life. Either we have one as our basic nature, or we have the other. The great importance of meekness is seen in the following Scripture.

NOTES

THE CAUSE OF ANGER: PERSONAL RIGHTS

- **The meek will have good judgment** — The meek will He guide in judgment. Psalm 25:9
- **The meek will learn the way of God.** — The meek will He teach His way. Psalm 25:9
- **The meek will inherit the earth.** — The meek shall inherit the earth. Psalm 37:11
- **The meek will respond to the Gospel.** — He came to preach good tidings to the meek. Isaiah 61:1
- **The meek will have special joy.** — The meek also shall increase their joy. Isaiah 29:19
- **The meek will understand Christ's nature.** — For I am meek and lowly in heart. Matthew 11:29
- **The meek will radiate inward beauty.** — The adornment of a meek and quiet spirit. I Peter 3:4
- **The meek will have power in witnessing.** — Be ready to give an answer...with meekness. I Peter 3:15

RIGHTS

ANGER OR MEEKNESS

It would not be possible to have a conflict with someone unless personal rights were involved. Notice the rights involved in the following:

"My conflict is with my sister. She took my clothes out of my closet without asking me. I got very perturbed, and I asked her why she didn't ask me. I would have considered lending something to her if she would have requested it. Then I lost control of my temper and started yelling—kind of."	The right to control personal property The right to have personal respect from her sister
"Today my brother was cleaning our room (his side). He found my junk on his side. I had thrown it away but someone had gotten it out. He hates me and had been throwing junk on my side that wasn't mine. I hadn't read my Bible and, being out of fellowship, I hit him on the head with some cardboard. That's how it started. During our fight, he swore and used bad language. He hates me more now. My parents don't spank him like they should. If they used more discipline, he wouldn't be like this at all."	The right to be responsible only for his side of the room The right to evaluate and pass judgment on his parents' discipline of his brother

NOTES

One evening five members of one family silently sat around a table. For many years they had not been able to achieve harmony among themselves. They had come to ask how this could be done.

THE BASIS OF MEEKNESS

YIELDING PERSONAL RIGHTS

A. IDENTIFYING ANGER

Each one was given a sheet of paper and asked to describe the last three situations in which they lost their temper. The ten-year-old son raised his hand and hesitatingly asked, "Should I choose three from today or one from the last three days?"

B. LISTING PERSONAL RIGHTS

After each one wrote out these situations, we made a list of all the rights each felt he had as a member of the family. Here are some of the rights:

RIGHTS

1. **The right to express personal opinions without being "jumped on"**
2. **The right to be accepted as an individual**
3. **The right to plan how free time will be used**
4. **The right to privacy**
5. **The right to earn and spend money**
6. **The right to choose friends**
7. **The right to control the use of personal belongings**

C. SEEING HOW RIGHTS CAUSE ANGER

Each one then reviewed the recent situations in which he lost his temper and was able to identify a personal right which had been violated.

Based on this discovery, each one realized that a significant key to the solution of his family conflicts would come if he would learn how to properly deal with his personal rights. Each one considered and accepted the following ideas:

NOTES

4 STEPS IN YIELDING PERSONAL RIGHTS

1. IDENTIFY PERSONAL RIGHTS

In the case of the girl whose sister takes her clothes, there are at least two rights involved. They are defined in her further explanation of the problem.

RIGHTS INVOLVED:

THE RIGHT TO CONTROL THE USE OF HER CLOTHES

"My sister is in eighth grade. She really doesn't wear the same size clothes as I, but she borrows mine anyway. Then, instead of hanging them up, she crumples them up in a ball and throws them under the bed. This gets me so mad that we're almost always fighting."

THE RIGHT TO HAVE HER MOTHER UNDER-STAND HER POSITION

"To make matters worse, my mother sides with her whenever I say anything. One day I bought a new pair of slacks, and my sister wore them. After she got home, she folded them up and put them away. I thought that was rather strange until I went to wear them. She had fallen while wearing them and one whole knee was ripped out."

RIGHTS

2. TRANSFER RIGHTS TO GOD

In the discussion that followed, this teen-ager learned that the rights to her clothes could not be transferred without also transferring the ownership of the clothes.

RIGHTS AND RESPONSIBILITY ACCOMPANY OWNERSHIP OF PERSONAL PROPERTY

Since the girl owned the clothes, she maintained the rights and all the responsibility for her clothes. If she transferred the ownership to God, then God would assume the chief responsibility to protect her clothes as well as the rights to their use.

Here is part of our conversation:

"This may sound strange, but have you ever thought about dedicating your clothes to God?"

NOTES

She replied, "That does sound strange. I've never heard of doing that."

I explained, "An effective Christian will dedicate whatever he acquires to God so that the real responsibility of protection and effective use will rest with the Lord and not with his own abilities."

God will always take good care of His own property

After a moment she said, "What if I dedicate them to God and my sister still borrows them and ruins them?"

I assured her, "When you dedicate your clothes to God and she continues to take them, she is not taking your clothes. She is actually taking God's clothes. When this occurs, and you share the problem with the Lord, you will see how powerful He really is. He is bigger than your sister. He can place it in your sister's heart to take care of the clothes if she borrows them and even to hang them up after she wears them."

After some further thought she exlaimed, "This sure sounds strange."

But I asked, "Would you be willing to try it?"

RIGHTS

3. TRANSFER OWNERSHIP TO GOD

• This transfer of ownership was done through a sincere prayer of dedication.

• Before that teen-ager prayed, the example was given of Abraham dedicating his son, Isaac, upon the altar. (Genesis 22:1-10)

God may begin by asking us to give to Him our most cherished possession

The teen-ager was encouraged to picture herself kneeling at an altar and placing all her clothes upon that imaginary altar, just as Abraham placed his son upon the altar. The following prayer was suggested:

"Lord, right now I dedicate all my clothes to you. From this moment on, they don't belong to me anymore but to you. You have the right to the way they're used, and I'm responsible under you to take care of them."

The teen-ager sincerely prayed this prayer.

NOTES

• This concept of thanking God for whatever He allows to happen is the key to yielding rights. It allows for the possibility that God may test her sincerity by allowing her sister to wear and even misuse the clothes.

4. THANK GOD WHATEVER HAPPENS

If her sister misused her clothes, she would still be able to thank the Lord because this would be an opportunity for her to prove to Him that she really did give her clothes to Him. She would also have the confidence that the Lord would use this situation for His own glory—whether it would be to teach her new lessons in trust or to let her sister see a new attitude in her.

Four days after this teen-ager yielded her rights to the Lord, she returned with the following enthusiastic report:

"It works!"

I inquired, "What works?"

She replied, "Giving my clothes to the Lord. I can hardly believe what's happened! I didn't tell my sister or anyone else about our talk, but since that time I haven't had one fight with my sister. She only borrowed my clothes once, but for the first time, she actually came home and hung them up! She even ironed the blouse she wore. I just can't get over it!"

From this experience the teen-ager was able to apply these four steps in regard to other rights. Here are some of the rights which each one of us must carefully turn over to the Lord.

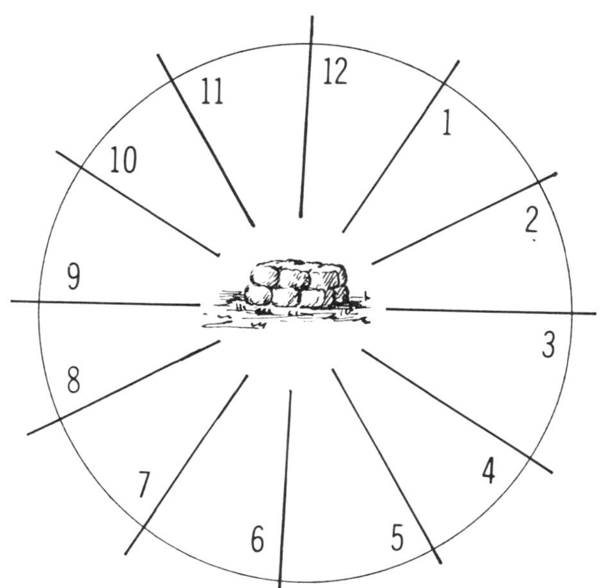

1. **Self-will**
2. **Dating**
3. **Clothes—Appearance**
4. **Money—Possessions**
5. **Knowledge**
6. **Friends**
7. **Music**
8. **Future**
9. **Health**
10. **Reputation**
11. **Schedule—Time**
12. **Activities**

RIGHTS

NOTES

RELATING RIGHTS TO LEVELS OF CONFLICT

JUST AS THERE ARE DIFFERENT LEVELS OF CONFLICTS, SO THERE ARE DIFFERENT LEVELS OF PERSONAL RIGHTS

IT IS ESSENTIAL THAT WE IDENTIFY AND YIELD OUR RIGHTS AT ALL LEVELS TO THE LORD.

• In order to determine the personal rights involved in home conflicts, we must be aware of the four possible levels of conflicts. To help a person yield a surface right when a deeper right is also involved is only going to produce a temporary solution. For example, a teen-ager called one day to report the following:

"I got a phone call from my girlfriend, and we were talking about two fellows. My mother was listening on the extension and at the supper table she repeated what I had said on the phone. I asked her if she had been listening. She said, 'yes.'

"I said she had no right to listen in on my conversation. She said she has a right to listen because she pays the bills and she's the boss. So I got mad and called her sneaky and told her she wasn't an understanding person. We really told one another what we thought. For two days things were strained, and then all of a sudden we both forgot it. But now I don't trust her and vice-versa."

LEVELS OF CONFLICT	RESULTING CONFLICTS	LEVELS OF RIGHTS
SURFACE PROBLEM	**SUSPICION** Mother listening in on phone conversations of daughter	The right to have privacy on the phone
SURFACE CAUSE	**ARGUMENT** Clash of wills resulting in each one distrusting the other	The right to make personal decisions apart from parents
ROOT PROBLEM	**MORAL IMPURITY** Daughter making the wrong choices of her friends and unwholesome dating habits	The right to date the boys she chooses The right to satisfy selfish desires
ROOT CAUSE	**RESISTING GOD'S GRACE** Daughter failing to yield self to the total disciplines of Christ through parents' counsel and authority	The right to resist God's authority in her life and be her own boss

NOTES

WHEN RIGHTS ARE YIELDED

DISTINGUISH BETWEEN RIGHTS AND RESPONSIBILITIES

In yielding rights, we must be careful not to yield responsibilities. For example, a student cannot say, "I gave my right to good grades to the Lord, and, therefore, I'm not studying as hard any more." A parent cannot say, "I gave my right to disciplining my children to the Lord and have stopped correcting them." There are responsibilities given by God and must not be confused with personal rights.

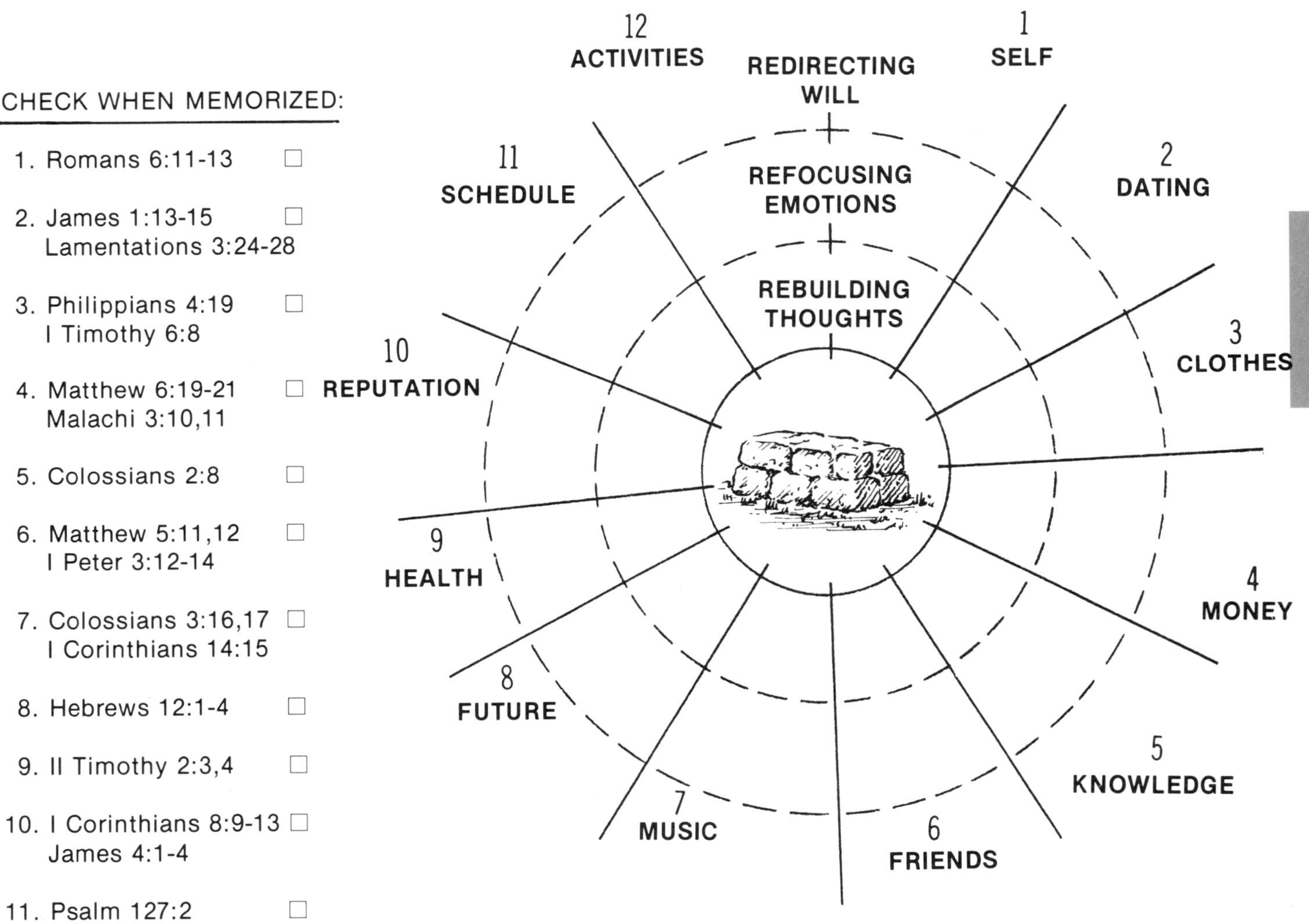

LEARN TO DEVELOP INWARD QUALITIES THROUGH LOSS OF RIGHTS

The deep inward feelings which result when our personal rights are withheld provide excellent motivation to personally identify with Scripture. This process is explained in the material on meditation. The following diagram illustrates how this procedure can be used with Scripture which deals with rights.

NOTES

EXPECT GOD TO TEST YIELDED RIGHTS

When God withholds from us a right that we have yielded to Him, we can expect that He will give corresponding insights into His Word.

In order to gain this insight, we must first learn what He says about the right that He is testing.

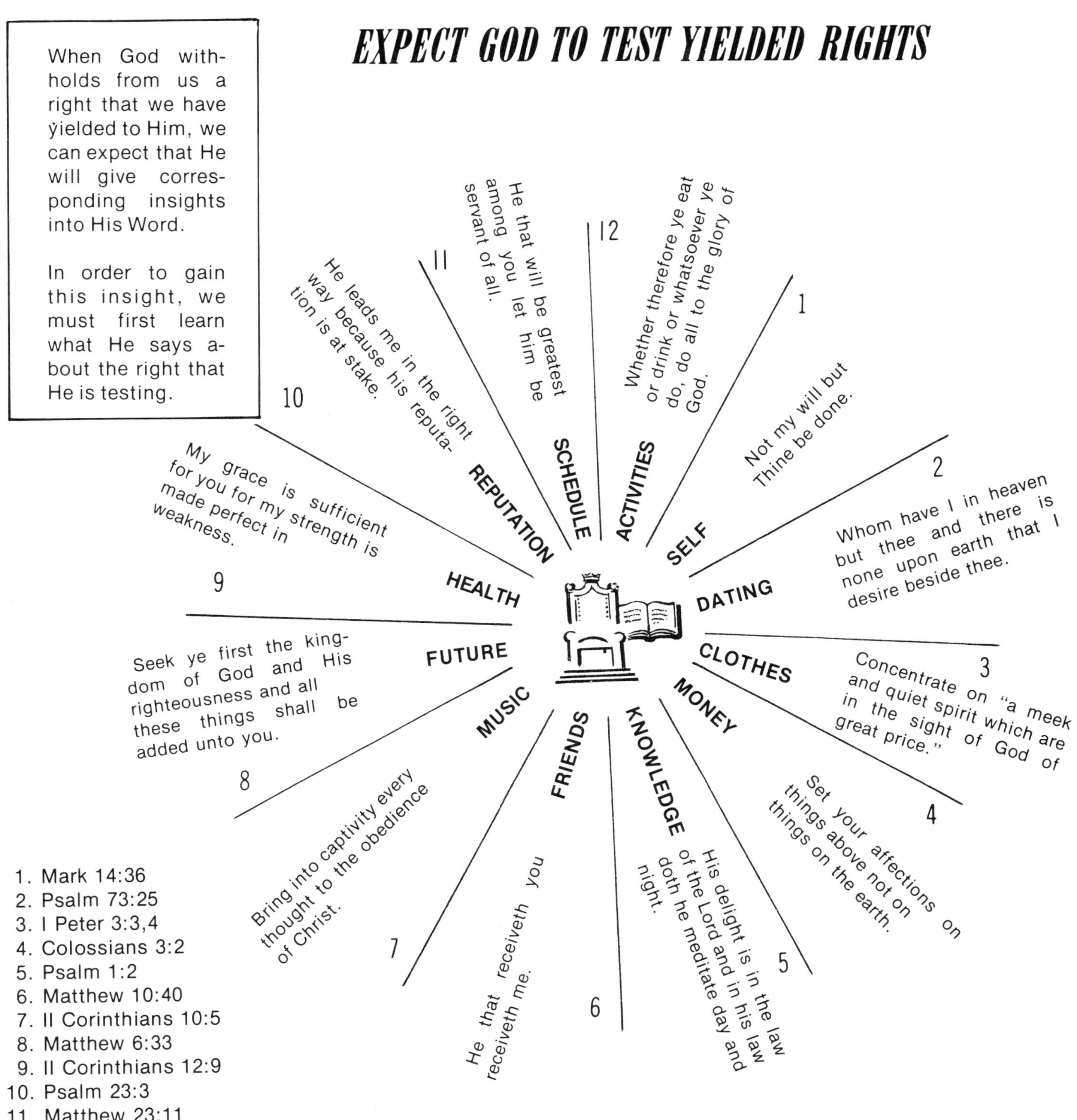

1. Mark 14:36
2. Psalm 73:25
3. I Peter 3:3,4
4. Colossians 3:2
5. Psalm 1:2
6. Matthew 10:40
7. II Corinthians 10:5
8. Matthew 6:33
9. II Corinthians 12:9
10. Psalm 23:3
11. Matthew 23:11
12. I Corinthians 10:31

EXPECT GOD TO TEST HIS RIGHTS

When we yield our rights to God, we can be sure that He will allow situations to develop in which these rights will be withheld from us. If we find ourselves becoming angry when this happens, we can be sure that our yielding of these rights was not complete in our own mind. Anger may also reveal related rights which were never identified and yielded.

NOTES

THE BASIS OF GENUINE LOVE

MORAL FREEDOM

- DISCERNING THE CAUSES OF MORAL IMPURITY

- DEFINING THE BASIC STEPS TO MORAL PURITY

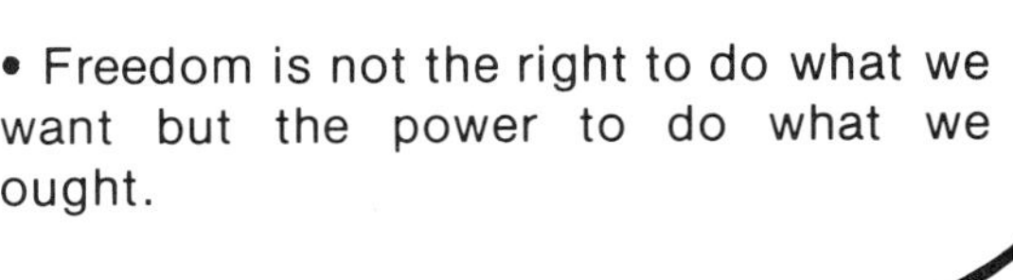

• Freedom is not the right to do what we want but the power to do what we ought.

NOTES

THE REQUIREMENT OF MORAL PURITY FOR GODLINESS AND LOVE

". . . use not liberty for an occasion to the flesh, but by love serve one another." Galatians 5:13

"Dearly beloved, I beseech you as strangers and pilgrims, abstain from fleshly lusts, which war against the soul;" I Peter 2:11

". . . see that ye love one another with a pure heart fervently:" I Peter 1:22

"For this is the will of God, even your sanctification, that ye should abstain from fornication. . . That no man go beyond and defraud his brother. . . For God hath not called us unto uncleanness, but unto holiness." I Thessalonians 4:3-7

"Abstain from all appearance of evil." I Thessalonians 5:22

• The essence of love is giving to the basic needs of another without the motive of personal gain. "God so loved that He gave..." The more free we are from personal desires, the more free we are to genuinely love others.

Love can always wait to give, but lust can never wait to get.

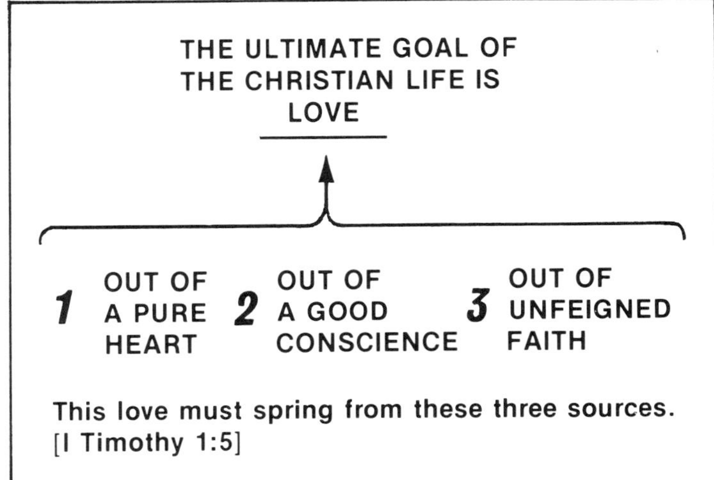

FREEDOM

THE RESULT OF IMPURITY TO OUR CONSCIENCE

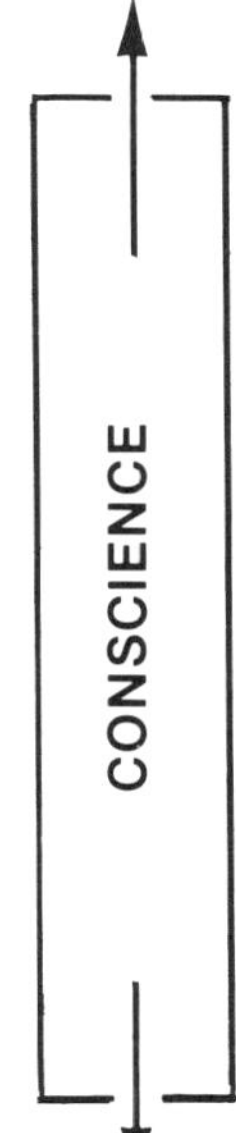

• God's will is that we increase the scope of our moral consciousness so that we are aware when we offend God and others.

• "Strong meat belongeth to them that are of full age, even those who by reason of use have their senses exercised to discern both good and evil." Hebrews 5:14

THE SCOPE OF OUR MORAL CONSCIOUSNESS

• When we allow moral impurity to exist in our lives, it soon becomes justified by our mind and conscience. At this point then, it doesn't bother our conscience.

• The tragedy to our relationships with both God and others is that in decreasing our moral consciousness in one area, we become unaware of how we are offending in many other areas—both by the things we do and especially by those things we fail to do and say.

OUR MORAL CONSCIOUSNESS DECREASED BY IMPURITY

NOTES

AN OUTWARD EXPRESSION OF IMPURITY

• One evening in a large suburban church, the Christian life was explained to a group of high school and college students. After the meeting the following event took place.

• Two college students—a fellow and a girl—edged their way through the church youth group until they stood directly in front of me. The girl nervously flicked at her cigarette and waited for an opening to say something. When it came, she inquired with studied sophistication,

"What would you say to someone who didn't believe in heaven or hell or the existence of God?"

The fellow nodded and waited for a reply. The entire group became strangely silent. I looked at her and said,

"Whether you believe in heaven or hell or in the existence of a God is not nearly as important to me as what has caused you not to believe in them.

"Your unbelief tells me some very significant things about you."

Her face reflected keen interest as she inquired, "What does it tell you about me?"

After looking around at all the curious bystanders, I explained to her,

"I don't think it would be fair to you to tell you in front of all these people. Let's make an appointment for this week, and I'll thoroughly explain what your unbelief tells me about you."

• Not only did she and the college fellow make appointments, but several others did as well. The following diagram was then explained to each one.

• A person's inner motivation will dictate outward actions. This inner motivation is determined by the relationship of the spiritual, psychological and physical drives.

NOTES

THE DEVELOPMENT OF REPROBATION

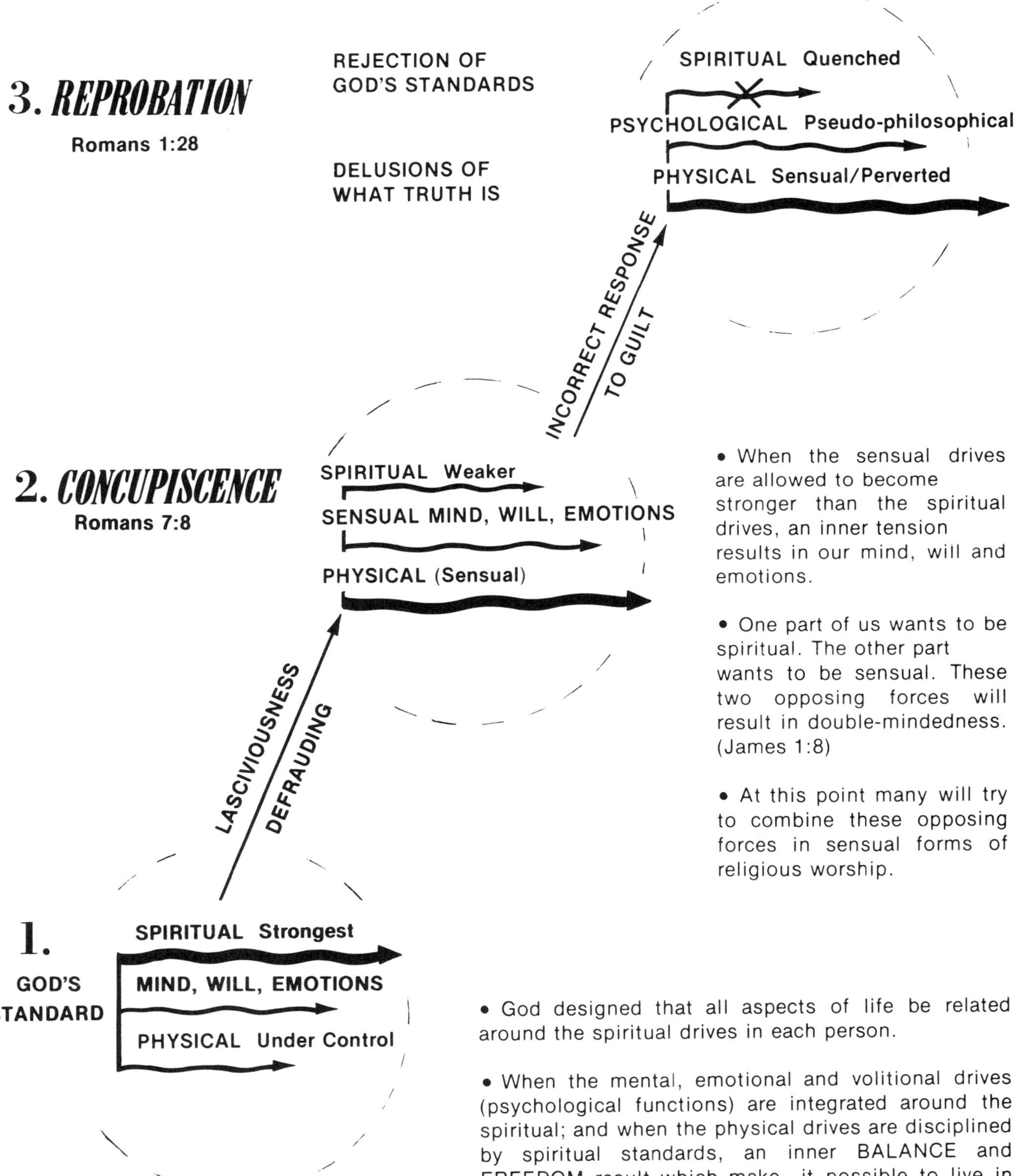

• When the sensual drives are allowed to become stronger than the spiritual drives, an inner tension results in our mind, will and emotions.

• One part of us wants to be spiritual. The other part wants to be sensual. These two opposing forces will result in double-mindedness. (James 1:8)

• At this point many will try to combine these opposing forces in sensual forms of religious worship.

• God designed that all aspects of life be related around the spiritual drives in each person.

• When the mental, emotional and volitional drives (psychological functions) are integrated around the spiritual; and when the physical drives are disciplined by spiritual standards, an inner BALANCE and FREEDOM result which make it possible to live in harmony with God's standards.

NOTES

DEFINING BASIC DEFINITIONS

SCRIPTURAL TERMS	AMPLIFICATION	REFERENCES
LASCIVIOUSNESS **Greek = Aselgeia** Other words used: Pernicious Wantonness	Preoccupation with bodily or sexual pleasure exhibited by excessive and unrestrained excitement of the physical senses for personal gratification.	"Now the works of the flesh are manifest, which are these: adultery, fornication, uncleanness, lasciviousness. . ." Galatians 5:19 "And many shall follow their pernicious ways; by reason of whom the way of truth shall be evil spoken of." II Peter 2:2 "For when they speak great swelling words of vanity, they allure through the lusts of the flesh, through much wantonness, those that were clean escaped from them who live in error." II Peter 2:18
CONCUPISCENCE **Greek = Epithumia** Other words used: Lusts Covet	A strong desire of any kind. Example: An abnormal sexual appetite.	"That every one of you should know how to possess his vessel in sanctification and honor; not in the lust of concupiscence, even as the Gentiles which know not God." I Thessalonians 4:4,5 "Let not sin therefore reign in your mortal body, that ye should obey it in the lusts thereof." Romans 6:12 ". . . for I had not known lust, except the law had said, Thou shalt not covet." Romans 7:7 ". . . thou shalt not covet thy neighbor's wife. . ." Exodus 20:17
DEFRAUD **Greek = Pleonekteo** Other words used: Covetous Greediness	Attempting to take advantage of another person in order to satisfy evil desires. Example: To arouse sexual desires in another which cannot be righteously satisfied.	"That no one go beyond and defraud his brother in any matter: (of concupiscence) because that the Lord is the avenger of all such..." I Thessalonians 4:6 "But now I have written unto you not to keep company, if any man that is called a brother be a fornicator, or covetous. . ." I Corinthians 5:11 "Who being past feeling have given themselves over unto lasciviousness, to work all uncleanness with greediness." Ephesians 4:19
REPROBATE **Greek = Apokimos**	Unprincipled, depraved, unable to discern evil.	"And even as they did not like to retain God in their knowledge, God gave them over to a reprobate mind, to do those things which are not convenient." Romans 1:28
FORNICATION **Greek = Porneia**	Unlawful sexual activity outside the marriage relationship.	"Flee fornication. Every sin that a man doeth is without the body; but he that committeth fornication sinneth against his own body." I Corinthians 6:18 "For this is the will of God, even your sanctification, that ye should abstain from fornication." I Thessalonians 4:3
LIBERTY **Greek = Eleutheria** Other words used: Free	Not the right to do what we want, but the new desire and power to do what we ought.	"Stand fast therefore in the liberty wherewith Christ hath made us free, and be not entangled again with the yoke of bondage." Galatians 5:1 "For, brethren, ye have been called unto liberty; only use not liberty for an occasion to the flesh, but by love serve one another." Galatians 5:13

NOTES

VISIBLE EVIDENCES OF MORAL IMPURITY

• A man's morality tends to dictate his philosophy and his theology. Because of this, it is important that we learn to be keen observers of the visible evidence of a man's life as well as discerners of the truth of a man's ideas.

1. CLAIMING THAT UNDER "GRACE" WE ARE FREE TO DO WHAT WE WANT.

"For there are certain men crept in unawares, who were before of old ordained to this condemnation, ungodly men, turning the grace of our God into lasciviousness. . ." Jude 1:4

"What shall we say then? Shall we continue in sin, that grace may abound? God forbid. . ." Romans 6:1,2

2. DESPISING SUBMISSION AND SPEAKING EVIL OF THOSE IN AUTHORITY.

"Likewise also these filthy dreamers defile the flesh, despise dominion, and speak evil of dignities." Jude 1:8

". . . to be punished: but (are) chiefly them that walk after the flesh in the lust of uncleanness, and despise government. Presumptuous are they, self-willed, they are not afraid to speak evil of dignities." II Peter 2:9,10

3. SCOFFING AT SPIRITUAL TRUTHS WHICH ARE BEYOND HUMAN REASONING

"But these speak evil of those things which they know not: but what they know naturally, as brute beasts, in those things they corrupt themselves." Jude 1:10

4. COMPLAINING ABOUT MORAL STRICTNESS AND DEVELOPING NEW AND FASHIONABLE PHILOSOPHIES.

"These are murmurers, complainers, walking after their own lusts; and their mouth speaketh great swelling words, having men's persons in admiration because of advantage." Jude 1:16

"For when they speak great swelling words of vanity, they allure through the lusts of the flesh, through much wantonness, those that were clean escaped from them who live in error." II Peter 2:18

"While they promise them liberty, they themselves are the servants of corruption. . ." II Peter 2:19

5. ARGUING IRRATIONALLY OVER PSEUDO-PHILOSOPHIES THAT CONTRADICT GOD'S WORD.

"But avoid foolish questions. . .A man that is an heretic after the first and second admonition reject; knowing that he that is such is subverted, and sinneth, being condemned of himself." Titus 3:9-11

6. USING THE GUISE OF RELIGION TO COVER PRIDE, LUST AND REBELLION.

"For men shall be lovers of their own selves, covetous, boasters, proud, blasphemers, disobedient to parents, unthankful, unholy, without natural affection, trucebreakers, false accusers, incontinent, fierce, despisers of those that are good:

"Traitors, heady, highminded, lovers of pleasures more than lovers of God; having a form of godliness but denying the power thereof: from such turn away." II Timothy 3:2-5

NOTES

DEVELOPMENT OF LASCIVIOUSNESS

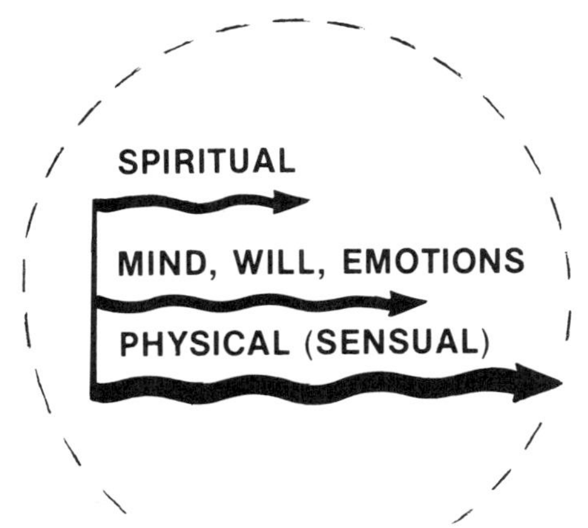

1. NATURAL CURIOSITY

God placed no restriction on curiosity except in the area of learning about evil (Romans 16:19). After creating man, God gave him freedom to eat of the fruit of every tree except of the tree of the knowledge of good and evil. (Genesis 2:17) God intended that we know evil, not by experience, but by discerning that it is foreign to His Spirit within us. (I John 4:1)

2. AWAKENING OF CONSCIENCE

When we follow curiosity into areas of knowing about evil, we are drawn away by our own lust and enticed. (James 1:14) Our conscience bears witness and our thoughts accuse us that this is not right. (Romans 2:15; I John 3:21)

3. SENSUAL FOCUS

". . . the woman saw that the (forbidden) tree was good for food (to satisfy the physical), and that it was pleasant to the eyes, and a tree to be desired to make one wise (in knowing evil)." It is significant that Satan tempts us after we are drawn away of our own lusts. (James 1:13-14)

4. QUESTIONING OF SCRIPTURE

His first approach was to cause Eve to question the Word of God, "Hath God said?" (Genesis 3:1) In his question, he implied that God was withholding the best from her. "God knows that. . . you will be as gods, knowing good and evil." (Genesis 3:5)

5. VIOLATION OF CONSCIENCE

As the sensual focus continues, lust conceives and brings forth a violation of God's law. (James 1:15) This violation may vary greatly from one person to the next, yet the result in each person is the same—a keen awakening of guilt.

6. AWAKENING OF GUILT

After Adam and Eve reached out and ate the forbidden fruit, they hid from God. A violation of conscience produces the awareness of personal responsibility before God and forces a person to respond either negatively or positively toward this guilt. This awakening of guilt is even reflected in the facial expressions of a child when he has done something which he instinctively knows is wrong. (Romans 2:15)

7. RESPONSE TO GUILT

The human system was not made to carry the emotional strain of guilt. We must respond to the guilt. We can attempt to appease God by doing good to make up for it, or we can rationalize the offense away, or we can follow God's way and repent of the transgression which produced the guilt. Confession enables us to receive His cleansing according to I John 1:9.

NOTES

DEVELOPMENT OF REPROBATION

• The following development of the wrong response to guilt explains how the spiritual system deteriorates so that it is not able to or does not wish to comprehend a heaven or hell or God. "For this cause God shall send them strong delusion." (II Thessalonians 2:11)

8. INCOMPLETE REPENTANCE OF LASCIVIOUSNESS

Incomplete repentance takes place when there is sorrow over the consequences of sin but not over the sin itself. The beginning of wisdom is to hate evil. (Proverbs 8:13; 9:10) Repentance for only the consequences of sin soon produces the secret envy of those who can "get away with it" and also gives rise to a world of fantasy in which secret, sensual desires are fulfilled.

9. COMPENSATION IN RELIGIOUS ACTIVITY

Since incomplete repentance does not remove the guilt, there is an attempt to personally make up for the sin by performing some religious or humanitarian service. This also prompts self-inflicted hardships.

10. FRUSTRATION OVER CONCUPISCENCE

Even though there is a sincere attempt to "turn over a new leaf," the sensual appetites which lasciviousness has stimulated now demand fulfillment. This produces frustration and double-mindedness. (James 1:8, 15)

11. "REDEFINING" MORALITY

There is a continuous mental effort to justify personal moral behavior on the basis of the existing moral code. Thus, if that code can be "reinterpreted" to include as "moral" what was previously immoral, the mind is eager to accept this and to reject previous codes as "straight-laced," "mid-Victorian," "too narrow," "rigid righteousness," etc.

12. ARGUMENTATION OVER SCRIPTURE AND DOCTRINE

Those who have "redefined" Scripture or God to fit in with their immorality will be quick to advance their ideas in order to "enlarge their world." In their world they have decided what is right and what is wrong. They are men of corrupt minds. (Titus 3:10,11) They willingly believe a lie. (II Thessalonians 2:II)

NOTES

THE EFFECT OF CONCUPISCENCE IN DATING

• Many teen-agers are looking for or reacting against a list of do's and don'ts on dating standards. As important as a list of guidelines is, it is even more important for each one to understand what the inner motivations and needs of the one being dated are.

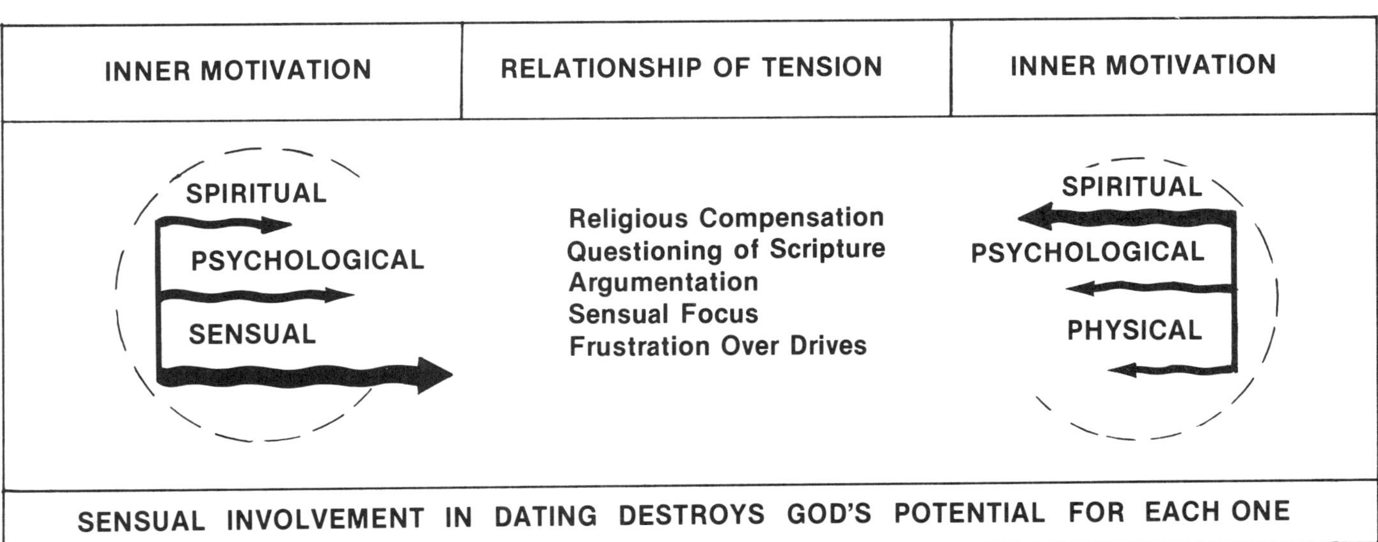

FREEDOM

BASIC STEPS TO CONQUER IMPURITY

1. LEARN TO "HATE" EVIL

A. MINIMIZE THE BENEFITS OF EVIL

The pleasures of sin last only for a season. (Hebrews 11:25)

B. MAGNIFY THE CONSEQUENCES OF EVIL

The sins of the parents are visited upon the third and fourth generations. (Exodus 34:7)

C. MAKE NO PROVISION FOR THE FLESH

". . . make not provision for the flesh, to fulfill the lusts thereof." (Romans 13:14)

D. TEST YOUR HATRED OF EVIL

The more we hate sin, the more we are able to love the sinner. The less we hate sin, the less we are able to love the sinner. (Christ's examples)

NOTES

2. MANIFEST COMPLETE REPENTANCE

A. AGREE WITH GOD

If we "fall into immorality" and still insist that we really aren't that type of person but we just slipped, we are disagreeing with God. He states, "The heart is deceitful above all things, and desperately wicked: who can know it?" (Jeremiah 17:9) Our response if we sin should be, "Lord, what I just did proves how accurate your Word really is."

B. IDENTIFY THE ROOT CAUSE OF SIN

The root cause of all our sins is the sin of being the boss and rejecting Christ. All impurity is only a by-product and evidence that Jesus Christ was not in control. The word "Lord" means "boss."

C. VISUALIZE THE SPIRITUAL CONSEQUENCES OF SIN

When we sin, we are really nailing Jesus Christ to the cross. We are also saying with those who crucified Him, "We will not have this man to reign over us." "He was wounded for our transgressions, he was bruised for our iniquities." (Isaiah 53:5) It is essential that we superimpose this picture over each transgression that comes to mind.

D. INTEGRATE PAST CONFLICTS INTO MEANINGFUL THOUGHT PATTERNS

The degree of inward peace which we experience is directly determined by the degree to which we are able to integrate all past experiences into meaningful thought patterns, such as the following:

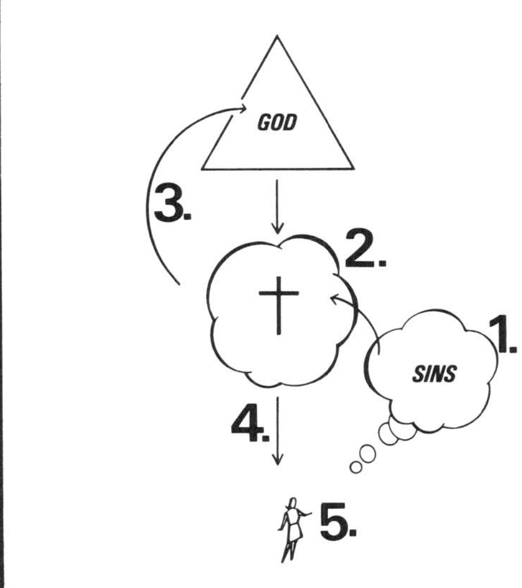

1. Remembrance of past failure.
2. That failure helped nail Christ to the cross.
3. Christ's death became payment for my sin.
4. I have asked God to cleanse me through the blood of Christ.
5. Now I belong to God, and my life is committed to Jesus Christ and His will for me.

FREEDOM

NOTES

THE STRUGGLE OF PRIDE IN COMPLETE REPENTANCE

• The very first step toward genuine repentance is to recognize the basic sin for which we are repenting. This basic sin is not the action of moral impurity or any of a number of other sins. They only reveal the deeper violation.

• THE PROBLEM OF PRIDE

"A woman came by appointment to discuss her problems. Reared in a thoroughly respectable home, she had attended church regularly during her youth. An unfortunate friendship had led to a way of life with which she herself was unhappy, and which had severed her from her friends.

"Soon the moral pillars of her life began to crumble, and she lost her self-respect. Her marriage failed through her own unfaithfulness, and every new turn of events seemed to bring temptations she could not overcome, until she had lost all incentive to resist. She was now adrift and subject to whatever influences were closest at hand. Her story was really quite shocking.

• PRIDE ASSURES US WE'RE NOT SO BAD

"She knew how wrong she was, how out of touch with God and humanity, and how much of an enemy she was to herself. Her conscience was obviously troubling her, and she was laboring under a sense of heavy guilt. Therefore, the statement she made when she finished with her story was quite surprising: '**People seem to think that I am such a terrible sinner. I can't see that I am such a bad person.**'

• PRIDE WILL AGREE TO ASSISTANCE BUT NOT TO SURRENDER

"She wanted prayer for the improvement of her morals and her fortunes, and she felt quite distressed about the failure she had made of life, but she could not see herself as a sinner. Her attitude was typical.

"There are few things more difficult to accept than God's appraisal of all men as sinners. Even those who are obvious sinners find it difficult to see their sinfulness. There are others who seem to be nothing but personified goodness through and through. It seems even more difficult to look upon them as being sinners. What is the Biblical definition of sin? Just what does the New Testament mean when it says, 'None is righteous, no, not one;' and that, 'all have sinned'?

NOTES

• PRIDE CAN BE VERY RESPECTABLE AND MORAL

"The fact that evil-doing results in social disapproval and unhappiness does not in itself make it sinful. On the other hand, the person who is law abiding and well-adjusted socially because he knows that evil-doing and crime do not pay is thereby not righteous. Those who disregard established moral laws are a menace and a problem to society and must be dealt with accordingly. However, they are not necessarily more sinful than the most respectable citizens.

"People are often troubled about the results of their misconduct and by what others think of them. They may have aspirations to do better, which may be more or less thwarted by temptations to do worse. Many times they will have great emotional disturbances as a result of their concern about their conduct.

• PRIDE WILL STRUGGLE TO DO BETTER

"They may even pray to God to help them, and they may perform religious exercises and attend religious services because of the strength that religion promises. None of this is necessarily due to a sense of sinfulness. It may be the result of an intense desire to achieve a happy and well-adjusted life and to be accepted and approved by others.

"Such distressing feelings, which result from the lack of social adjustment and approval, are often thought of as a sense of sinfulness. However, we must make it clear that the New Testament means something different from this when it speaks of confessing that we are sinners. A deep sense of sin will have a very sobering effect upon a person, but the New Testament never presents sin in such a way that recognizing it in ourselves should lead us to despair.

• PRIDE DOESN'T UNDERSTAND THE REASON GOD CALLS US SINNERS

"Jesus never condemned anyone who recognized that he was a sinner. In fact, it was for just such people that He offered hope. Introspective examination and hopeless depression over our failings are the result of an unwillingness to recognize that we are really sinners. Once having accepted God's verdict that we are sinners, we can turn our attention to the good news that Christ offers to sinners."

"Man's sinfulness consists in his REFUSAL TO HONOR GOD AS GOD. It is not necessarily a denial of the existence of God. It is not a rejection of the philosophical or religious concept of God. We are sinners even though we believe in God and worship Him.

• PRIDE WILL NOT GIVE GOD HIS RIGHTFUL PLACE

"If God is God, His rightful place is at the very center of all existence, so that all of life revolves around Him. Our sinfulness consists in that God is not given this place. Life for us does not revolve around God. It revolves around ourselves.

"Men have even gone so far as to make gods of their own choosing in order to make God conform to their own desires. Someone has correctly likened sin to anarchy. Crime is breaking the laws of the State, but anarchy challenges the very right of the State to make laws. Sin is more than breaking God's commandments. It challenges the very right of God to rule as God.

NOTES

• PRIDE ALLOWS LIFE TO REVOLVE AROUND OURSELVES

"The New Testament, therefore, defines sin as something more than mere wrong-doing. It is allowing life to revolve around ourselves instead of God. The life of everyone of us revolves around himself, and God does not occupy the place of God to any of us. Therefore, we are all sinners. The power of sin over us is such that it is impossible for us to change this situation.

"This rejection of God as God, so that life revolves around ourselves instead of Him, is behind all moral and spiritual evil. One kind of moral evil is described in the first chapter of Romans where it is stated three times that 'God gave them up' to all forms of degradation. (Romans 1:24,26,28)

• PRIDE KEEPS SELF ON THE THRONE

"Envy, murder, sexual immorality and perversion, gossip, insolence, ruthlessness, etc. are described as symptoms of man's refusal to allow God to be God to him. When men refused to honor God as God, they removed themselves from His dominion. He merely let them go. They became subject to overpowering passions which produced all forms of immorality. Sin has become a power dominating man.

"Sin rules by keeping self, instead of God, in the center of our lives. Therefore, salvation from sin is to a certain extent salvation from ourselves. This is something which has been missed by some Christians who go about seeking ways to improve themselves when they really need to be saved from the self they are trying to improve.

• PRIDE LEADS TO A REPROBATE MIND

"When men have once dethroned God and put self in His place, sin ceases to exist for them except as an abstract concept. Since God is no longer at the center of life, and men do not recognize His right to be there, they are no longer conscious of any rebellion against Him, and sin ceases to be sin for them.

"When God is no longer honored as God, sin ceases to be sin in the eyes of the sinner. Sin makes it impossible for us to see that we are subjects of a spiritual kingdom that refuses to honor God as God, and that is completely at odds with God. Sin rules over us by making it impossible for us to see that we are enemies in active rebellion against God, and that in this controversy He is right and we are wrong.

• PRIDE ENSLAVES US IN THE SIN CHRIST CAME TO FREE US FROM

"Sin has the power to convince those who are its most obedient slaves that they themselves are free. When Jesus spoke to certain people of freedom, they replied, 'We are descendants of Abraham and have never been in bondage to anyone. How is it that you say, 'You will be made free?' (John 8:33) They were full or resentment, ill will and pride. Yet they considered themselves to be perfectly free.

"God and man cannot be reconciled simply by God being gracious and loving enough to overlook our faults and forgive our sins. Release must be something more than ordinary forgiveness. It must be something which will redeem us from the power of sin so that God may again become God to us." (From Captivated by Christ, Wesley Nelson, Christian Literature Crusade, Fort Washington, Pennsylvania, 1956)

NOTES

THE IMPORTANCE OF REPENTING OF PRIDE

• Receiving God's grace, (His power within us to follow His will - I Corinthians 15:10), is the only way we will overcome moral impurity or any other sin. And the way we receive His grace is by humbling ourselves before God. "God resisteth the proud but giveth grace unto the humble." James 4:6

THE STEPS GOD GIVES TO REPENT OF PRIDE James 4

1. "SUBMIT YOURSELVES TO GOD"

This means total, unconditional acceptance of Jesus Christ as Lord and Savior. It means finding His will for daily living. It means no longer leaning on our own understanding. It means getting back under the authority He has placed over us. This is especially important for the next step.

2. "RESIST THE DEVIL"

This involves purposing in our hearts that we will not defile ourselves. (Daniel 1:8) It means learning and quoting Scripture when temptations come, as Christ did to Satan. It also involves learning how to intercede for those in authority over us. By doing this, we assist them to resist temptation, and they then become better "umbrellas of protection" for us. (I Timothy 2:1,2; James 5:16)

3. "DRAW NEAR TO GOD"

We draw near to God by spending time in His Word and in prayerful meditation of its application to our lives—beginning with a thorough self-examination of the past. As we examine all the prideful actions and motives of the past we will see how we have sinned and hurt others. We will see how disloyal we have been to God and others.

As a result of this activity, we should "be afflicted, and mourn, and weep:" our "laughter will be turned to mourning and our joy to heaviness." (James 4:9)

4. "CLEANSE YOUR HANDS OF SIN"

This means ceasing any activity of impurity and getting rid of any possessions of impurity. It also means cleaning our "hands" of any guilt that is on them from offending others. This involves humbling ourselves and going to them to gain forgiveness and a clear conscience.

5. "PURIFY YOUR HEARTS OF DOUBLE-MINDEDNESS"

We are warned in James, chapter one, not to ask God for things we're really not sure we want Him to give us. Do we really want Him to humble us? Do we really want to be holy? Do we want to hate sin and love the things of God?

NOTES

3. LEARN TO WALK IN GOD'S SPIRIT

"This I say then, walk in the Spirit and ye shall not fulfill the lust of the flesh."
Galatians 5:16

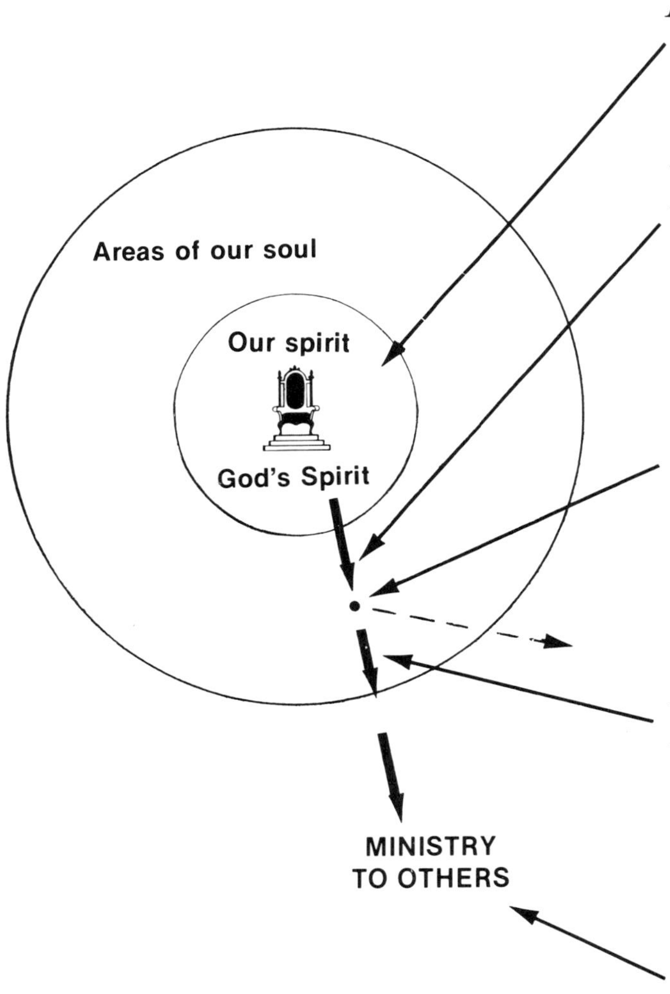

A. INDWELLING

When we receive Jesus Christ as our personal Savior, His Spirit indwells our life. His specific home in us is our spirits. (Ephesians 1:13,14)

B. FILLING

The Spirit of God desires freedom to fill all the inward parts of our souls (mind, will and emotions). He wants to transform them into the image of Christ. (Ephesians 5:18,19; Romans 12:2)

C. TESTING

When the Holy Spirit reveals thoughts, words, actions, or attitudes which need changing, a test results—God's Spirit versus our spirit. If our willful spirit prevails, God's Spirit is grieved and His effectiveness in us is quenched. (I Peter 1:6; James 1:2; I Peter 4:12; Luke 4:1)

D. RESISTING

Just as Jesus Christ resisted Satan with the sword of the Word, so we must determine the precise Scriptural principles to quote to Satan with each temptation. (James 4:7; I Peter 5:9; Ephesians 6:17)

E. MATURING

To the degree that we cooperate with the Holy Spirit in resisting Satan with the Word of God, we develop spiritual maturity. Jesus went to the wilderness in the fulness of the Spirit, but He returned in the power of the Spirit. (Luke 4:14; Colossians 1:29)

NOTES

4. INCREASE SPIRITUAL ALERTNESS

• Our ability to perceive God's direction in life is directly related to our ability to sense the inner promptings of His Spirit. God provides a specific activity to assist us in doing this.

A. LEARN WHY FASTING INCREASES SPIRITUAL ALERTNESS

If we eat, an increased amount of blood is needed for our digestive processes; if we exercise, a greater amount of blood is used in building up our muscles; but if we neither eat nor exercise, a greater amount of blood is available for mental and spiritual concentration.

B. DISCERN WHEN TO FAST

Fasting is a voluntary abstinence from food for one or more meals.

Fasting must be combined with Scripture memorization and meditation.

Fasting should focus on reaching specific spiritual objectives.

Fasting is most efficient when practiced regularly one day a week.

Fasting should be preceded by nutritional eating habits and medical counsel if physical ailments exist.

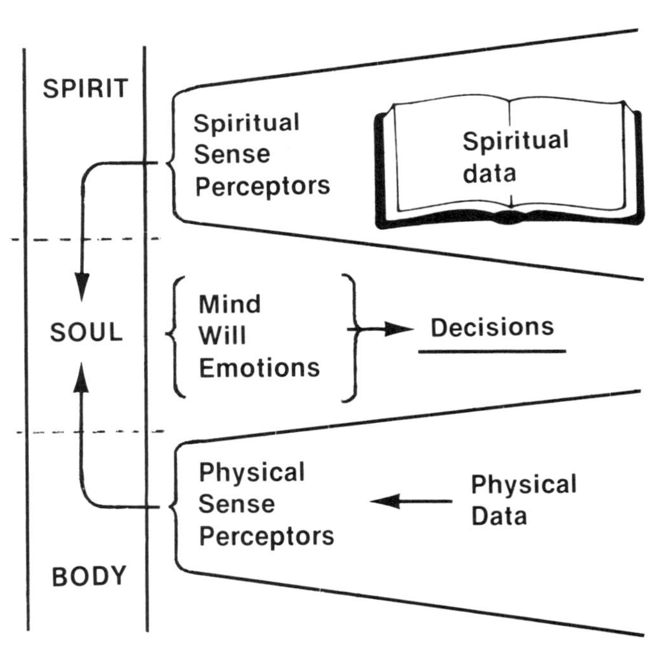

C. TURN NEEDS INTO MOTIVATION FOR FASTING

	READ, MEMORIZE, MEDITATE
☐ Detecting temptation	James 1; Galatians 5; Psalm 25
☐ Conquering moral impurity	Colossians 3; Romans 6,7 & 8
☐ Discerning God's will	I Thessalonians 4; Romans 12
☐ Identifying genuine love	Philippians 2; I Corinthians 13; I John
☐ Increasing spiritual growth	John 15; I Peter 2; Matthew 5,6 & 7

NOTES

GUIDES FOR A DAY OF FASTING

• Men through whom God has worked greatly have emphasized the significance of prayer with fasting. One such man used the following schedule for a day of prayer and fasting.

• Whenever this Christian leader had an important decision to make, or whenever he was asked to bring an important message, he would set aside a twenty-four hour period prior to the meeting or to the time the decision had to be made. The twenty-four hours went from evening to evening. Here are the items included in his day of prayer and fasting.

***EVENING**

• **READING LARGE SECTIONS OF SCRIPTURE**

He read or scanned as many significant sections of Scripture as possible for general content and key ideas related to the subject of his needs.

• **MARKING SIGNIFICANT SECTIONS FOR FURTHER STUDY**

When a particular section seemed significant to him, he would make a special notation of it for the purpose of studying it further the following morning.

— SLEEP —

MORNING

• **STRENGTHENING PERSONAL SPIRITUAL COMMUNION**

His first job in the morning was to enjoy a time of personal edification from the Psalms and Proverbs. These sections were used to put his own heart in tune with the Lord.

• **STUDYING SIGNIFICANT SECTIONS**

He would then reread the significant sections marked this evening before and begin study in each one. The study involved outlining the section, making special word studies, looking up cross-references, etc.

*God created the evening as the beginning of the day. "The evening and the morning were the first day." (Genesis 1:5, etc.) The significance of this is that the important thoughts in the evening are upon our minds throughout the night hours, and they set our mental attitudes for the following day.

NOTES

• TURNING SCRIPTURE INTO A PERSONAL PRAYER

As each insight was gained in his study of the Scripture, he would turn it into a personal response to the Lord. As he did this, he would analyze his life and evaluate it on the basis of the principles of each section.

AFTERNOON

• SELECTING KEY VERSES TO MEMORIZE

In the course of his study and prayer, key verses would stand out as those which should be committed to memory. He would begin to memorize these, a few verses at a time.

• MAKING MELODY IN HIS HEART

For meaningful variation during memorizing, he would read related excerpts of Christian classics or read and hum related hymns.

• DISCOVERING PRINCIPLES THROUGH MEDITATION

The word "meditation" is based upon rumination—as a cow chewing its cud. In the same way, this missionary would mentally, emotionally and volitionally think and rethink all that which he had studied for the purpose of identifying key Scriptural principles to be used in the solution of his problem or in the preparation of his message.

During this time of meditation, he sometimes would become weary. If so, he would put himself to sleep meditating on Scripture. By doing this, he often discovered that his mind was clearer after a short nap so that his meditation on the Word was even more meaningful.

• After preparing a message by use of this schedule, he would go directly to the platform to bring the message. Those who listened to him speak marvelled at the depth of his message and the preciseness of his words in meeting their needs.

One man made the comment, "It was as though we were listening to the very oracles of God!"

• ADDITIONAL POSSIBLE PROJECTS

It is very beneficial to spend some time during a day, or especially during days of fasting, in reading the biographies of the men and women down through history who are in "God's hall of fame."

It is also important to write down ideas and insights not only on Scripture, but on ways of expressing God's love to those under our care and those around us. These pages will be significant parts of our life notebook.

NOTES

BASIC PURPOSES FOR FASTING

• DEFINITION: FASTING, NESTEUO

To fast; to abstain from eating; is used of voluntary fasting. Fasting was an established practice in Christ's day (Matthew 9:14,15; Mark 2:18-20; Luke 5:33-35) and was practiced in the early church. It is important to remember that it is to be a voluntary activity and not a forced activity.

• In an extended fast of over three days, one quickly experiences a great decrease in sensual desires and soon has a great new alertness to spiritual things. In addition to this, the following are further purposes of fasting listed in Scripture.

FREEDOM

• FASTING TO GAIN SPIRITUAL ALERTNESS TO OVERCOME TEMPTATION

Jesus Christ was led to fast forty days - Matthew 4:2

• FASTING TO SEEK GOD'S WILL IN A SPECIFIC MATTER

The Israelites fasted to determine direction in battle - Judges 20:26
Paul and Barnabas prayed with fasting before choosing elders - Acts 14:23

• FASTING IN REPENTANCE FOR SIN

The Israelites fasted and repented and put away false gods - I Samuel 7:6
David fasted and repented of his sin - II Samuel 12:16; 21-23
Ahab fasted and repented after causing Naboth's death - I Kings 21:27
Hearing God's Word, Israel fasted, confessing their sins - Nehemiah 9:1-3
Daniel fasted and repented for himself and the people for not having walked in the laws of the Lord - God's chastisement was to come - Daniel 9:3
Joel called for a fast because of the Lord's chastening - Joel 1:14; 2:12, 15
The people of Nineveh repented in fasting - Jonah 3:5

• FASTING FOR CONCERN FOR THE WORK OF GOD

Nehemiah fasted over the condition of Jerusalem - Nehemiah 1:4

NOTES

• FASTING FOR DELIVERANCE OR PROTECTION

Jehoshaphat and all Judah fasted for deliverance in battle - II Chronicles 20:3
Ezra and the people fasted for the Lord's deliverance - Ezra 8:21-23
The Jews fasted and grieved after King Ahasuerus' decree - Esther 4:13,16
God delivered the Jews from Haman's plot - they fasted and rejoiced - Esther 9:31
People fasting for repentance and deliverance but God will not hear - Jeremiah 14:12

• FASTING TO HUMBLE ONESELF BEFORE GOD

David humbled himself before God - Psalm 69:10,11,13

• FASTING AS PART OF WORSHIP

Anna served God through prayers and fastings daily - Luke 2:37
The early church was fasting and worshipping God - Acts 13:2,3

• FASTING WHEN IN DEEP SORROW

Sorrow over the death of Saul and his sons - I Samuel 31:13; II Samuel 1:11,12
David grieved over the life of his child - II Samuel 12:16; 21-23
David prayed and fasted for his enemies' troubles - Psalm 35:13
King Darius fasted when Daniel was in the lions' den - Daniel 6:18

GUIDES FOR PROPER USE OF FASTING

Fast for the purpose of greater effectiveness in discerning and achieving God's purposes Isaiah 58:6

Fast secretly and God will reward you openly - Matthew 6:16-18

WARNINGS AGAINST IMPROPER USE OF FASTING

Don't fast to achieve selfish purposes - Isaiah 58:3-5

Don't fast to impress others with your spirituality -Zechariah 7:5; Matthew 6:16-18; Luke 18:12

NOTE: In addition to the above verses, some Greek manuscripts mention fasting in connection with the following references:

Matthew 17:21
Mark 9:29
Acts 10:30
I Corinthians 7:5

NOTES

5. DISCERN CYCLES OF LIFE

• God warns, "He that covereth his sin shall not prosper," and, "Whatsoever a man sows he shall also reap." The following diagram illustrates how this works.

THE FOLLOWING IS BASED ON ROMANS 5-8 AND GALATIANS 5,6

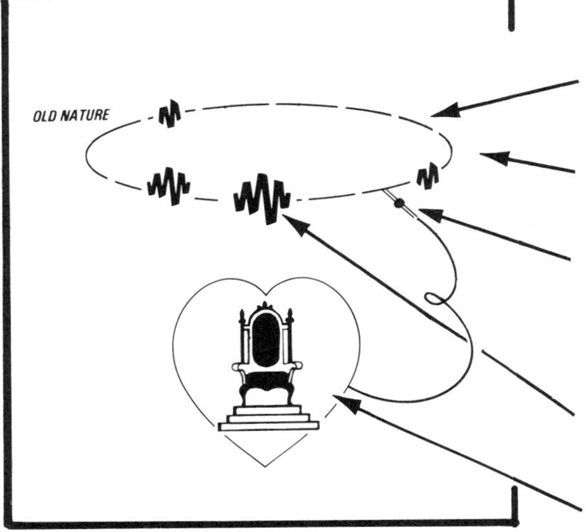

- A cycle of life can be days, weeks, months, years, seasons, circumstances or weather conditions.
- One cycle of life involves impressions of sensuality in our lower nature.
- Obeying an impulse of our lower nature establishes a permanent sin pattern. Unless it is confessed and forsaken, it will reappear when the cycle returns as a motivation to be sensual or to compensate for guilt.
- When sin patterns are reinforced, they become deeper and stronger and are soon sin habits.
- Retaining the right to be our own boss increases and complicates the destructive power of the lower nature.

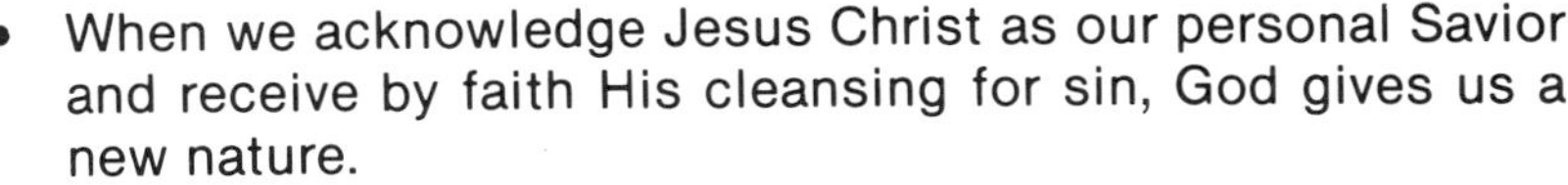

- When we acknowledge Jesus Christ as our personal Savior and receive by faith His cleansing for sin, God gives us a new nature.

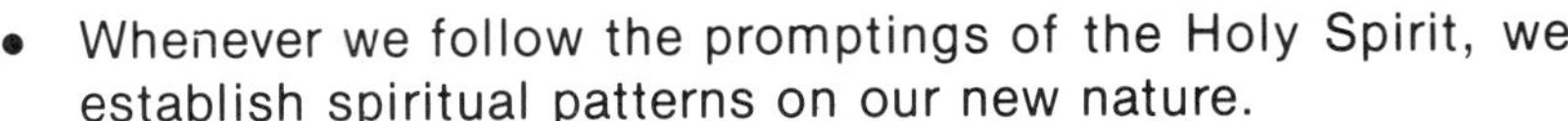

- Whenever we follow the promptings of the Holy Spirit, we establish spiritual patterns on our new nature.

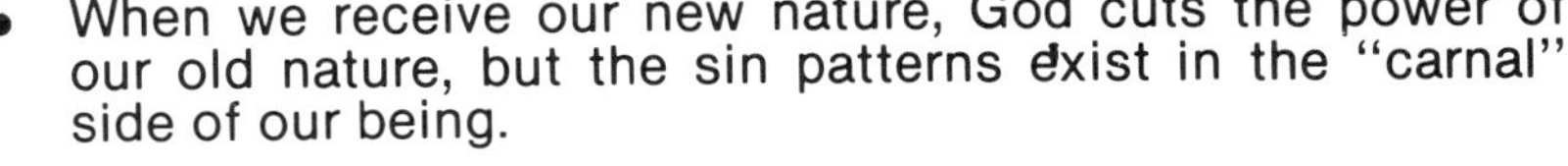

- When we receive our new nature, God cuts the power of our old nature, but the sin patterns exist in the "carnal" side of our being.
- When we are over a previous sin habit, there is a pull from the lower nature to fulfill it. If we surrender to sensuality, we create new pressures of resisting the Holy Spirit and quench His power in us. When we resist these impulses by internalizing Scripture, especially the Psalms, we soon build spiritual patterns equal to the sin patterns.
- When the spiritual patterns are stronger than the former sin patterns, we have a greater desire to do what is right than to do what is wrong. This is the basis of moral freedom.

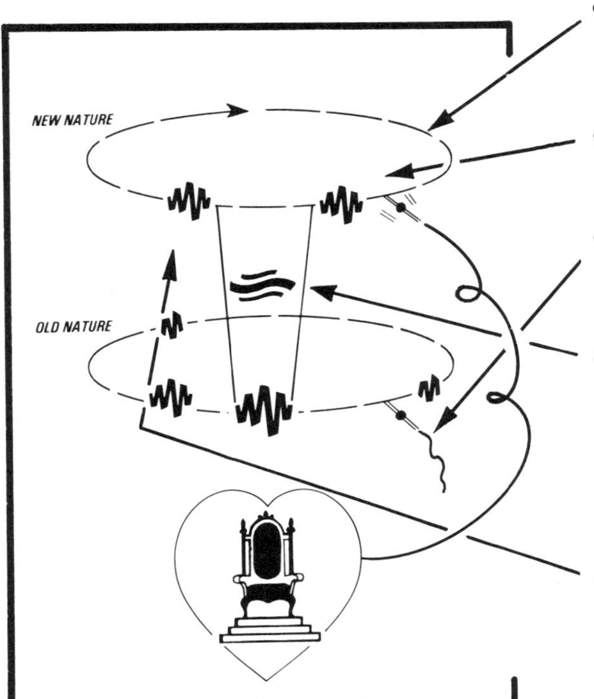

NOTES

6. TRANSFORM THOUGHT PATTERNS

• Since our natural inclinations to do evil are more powerful than our will and emotions to resist them, it is essential that we learn how to cast down every imagination by internalizing Scripture.
II Corinthians 10:4,5

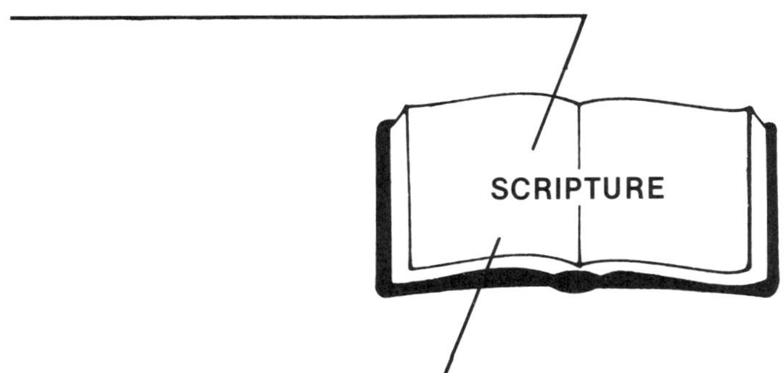

• When we confess Jesus Christ as Lord and Savior, our spirits are reborn by His Spirit. (John 3:6)

• God's Spirit then desires to transform our souls by taking sections of Scripture through the mind, will, and emotions in the following steps. (Romans 12:2)

Emotions

Will

Mind

SOUL

GOD'S SPIRIT

Our Spirit

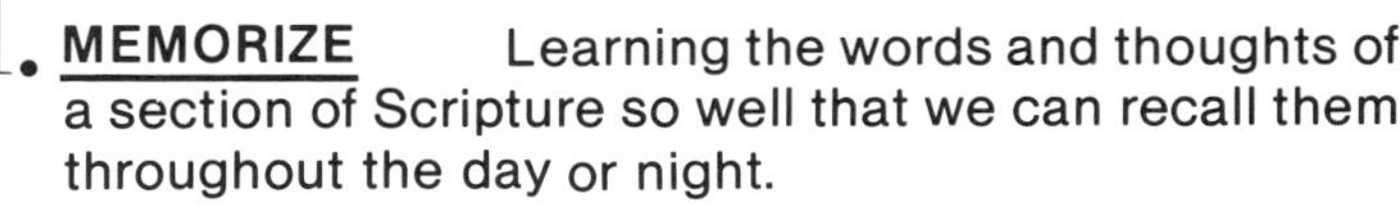

1. <u>MEMORIZE</u> Learning the words and thoughts of a section of Scripture so well that we can recall them throughout the day or night.

2. <u>VISUALIZE</u> Picturing each important word and listing what should be evident in our lives but isn't. If we live our lives in Christ and His words live in our hearts, we may ask for whatever we like (these qualities) and they will come true for us. (John 15:7)

3. <u>PERSONALIZE</u> Changing pronouns of "you," "they," and "his" to "I," "me," and "my" so that the Scripture becomes a personal expression to God of our inward thoughts, decisions, and emotions.

4. <u>HARMONIZE</u> Putting the words of Scripture to creative melody as we express them to the Lord, "Singing and making melody in our hearts (with Scripture) for the ears of God." "The Father seeketh such to worship Him." (Ephesians 5:18; John 4:23)

• This process constitutes meditation. God assures us that whatever we do will prosper if we meditate day and night. It is the ultimate activity by which we gain moral freedom.

NOTES

TRANSFORMING THOUGHTS

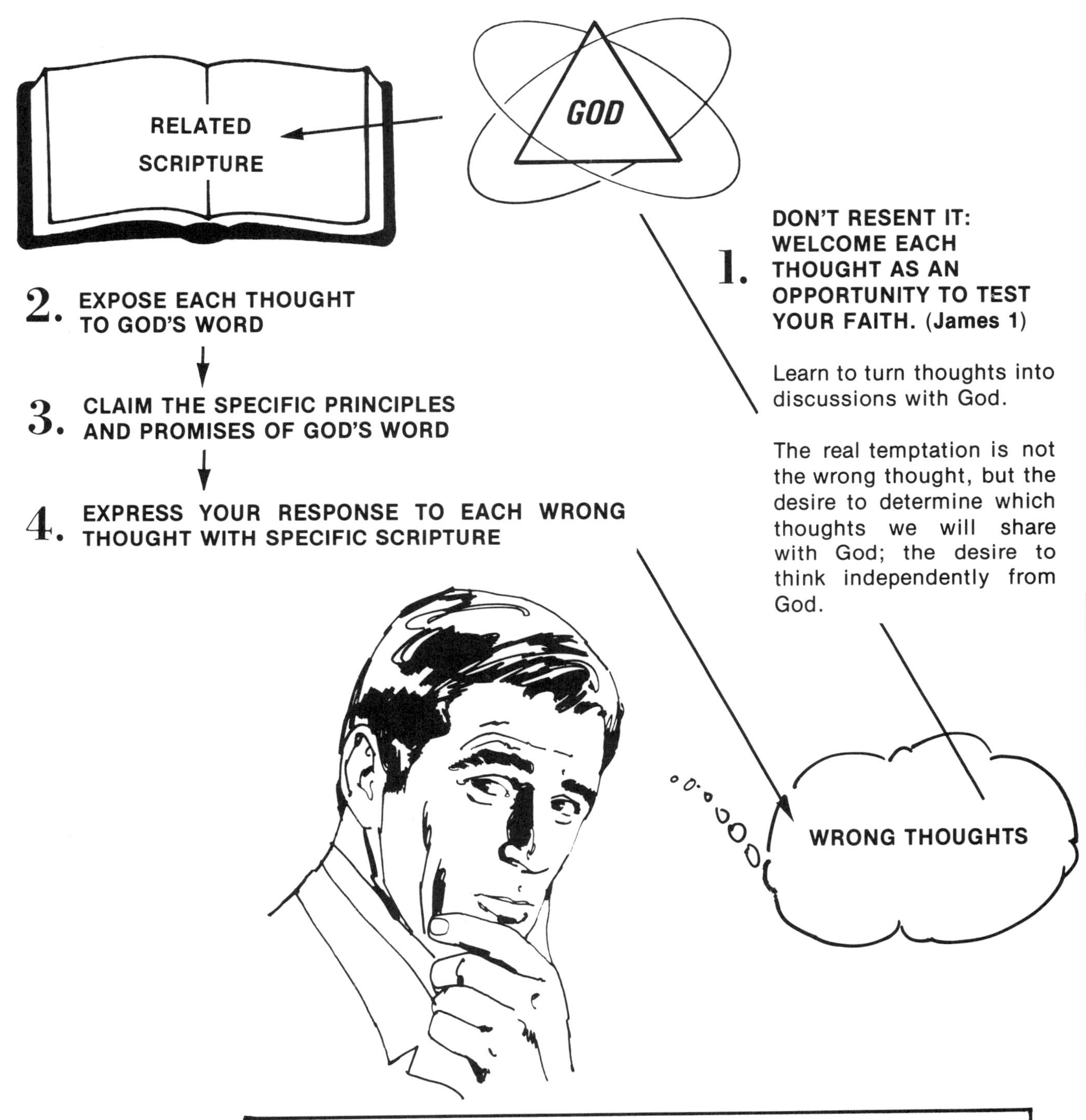

FREEDOM

- "For the weapons of our warfare are not carnal, but mighty through God to the pulling down of strong holds; casting down imaginations, and every high thing that exalteth itself against the knowledge of God, and bringing into captivity every thought to the obedience of Christ." II Corinthians 10:4,5

NOTES

SUCCESSFUL
Living

NOTES

TABLE OF CONTENTS

NOTES

THE FOUNTAIN OF TRUE SUCCESS

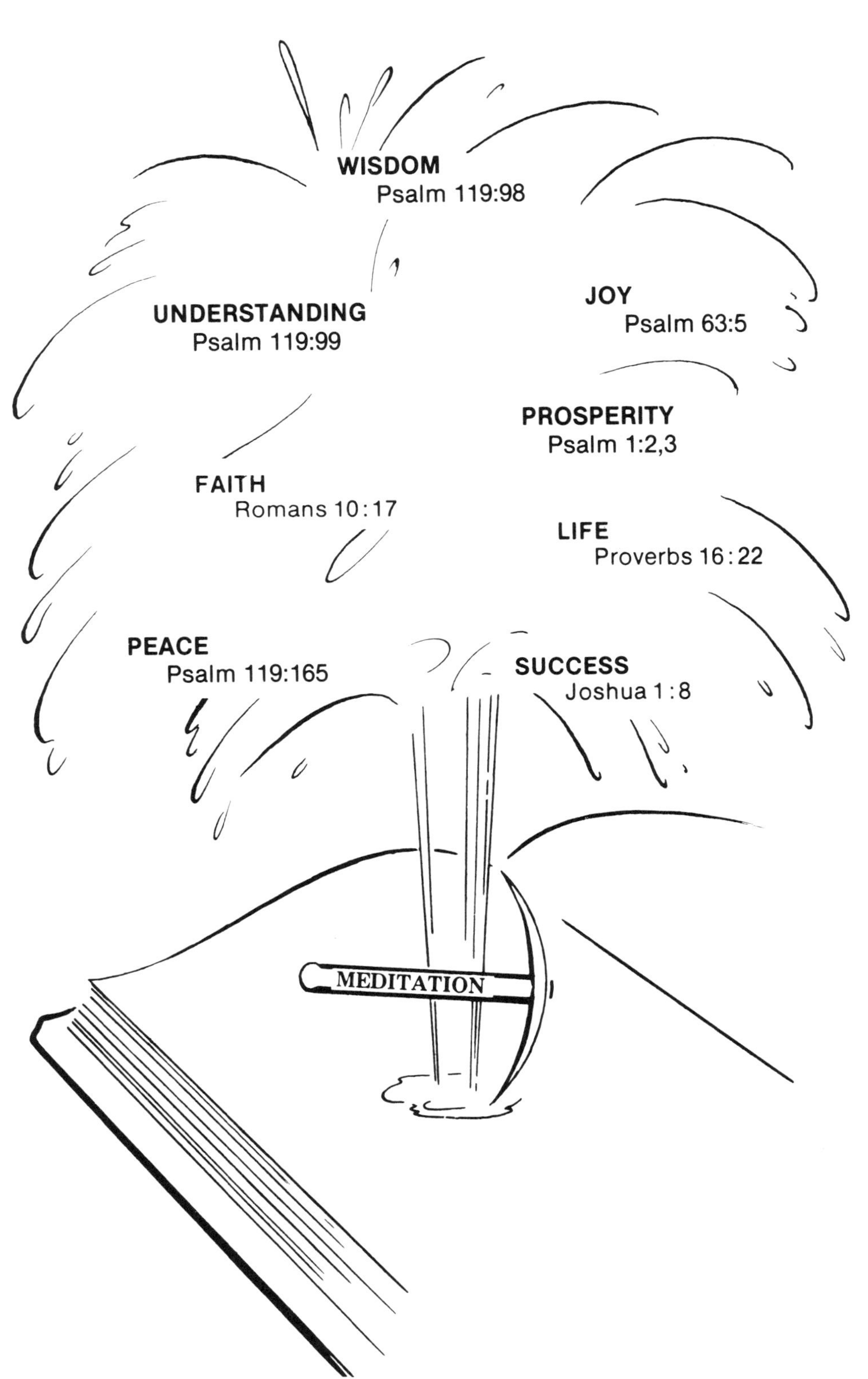

• My lack of scholastic ability became quite obvious to my teachers and to me as far back as the first grade.

It required nine years and a lot of teachers' patience and sympathy to get me through the first eight years of school. At the bottom of those eight passing report cards were those familiar words, "PASSED ON PROBATION."

Prior to my entering high school, I sincerely purposed to make good grades; but with four to six hours of study each night, I only managed to "achieve" average grades.

Then a Christian friend challenged me to begin a certain "project" in my Christian life which at first seemed quite impossible.

However, I diligently worked on this "project" for a semester. At the end of that semester the school grades rose to an A- average!

The "project" was continued during the remaining years of high school whereupon I graduated as a member of the National Honor Society.

This "project" was maintained "off and on" during college and graduate school. To my amazement, in direct proportion to my faithfulness in this "project", my grades went either up or down.

NOTES

THE BASIC REQUIREMENT

WHICH GOD HAS ESTABLISHED FOR LIFE, WISDOM AND SUCCESS

• Whenever God speaks of success in Scripture, He relates it to the continuous inner activity of meditation.

- **YOU WILL HAVE GOOD SUCCESS**

"This book of the law shall not depart out of thy mouth, but thou shalt meditate therein day and night, that thou mayest observe to do according to all that is written therein: for then thou shalt make thy way prosperous, and then thou shalt have good success." (Joshua I:8)

- **WHATEVER YOU DO WILL PROSPER**

"But his delight is in the law of the Lord; and in his law doth he meditate day and night. And he shall be like a tree planted by the rivers of water, that bringeth forth his fruit in his season; his leaf also shall not wither; and whatsoever he doeth shall prosper." (Psalm 1:2,3)

- **YOU WILL EXCEL IN WISDOM AND UNDERSTANDING**

"O how love I thy law! It is my meditation all the day. . . I understand more than all my teachers: for thy testimonies are my meditation." (Psalm 119:97,100)

- **YOU WILL HAVE NEW POWER OVER SIN**

"Wherewithal shall a young man cleanse his way? By taking heed thereto according to thy word. . . Thy word have I had in mine heart that I might not sin against thee." (Psalm 119:9,11)

- **YOU WILL DISCOVER HOW TO LIVE**

"He taught me also, and said unto me, Let thine heart retain my words; keep my commandments and live." (Proverbs 4:4)

- **YOUR SUCCESS WILL BE OBVIOUS TO ALL**

"Meditate upon these things; give thyself wholly to them; that thy profiting may appear to all." (I Timothy 4:15)

• The project that this Christian friend introduced to me was memorizing and meditating on a chapter of Scripture each week.

God does not promise success for memorizing Scripture, but He does promise success for anyone who will meditate in His Word day and night.

The continuous mental discipline of memorizing and meditating on Scripture rebuilt my thought structures, refocused my emotions, and redirected my goals.

Very logical by-products of this activity were increased memory span, greater ability to concentrate and an improved reading rate.

The absence of these had been some of the major causes for poor grades in school.

As this project continued many other beneficial by-products began to appear. When it was discontinued there was a noticeable decline in the success of what I attempted to accomplish.

One of the reasons God is able to guarantee success in whatever we do if we meditate on His Word (Psalm 1:3) is that meditation brings a greater ability to discern ahead of time which ventures will be successful and which ones will not be successful.

NOTES

THE PRICE OF SUCCESS

PERSONAL DISCIPLINE

- **THE PROBLEM OF GETTING INTO GOD'S WORD DAILY**

My good intentions defeated me. I knew how important it was to read God's Word daily and wanted to spend at least one hour, but since I didn't have this much time in the morning, I purposed to do it after school.

After school, interruptions came and I decided to put it off until after dinner. But the pressure of homework caused me to postpone it until right before going to sleep. Then I was too tired so I resolved to get up earlier the next morning. But the next morning I reasoned that sleep was important and I'd do it right after school. This discouraging routine was repeated over and over again. It caused me to wonder if it really was important to read God's Word every day.

- **THE IMPORTANCE OF BEING IN GOD'S WORD DAILY**

> "Blessed is the man that heareth me, watching daily at my gates, waiting at the posts of my doors." (Proverbs 8:34)
>
> ". . . he wakeneth morning by morning, he wakeneth mine ear to hear as the learned." (Isaiah 50:4)
>
> "My voice shalt thou hear in the morning, O Lord; in the morning w1ll I direct my prayer unto thee, and will look up." (Psalm 5:3)

- **A CAUTION BEFORE MAKING A VOW TO READ DAILY**

"When thou vowest a vow unto God, defer not to pay it; for he hath no pleasure in fools: pay that which thou hast vowed. Better it is that thou shouldest not vow, than that thou shouldest vow and not pay.

"Suffer not thy mouth to cause thy flesh to sin; neither say to the angel, that it was an error: wherefore should God be angry at thy voice, and destroy the work of thine hands?" (Ecclesiastes 5:4-6)

• Even before that Christian friend introduced me to the inward exercise of meditation, another friend suggested that I make a decision which would be a big step toward helping me include God's Word in my daily schedule.

He suggested that I make a vow to God that I would spend at least ten minutes every day reading His Word. Previously I had made many promises and resolutions to myself that I would be more faithful in reading Scripture, but these never carried the same weight as did a vow to God.

A vow to God is a very serious matter - as emphasized in Ecclesiastes 5:4-6. I was urged to consider this before making it.

Shortly after making that vow, I discovered that it did remove one of my biggest hindrances to consistent Christian living - that of getting started in God's Word every day. Once I started reading the Word, the time usually went well beyond the ten-minute minimum.

The first big test to this vow came during the week after making it. One day I completely forgot about it until I was in bed and almost asleep. All of a sudden God reminded me about it - as He has faithfully done every day since. I realized that if I debated for even one minute, I'd fall asleep, and the words of Ecclesiastes 5:4 quickly came to mind.

After jumping out of bed I struggled to keep my eyes open for the ten minutes. I didn't get too much from the reading that night, but this taught me a big lesson. Up to that point I was trying to fit God's Word into my schedule rather than building my schedule around God's Word. This became an important turning point in my whole outlook on life.

NOTES

TRUE SUCCESS DEFINED

Success is not determined by what we are but rather by what we are compared to what we could be. It is not measured by what we have done but rather by what we have done compared to what we could have done.

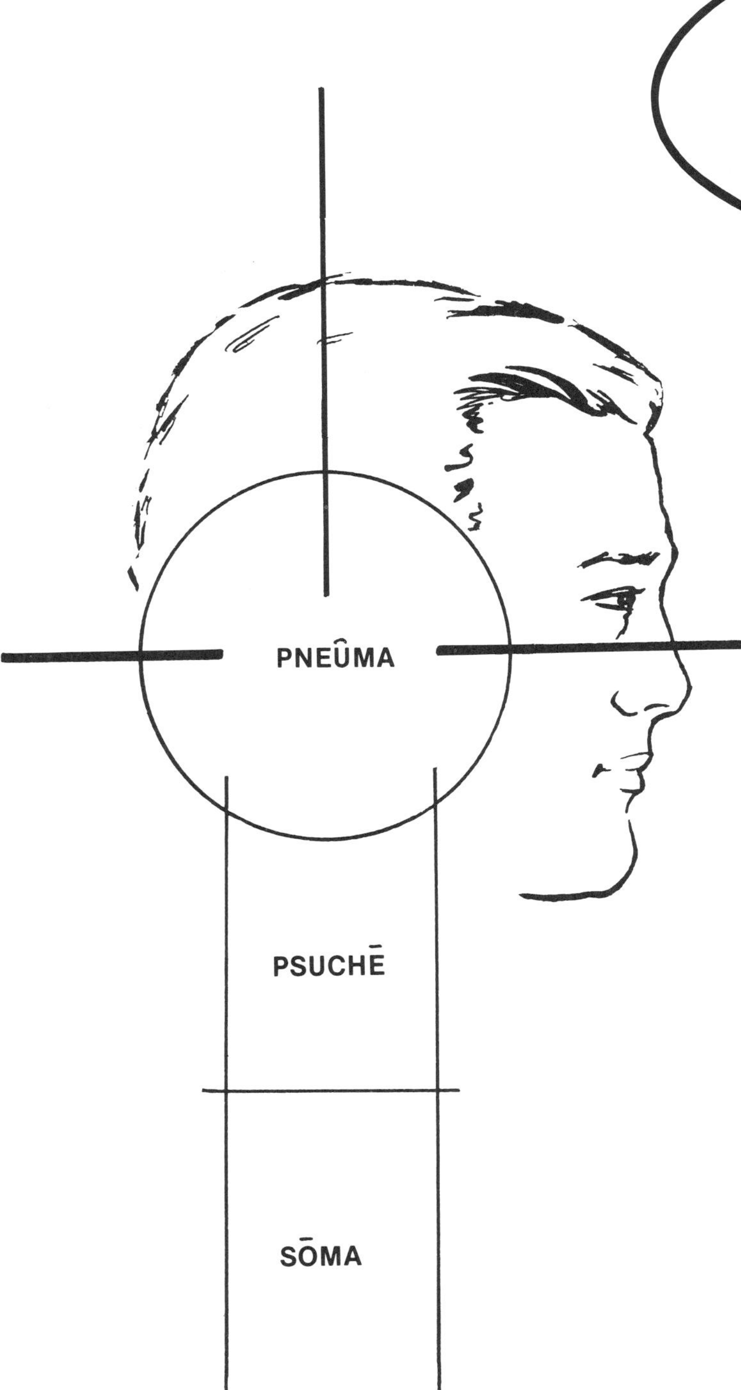

- **OUTWARD SUCCESS BUT INWARD FRUSTRATION**

A bewildered and very concerned young man revealed deep inward frustration which was becoming heavier by the day. His friends considered him to be very successful since he had achieved the high educational, social and financial goals he had set for himself. Inwardly, however, he was becoming more and more perplexed over a deep sense of unfulfillment. He was unaware of its cause.

- **THE PROBLEM OF NOT BEING A "WHOLE PERSON"**

The first step toward an answer came when he learned that one of the basic parts of his total being had never been made alive and integrated with the other parts of his being.

He had taken care of the needs of his body and the needs of his mind, but life was designed to be lived on three levels, and he had neglected his spirit (pneuma). In spite of his accomplishments, he had not yet become a whole person. His life was lived on a dull "two-dimensional" plane rather than on a dynamic "three-dimensional" one. He was outwardly successful but inwardly dissatisfied. He was outwardly busy but inwardly bored.

- **SUCCESSFUL LIVING RESULTS FROM SUCCESSFUL DEVELOPMENT OF SPIRIT, SOUL AND BODY.**

- **THE FOLLOWING MATERIAL WAS THEN EXPLAINED TO HIM.**

NOTES

THE CAUSE OF BOREDOM

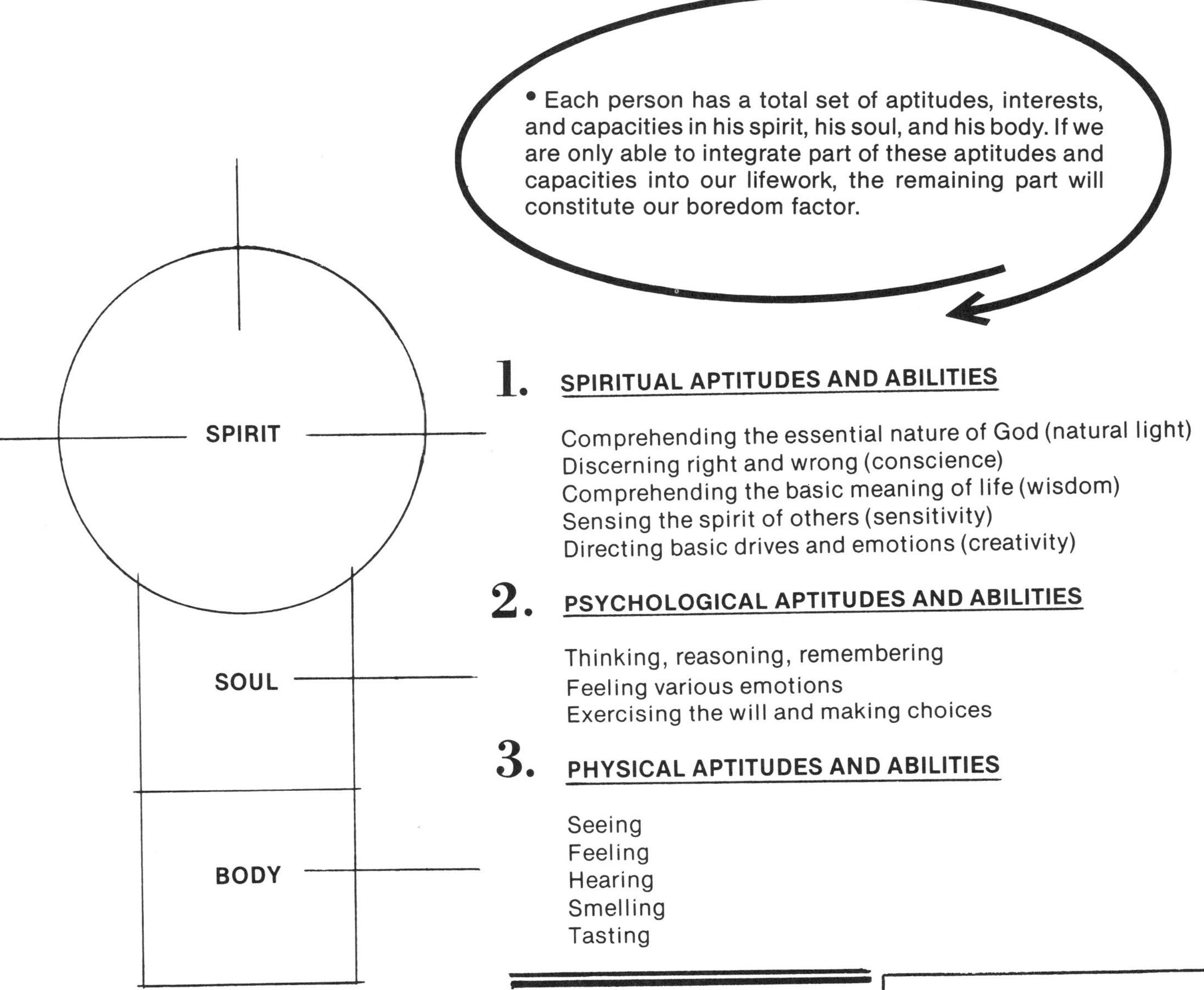

• In determining the total potential of our lives, we must add up all the above aptitudes and abilities.

• If we only develop and integrate 30 per cent of our total aptitudes and capacities into our lifework, then we will have a 70 per cent boredom factor in our lives.

NOTE:

The above divisions are designed as a teaching aid. Man is a unity and is difficult to divide into parts; however, in I Thessalonians 5:23 we have a three-fold division. ". . .and I pray God your whole spirit and soul and body be preserved blameless. . ." The Greek word "KAI" which is translated "and" is used between spirit and soul as well as between soul and body. This grammatical construction clearly shows that the spirit differs from the soul and the soul differs from the body.

NOTES

THE BASIS OF MAKING CORRECT DECISIONS

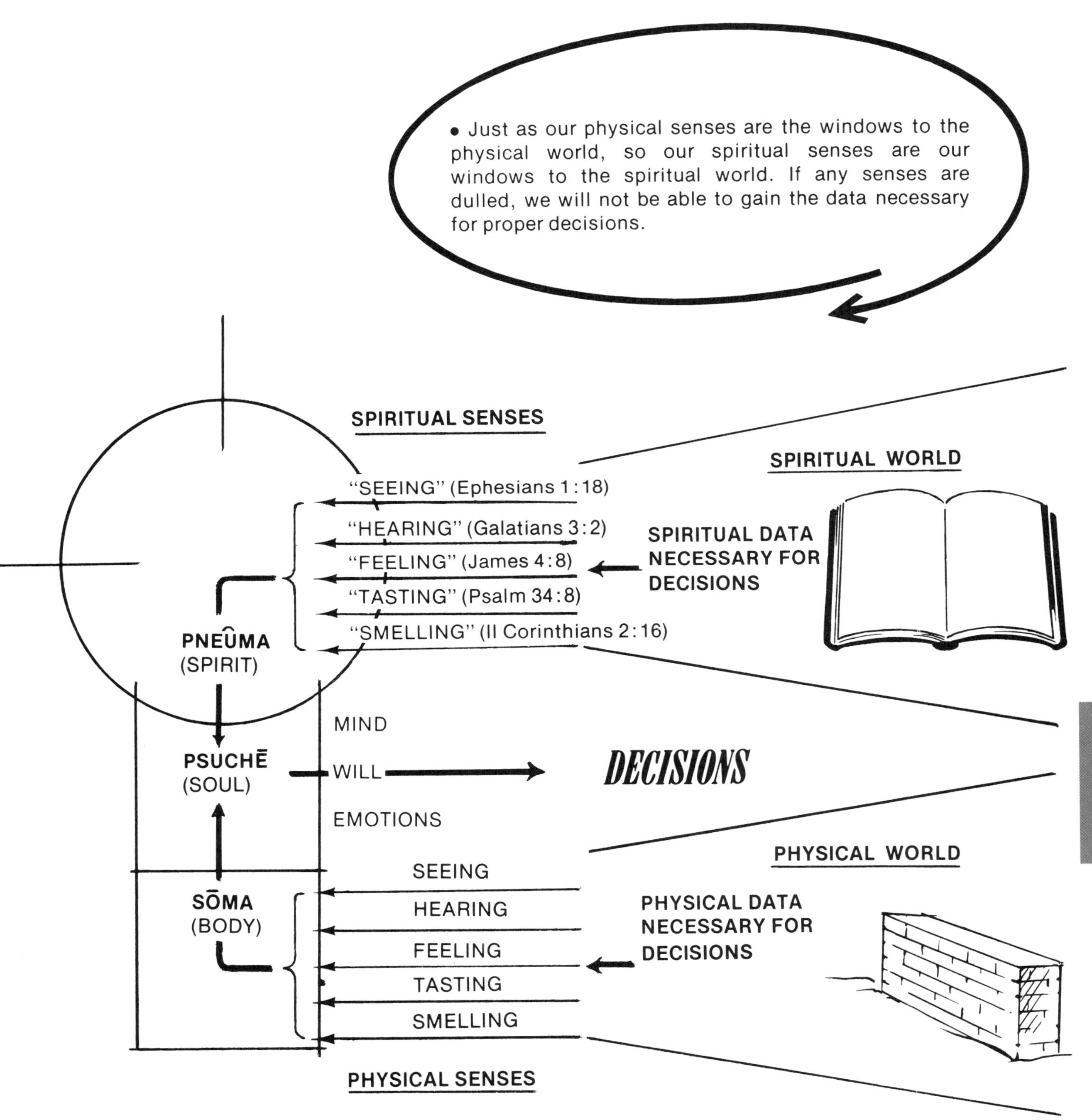

SUCCESS

NOTES

5 BASIC STEPS TOWARD BECOMING A "WHOLE PERSON"

• In order to become a whole person, we must first be made alive in our spirits and then allow our spirits to become the center our lives. This objective is incorporated in the following five steps:

1. BE REBORN IN YOUR SPIRIT

2. REBUILD YOUR THOUGHTS

3. REFOCUS YOUR EMOTIONS

4. REDIRECT YOUR GOALS

5. REPRODUCE YOUR LIFE IN OTHERS

• Only through our spirits can we discover that third dimension of life and gain the personal fulfillment which our beings long to achieve. The following pages illustrate the potential development of these objectives.

NOTES

THE BASIC CONFLICT OF INNER NATURES

• Two forces within us become quite obvious as we attempt to fulfill that which we know to be right. One force seeks to draw our attention to the wrong impulses; the other seeks to draw our attention to the right impulses. The resulting struggle is well-described in the words of Romans 7:15-25.

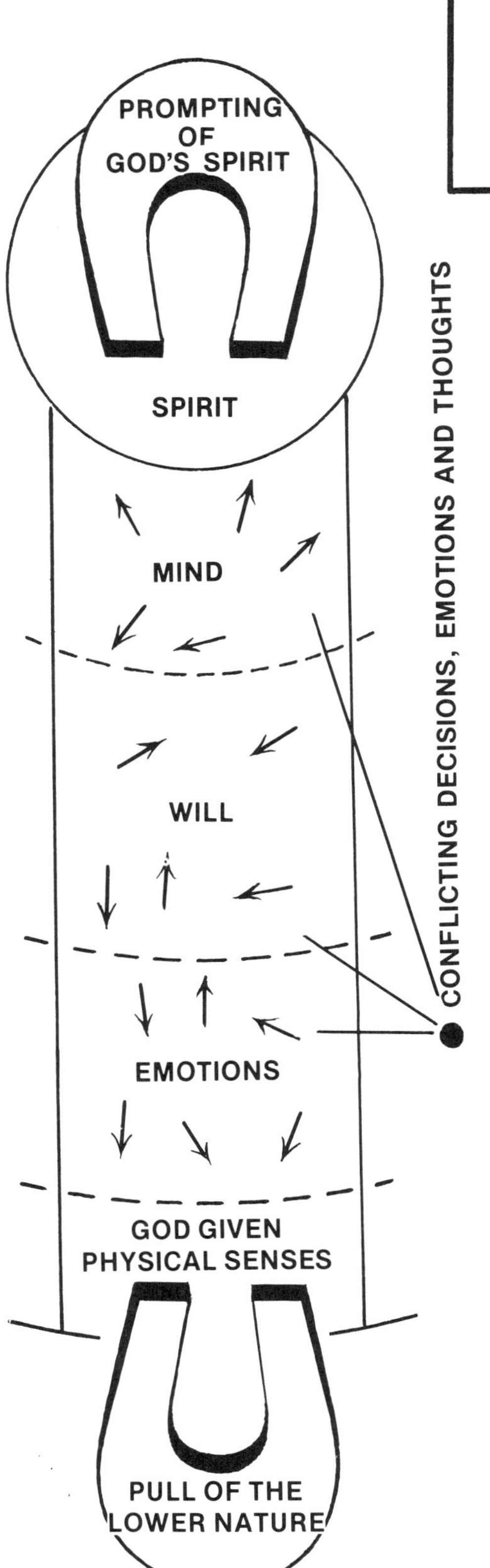

• "For that which I do I allow not: for what I would, that do I not; but what I hate, that do I. If then I do that which I would not, I consent unto the law that it is good.

"Now then it is no more I that do it, but sin that dwelleth in me. For I know that in me (that is, in my flesh,) dwelleth no good thing: for to will is present with me; but how to perform that which is good I find not.

"For the good that I would I do not: but the evil which I would not, that I do. Now if I do that I would not, it is no more I that do it, but sin that dwelleth in me.

"I find then a law, that, when I would do good, evil is present with me. For I delight in the law of God after the inward man: But I see another law in my members, warring against the law of my mind, and bringing me into captivity to the law of sin which is in my members.

"O wretched man that I am! Who shall deliver me from the body of this death? I thank God through Jesus Christ our Lord."

NOTES

HOW TO BE "REBORN" IN YOUR SPIRIT

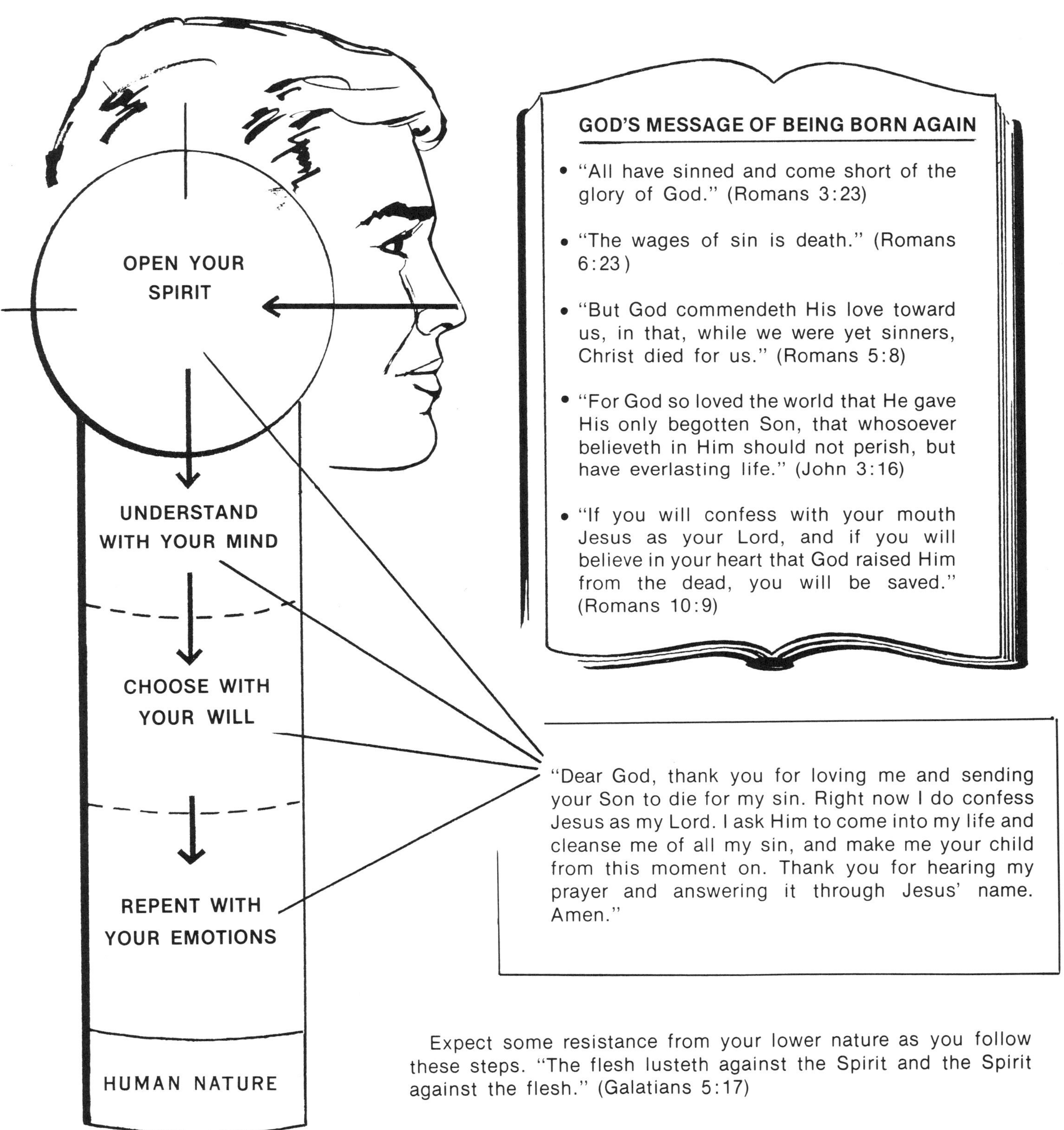

Expect some resistance from your lower nature as you follow these steps. "The flesh lusteth against the Spirit and the Spirit against the flesh." (Galatians 5:17)

NOTES

STEPS TO TRANSFORM YOUR SOUL

• Once we have been born again by the Spirit of God, we will continue to experience conflicting struggles in our mind, will and emotions. But now the Spirit and Word of God make it possible to "Be transformed by the renewing of our minds." (Romans 12:2)

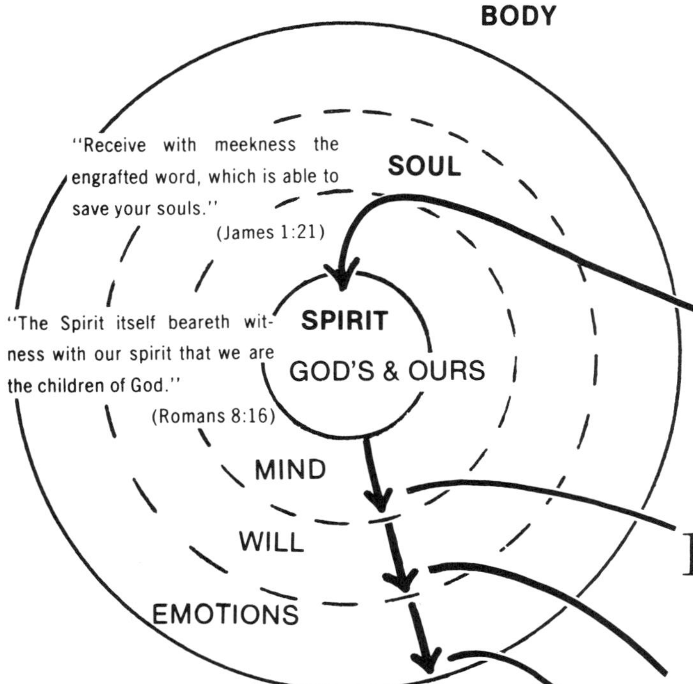

BODY

SOUL

"Receive with meekness the engrafted word, which is able to save your souls." (James 1:21)

SPIRIT
GOD'S & OURS

"The Spirit itself beareth witness with our spirit that we are the children of God." (Romans 8:16)

MIND

WILL

EMOTIONS

• Determine areas of personal character deficiency and find large sections of Scripture relating to them.

Take these sections through the following steps of action.

1. MEMORIZE

"The entrance of thy words giveth light." (Psalm 119:130) "It is a pleasant thing if you keep them within you." (Proverbs 22:18)

2. VISUALIZE

Picture each word. "If you cry after knowledge and lift up your voice for understanding: If you seek her as silver and search for her as for hidden treasures; then shall you understand the fear of the Lord and find the knowledge of God." (Proverbs 2:3-5)

3. PERSONALIZE

Put Scripture into the first-person and quote it back to God. "If you abide in me and my words abide in you, you shall ask what you will and it shall be done unto you." (John 15:7)

• MEDITATION INVOLVES ALL THREE OF THESE STEPS

"This book of the Law shall not depart out of your mouth, but you shall meditate therein day and night; for then shall you make your way prosperous and then shall you have good success." (Joshua 1:8)

"But his delight is in the Law of the Lord and in his Law does he meditate day and night. . . Whatsoever he doeth shall prosper." (Psalm 1:3)

NOTES

HOW TO REBUILD THOUGHT STRUCTURES

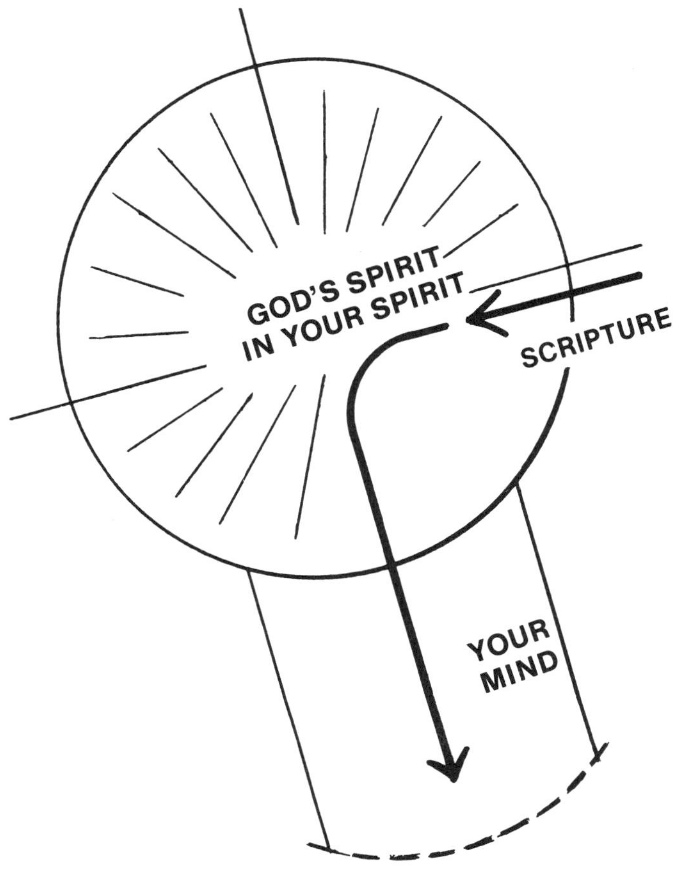

• God's Spirit is the author and interpreter of Scripture. Once He enters our spirit, He is able to rebuild our thoughts, emotions and will around a comprehension of His Word. John 16:13; 14:26.

1. MEMORIZE GOD'S THOUGHT STRUCTURES

If we are to think God's thoughts after Him, we must be able to comprehend and appreciate His structure of thinking as presented in Scripture. The best way to do this is to memorize whole thoughts and ideas from Scripture.

The very fact that many sections are hard for us to understand underscores the truth of Isaiah 55:8 & 9, "For my thoughts are not your thoughts..."

BASIC SECTIONS TO BEGIN MEMORIZING:

- James 1 - How To Prepare For Temptations
- Matthew 5, 6, 7 - How To Find Happiness
- Hebrews 12 - How To Appreciate God's Chastening
- John 15 - How To Grow Spiritually
- Colossians 3 - How To Refocus Affections
- Romans 5-8 - How To Conquer The Lusts Of
- Galatians 5, 6 The Lower Nature
- I Corinthians 13 - How To Develop Genuine Love
- Psalms 1, 15, 34, 63, 139

2. SATURATE YOUR MIND WITH SCRIPTURE

The literal concept behind the word, "meditation," is that of a cow chewing its cud. Just as it brings up again and again that which it has eaten, so we should recall in our minds over and over again that which we have memorized.

One day a family living on the edge of a desert was amazed to see that seeds had sprouted in the salty desert sands behind their home. No one could figure out how this happened, since they had often tried to grow things there with no results. The mystery was solved when they discovered that every day the mother had thrown her dishwater out the back door. After months and months, the salt which had hindered any growth was washed out of the sand. Then one day she threw some seeds out the back door. A short time later the plants began to sprout.

In the same way, as we saturate our minds with God's Word, it will wash out thoughts opposed to Scripture and will reconstruct other ideas around God's principles. "Sanctify them through Thy truth, Thy Word is truth." (John 17:17) "Now you are clean through the Word that I have spoken unto you." (John 15:3)

NOTES

HOW TO REDIRECT YOUR WILL

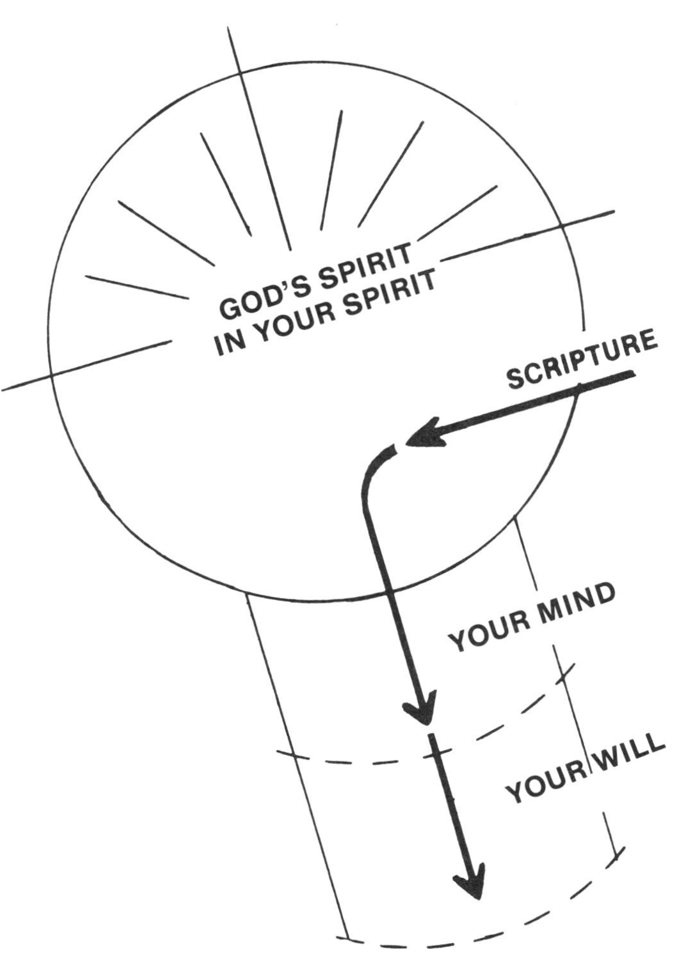

• The second step is to visualize each word and then ask God to show you how to turn that word into action which will build Christian character and lead others to salvation.

1. PURPOSE TO BECOME A LIVING TRANSLATION OF GOD'S WORD

In every age and within every society God has certain specific goals which He wants to accomplish. He looks for men through whom He can reach these objectives.

As we live in Scripture and compare the needs of our society with similar situations in Scripture, we will gain an understanding of some of the goals which God wants to accomplish.

2. ASSUME RESPONSIBILITY FOR GOD'S WORK AND REPUTATION

Just as there are many physical members within one person, so there are many Christians within the body of Christ. Each one is to be sensitive to certain needs within and without the body which he can become personally responsible for.

As we begin laying down our lives for the brethren, the Word of God will become a living force through us.

3. EXPAND THE MEANING OF KEY WORDS - THEN TRANSLATE THEM INTO ACTION

One of God's greatest problems in using words to communicate His ideas is our inability to comprehend the thought concepts behind the words. Several helps can be used in expanding key words - a concordance to look up other verses in which the word is used, an expository dictionary to express the meaning of the word as used in the original language, a dictionary to look up the full meaning of the English word.

NOTES

HOW TO REFOCUS EMOTIONS

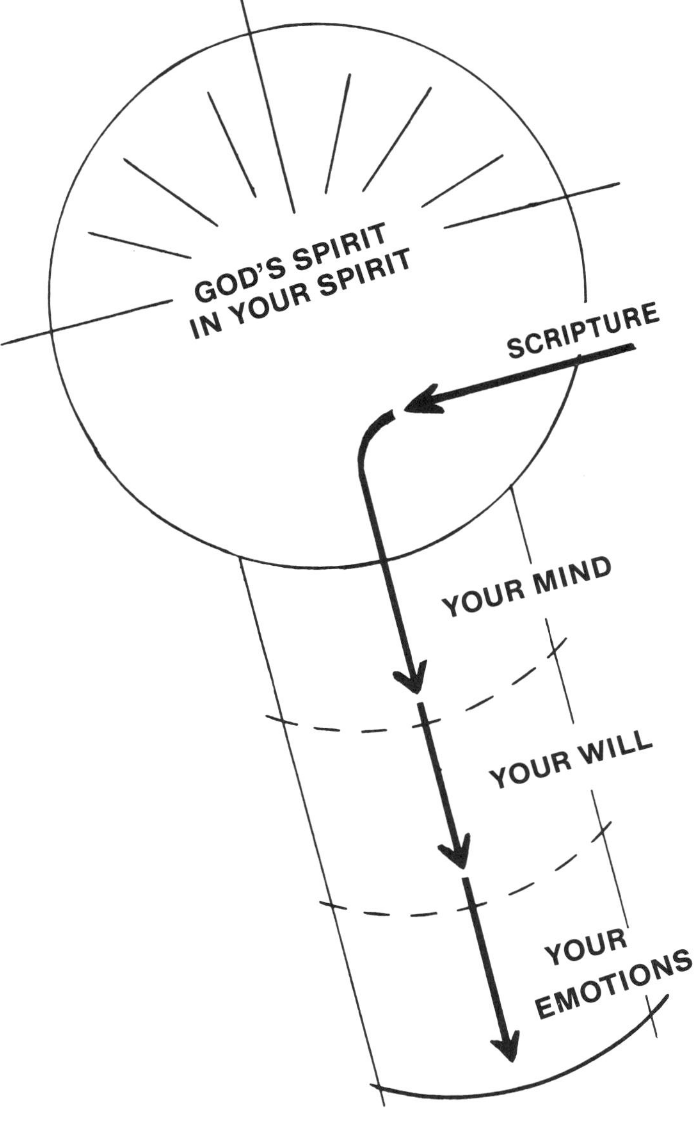

- The third step toward making God's Word live in our hearts is allowing it to become the full expression of our emotions.

1. PERSONALIZE THE SCRIPTURE YOU HAVE MEMORIZED

God delights to hear His own Word, especially when we are using it to express our own desires and emotions. To do this, we can take the same sections which we have memorized and add personal pronouns wherever possible. This process is illustrated in the following verse.

JOHN 15:7	JOHN 15:7 (Personalized)
"If you abide in me and my words abide in you, you shall ask what you will and it shall be done unto you."	"Lord, I will abide in you and allow your words to abide in me. Then, whatever I ask shall be done unto me."

2. EXPRESS IRRITATIONS, DISAPPOINTMENTS, HEARTACHES THROUGH SCRIPTURE

The book of Psalms was written by a man after God's own heart. It expresses the very heart of God and should express our hearts. However, there is a wide spectrum of emotions within Psalms, and much of this spectrum we may not yet have experienced.

Therefore, God will allow certain situations in our lives to expose us to new sections of this spectrum, and thereby gain a wider sensitivity and insight into the nature of God and the feelings of others. Many sections in Psalms are already written in the first person, and therefore become excellent material to help us refocus our emotions.

NOTES

HOW TO GET STARTED

• If we desire to build Scripture into our lives, we must realize that it demands the central focus of our concentration. The very nature of its operation requires that we build our schedules around it rather than trying to fit it into our present routine.

1. SELECT A MEANINGFUL SECTION OF SCRIPTURE

A meaningful section of Scripture is one that relates directly to a question or a problem or a particular interest which you have. The Scripture on page 144 is recommended for this purpose.

2. GIVE GOD THE DAY THAT BELONGS TO HIM

One of the first questions in regard to memorizing is, "When will I ever find time?" The best time to invest in this project is the time that already belongs to God. This involves one day a week.

3. BEGIN THE DAY IN THE EVENING

The significance of our day beginning in the evening is that the last important thoughts on our minds in the evening remain on our subconscious minds throughout the night and consciously or unconsciously set our mental attitudes for the day.

Thus, God emphasizes the need to go to sleep while meditating on His Word. "My soul shall be satisfied as with marrow and fatness; and my mouth shall praise thee with joyful lips: when I remember thee upon my bed, and meditate on thee in the night watches." (Psalm 63:5,6)

NOTES

PURPOSE IN LIFE

One of the most persistent questions in the minds of both youth and adults is: "What is my purpose in life?"

In order to understand why God made us and what His will is for our lives, it is essential to know the ways and callings of God.

NOTES

THREE BASIC ASPECTS OF

THE WAYS OF GOD

• Each of us can expect that God's major dealings with us will be in harmony with His basic ways. He wants us to know these ways so we can properly respond to the events He brings into our lives.

BIRTH OF A VISION	DEATH OF THE VISION	SUPERNATURAL FULFILLMENT OF THE ORIGINAL VISION
Each one of us has special purposes for being here. God wants to reveal them to us. ILLUSTRATIONS:	The expectations God gives are powerful motivations to continue during discouragement.	He usually fulfills our expectations in ways that we never would have thought.
ABRAHAM had a vision of being the father of a great nation.	**SARAH** was barren and became too old to have children.	**GOD** gave Abraham and Sarah a son in their old age who became the father of a great nation.
JOSEPH had a vision that he would be a great leader and that many would bow down to him.	**JOSEPH'S BROTHERS** sold him to some merchants and he became a slave. Later he was falsely accused and condemned to spend his years in prison.	**GOD** allowed Joseph to interpret the dreams of the butler and baker and later the king, whereupon, he was made a ruler in the land.
MOSES had a vision of leading his people out of the bondage of Egypt.	**PHARAOH** as well as his own people drove Moses out of Egypt after his first attempt to relieve their bondage.	**GOD** gave Moses signs and wonders to convince Pharoah and his people that God was speaking through him to lead the nation to Canaan.
THE DISCIPLES of Jesus Christ had a vision of establishing and being an important part of the Kingdom of God.	**JESUS** was killed by the very ones He came to save, and the disciples saw Him buried in a tomb.	**GOD** raised Jesus from the dead, and great miracles were performed by the disciples until the Gospel had spread through all the world.
A GRAIN OF WHEAT has a "vision" of reproducing itself and many more grains of wheat.	**THE GRAIN** dies in the ground.	**A HARVEST** springs up out of the very process of "death" in the ground.

NOTES

THE NEED FOR THE DEATH OF A VISION

• God said of His own people, "Forty years long was I grieved with this generation, and said, it is a people that do err in their heart, and have not known my ways." Psalm 95:10.

When we begin to understand His ways, we see the great value in going through the Death of a Vision.

BIRTH OF A VISION	DEATH OF A VISION	FULFILLMENT OF A VISION
FAITH "Visualizing what God intends to do in my life."	**HOPE** "Anticipating and expecting God to work out His revealed will in my life even when it doesn't seem possible."	**LOVE** "The motivation to reproduce Christ's character in others as He has done in me."

A. GOD'S "BUILDING PROGRAM" DURING THE DEATH OF A VISION:

Since God is far more concerned with our becoming like Jesus Christ in character than He is with our doing good works to further His kingdom, He needs this time of "waiting" to accomplish character building.

The "vision" provides the motivation not to become discouraged. This time of "death" and character building prepares us for a greater ministry when He does fulfill the vision.

Notice the qualities that are sure to be developed during this time: Patience, in waiting God's time; Faith, in knowing what He will do; Meekness, in yielding personal rights; Self-control, in not running ahead of God, and many, many others.

B. SATAN'S "BUILDING PROGRAM" DURING THE DEATH OF A VISION:

Satan's purpose is to destroy God's work in our lives and also as much of the potential for achieving God's work as he can. To do this during this time he comes as an "angel of light" to deceive as many as possible. II Corinthians 11:14.

He prompts us to try in our own energy and wisdom to fulfill the original vision. He doesn't want us to learn God's qualities, and whenever we follow his leading, conflict results.

A classic example is Abraham trying to fulfill God's promise of a great nation by having a son by Hagar. Conflict has resulted ever since between their descendants.

NOTES

DEFINING GOD'S PURPOSE IN LIFE

• God's ultimate purpose for each one of us is that we become more and more like His Son, the Lord Jesus Christ. Then, His purpose is that we reproduce His life in the lives of those around us.

Paul travailed as in birth that those with whom he worked would have Christ formed in them. Galatians 4:19

A. GOD'S PURPOSE: SPIRITUAL MATURITY

Whatever our vocation in life may be, our primary life goal should be that of Colossians 1:28: "Warning every man, and teaching every man in all wisdom; that we may present every man perfect (or mature) in Christ Jesus."

B. WHAT DOES IT MEAN TO BRING EVERY MAN TO HIS FULL MATURITY?

It means building the principles of God's Word into a person's life so that he is equipped to understand and follow the promptings of the Holy Spirit in knowing how to respond to any situation with Christ-like attitudes.

C. HOW DOES GOD PREPARE US TO ACCOMPLISH THIS?

He allows problems, irritations, and responsibilities to come into our lives so that we are motivated to search out His Word and develop the full potential which He put within our lives.

SPIRIT	• God has given to us certain spiritual aptitudes, abilities and capacities.
SOUL	• He has also given to us mental, emotional and volitional aptitudes, abilities and capacities.
BODY	• We also have been given physical aptitudes, abilities and capacities.

• God knows that, left to ourselves, many of us would only develop a small portion of the aptitudes, abilities and capacities which He has put within us.

To the degree that we didn't develop the rest, we would experience boredom in our lives.

Therefore, in order to direct and motivate us in developing the rest, God chooses to bring into our lives certain problems, irritations and responsibilities.

NOTES

BASIC INSIGHTS ON KNOWING GOD'S WILL

1. GOD'S WILL INVOLVES PEOPLE

God so loved a world of people that He gave His Son... It is all too easy for us to become more concerned about things and organizations than people. If this happens we will miss the real joy of knowing God's will.

2. KNOWING BASIC NEEDS REMOVES FEAR OF PEOPLE

Many people have a fear of talking to other people. There is a way, however, of overcoming this fear. If we were walking down a neighborhood street and happened to see a gathering of people sitting in the front room of one of the homes, we would probably experience a certain fear about the idea of intruding in their gathering.

If, however, we saw that the roof of their home was on fire, we would overcome our fear. We would be sure that the message we had to give them was one which they needed to hear. We would also be quite confident that they would immediately recognize the importance of our message.

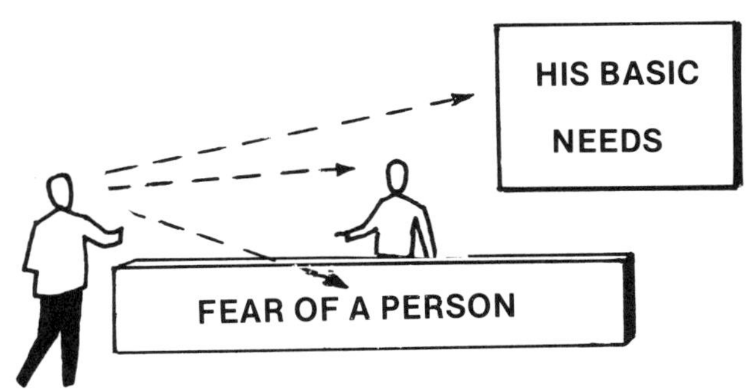

"Herein is our love made perfect, that we may have boldness . . .
There is no fear in love; but perfect love casteth out fear."
I John 4:17,18

3. GOD HAS A SPECIAL CONCERN FOR CHRISTIANS

It is quite easy for us to become discouraged with the spiritual immaturity of some Christians and decide that we will not bother with them but instead will concentrate on reaching those who have never heard the Gospel.

It is important for us to proclaim the Gospel to those who have never heard. But when there are already Christians in an area, it is also important to bring them up to their full maturity in Christ. If we don't do this, their immaturity will cause others to stumble, and we won't know how to solve similar immaturity in those we lead to Christ.

This is one reason we are to "do good unto all men, especially unto them who are of the household of faith." Galatians 6:10

In determining God's will for our lives, one of the most important questions we can ask ourselves is: " How can I help the Christians around me to mature and by so doing, beautify the body of Christ?"

NOTES

4. WE ARE TO ASSUME RESPONSIBILITY FOR THE REPUTATION OF THE LORD JESUS CHRIST

When one member of the body of Christ sins or displays spiritual immaturity, the reputation of Christ is damaged and the whole body of Christ then suffers. When David sinned with Bathsheba, Nathan the Prophet stated: ". . .by this deed thou hast given great occasion to the enemies of the Lord to blaspheme . . ." II Samuel 12:14.

Because of this, we are to "exhort one another daily...lest any of you be hardened through the deceitfulness of sin." Hebrews 3:13 Just as the corpuscles in our blood surround a wound in the skin and die in order to stop the infection from spreading, so we are to "lay down our lives for the brethren." I John 3:16

5. THREE TYPES OF CHRISTIANS EXIST IN MOST CHURCH GROUPS

When I had the privilege of working directly with many churches and youth groups, I could always expect to find three types of Christians: those who were cold, those who were spiritually hot, and those who were in between.

I soon learned why the in-between or "lukewarm" Christians are so nauseating to God.

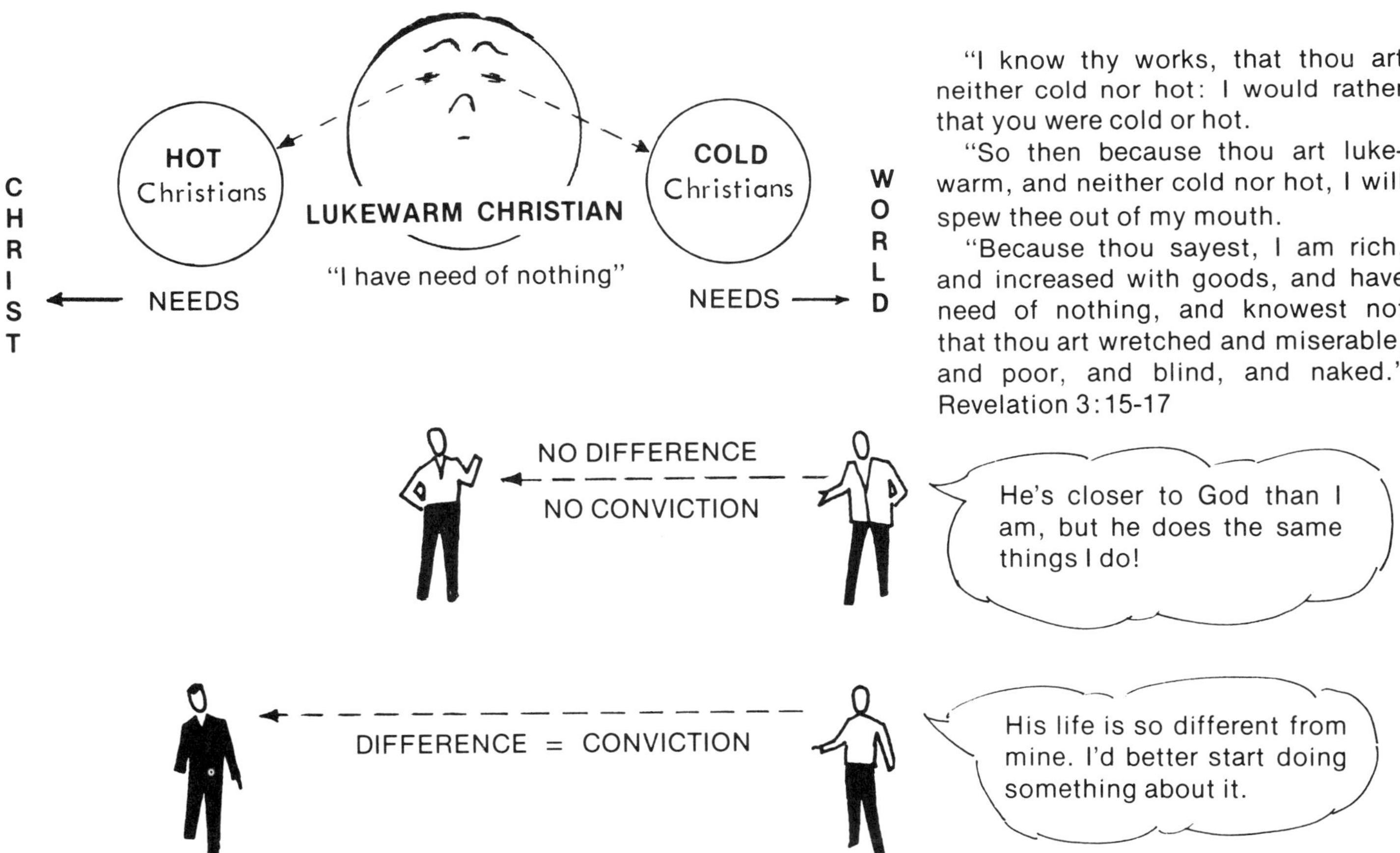

"If my people, which are called by my name shall humble themselves, and pray, and seek my face, and turn from their wicked ways; then will I hear from heaven, and will forgive their sin, and will heal their land." II Chronicles 7:14
"For the time is come that judgment must begin at the house of God." I Peter 4:17

NOTES

6. GOD'S WILL INVOLVES LEADING THOSE FOR WHOM WE ARE RESPONSIBLE TO SPIRITUAL MATURITY

When we determine which individuals are under our spiritual care and purpose to give ourselves to the high calling of leading them to spiritual maturity, we have established the basis for a fulfilling ministry in our lives. Then, as God allows us to experience death to our natural inclinations and discover His way of responding to life situations, we are "able to comfort them which are in any trouble, by the comfort wherewith we ourselves are comforted of God." II Corinthians 1:4

7. WE ARE RESPONSIBLE TO DEEPEN OUR MESSAGE. GOD IS RESPONSIBLE TO BROADEN OUR MINISTRY.

We are prone to be concerned with how many people we are reaching with the Gospel. But God is concerned that we bring those we reach to spiritual maturity. "That we may present every man perfect in Christ Jesus." Colossians 1:28 Those who become mature are then able to reproduce the life and character of Christ in others as well.

If we love Christ, we are to show it by keeping His commandments and feeding His sheep. John 14:15; John 21:15-17 Sheep reproduce sheep as the shepherd feeds them.

8. GOD'S WILL INVOLVES THE "MESSAGE" WE DEVELOP MORE THAN THE "JOB" WE ARE DOING

As each one of us dies to natural inclinations which are contrary to the Word of God, and as we experience the life of Christ by applying the principles of His Word to our daily lives, we build a "life message."

God desires that each one of us becomes a "living epistle." II Corinthians 3:2 As we do, we experience more and more joy. Proverbs 15:23

God has chosen us and ordained us that we should go and bring forth fruit and that our fruit should remain. John 15:16

PURPOSE

9. ACHIEVING SPIRITUAL MATURITY INVOLVES RESPONDING TO EIGHT CALLINGS

In II Peter 1:4 we learn that there are "given unto us exceeding great and precious promises, that by these ye might be partakers of the divine nature, having escaped the corruption that is in the world through lust."

Then we are given eight specific "callings" and told to give all diligence in following them.

NOTES

DISCOVERING PURPOSE THROUGH 8 CALLINGS

SPIRITUAL DEVELOPMENTS THROUGH SPECIFIC CALLINGS

Repentance of SALVATION	Separation from Darkness	Dedication to the Light	Investment in SERVICE	Endurance in SUFFERING	Humility in Responses	Alertness in Sharing	Reproduction of Maturity
1	2	3	4	5	6	7	8
Give the Lord Jesus Christ His rightful place at the center of your life.	Discern and turn from evil in all its forms.	Commit yourself to the light of Scripture.	Become involved in lasting achievement.	Expect to be misunderstood.	Respond as God would to those who wrong you.	Be alert to others who have been hurt.	Guide them through the same steps God has taken you.

Our **"WITNESS"** increases as we fully obey each **CALLING**

PURPOSE: TO BECOME THE MOST EFFECTIVE "TRANSLATOR" OF SPIRITUAL TRUTH

"STAR" WITNESS

One who has a vital message and must be available at all times to share it.

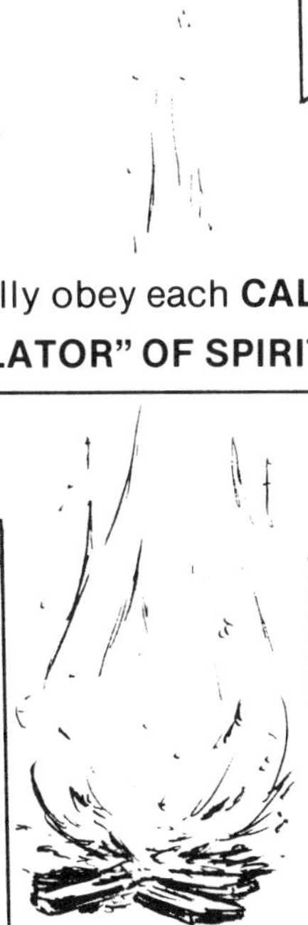

Romans 10:9	I Peter 2:9	Romans 12:2	Matthew 6:19	I Peter 4:12	Romans 8:29	II Cor. 1:4	Col. 1:29
FAITH	VIRTUE	KNOWLEDGE	SELF-CONTROL	ENDURANCE	GODLINESS	BROTHERLY KINDNESS	LOVE

NOTES

1. THE CALLING OF SALVATION

• To the degree that we respond to each of the 8 callings, we increase the scope of our "life message" and thereby experience the will of God for our lives.

The very first step is to receive eternal life through faith in the Lord Jesus Christ. John 3:3

A. RECEIVE SALVATION BY "GRACE" THROUGH FAITH . . .

Paul explains the "grace of God" as an active work of God within us to do His will, since all men are born sinners, and "there is none righteous, no, not one." Romans 3:10 God's first work of saving grace within us is to call us to repentance. "The goodness of God leadeth thee to repentance." Romans 2:4 "By grace are you saved." Ephesians 2:8

When we respond to His grace by confessing that we are sinners and receiving the Lord Jesus Christ as our personal Savior, we are born again by the Spirit of God and receive more "grace" to live the Christian life. "God is able to make all grace abound toward you." II Corinthians 9:8

Paul explains the work of God's grace in him as a Christian in I Corinthians 15:10. "But by the grace of God I am what I am; and His grace, which was bestowed upon me, was not in vain; but I labored more abundantly than they all: yet not I, but the grace of God which was with me."

B. NOT BY WORKS OF RIGHTEOUSNESS WHICH WE HAVE DONE

Whenever I ask a group of people the following question, some in the group say, "Yes," and other say, "No": "Can a non-Christian person sincerely believe that he can cast demons out of another person by the power of God?" Christ's answer startles those who say, "No."

"Many will say to me in that day, Lord, Lord, have we not prophesied in Thy name? And in Thy name have cast out devils? And in Thy name done many wonderful works? And then will I profess unto them, I never knew you: Depart from me ye that work iniquity." Matthew 7:22, 23

When the Chinese character for "sheep" is combined with the character for "me," the result (with a small alteration) is the character for "righteousness."

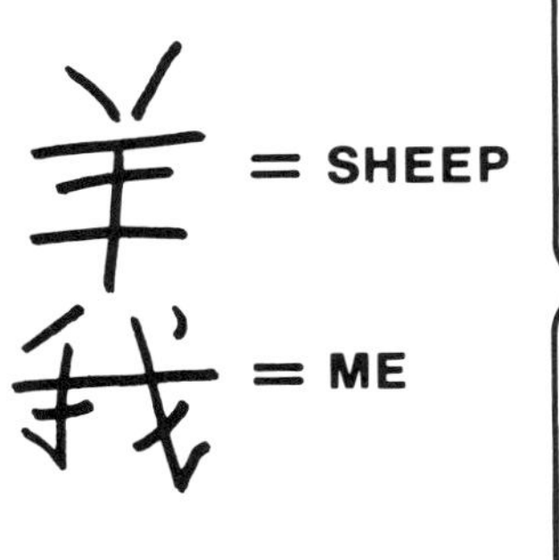

R
I
G
H
T
E
O
U
S
N
E
S
S

• The story is told of a shepherd who discovered that one of his sheep had died leaving an orphan lamb. He knew no other parent would take care of that orphan lamb, and it too would die.

This lamb was very special to him, so he killed another lamb with a living parent and wrapped the skin around the orphan lamb. The living parent responded to its own covering and began caring for the orphan lamb.

NOTES

5 CAUSES OF DOUBTING SALVATION

• Large numbers of those who have professed to receive Jesus Christ as personal Savior continue to have doubts from time to time as to whether or not they really are Christians. Here are some of the major causes of those doubts.

1. "SECOND THOUGHTS" ABOUT CHILDHOOD DECISIONS

It is very important to explain the Gospel to children and to encourage them to receive Jesus Christ as their personal Savior. However, it is also very important to encourage those same children to reaffirm their childhood decisions when they reach the teen-age years.

Questioning childhood decisions not only results in doubts about salvation, but may motivate some to doubt God's existence.

2. AN UNFORGIVING SPIRIT TOWARD AN OFFENDER

Bitterness toward one or more individuals has been a major cause of doubts about salvation. The words of Jesus Christ would certainly explain why. "But if ye forgive not men their trespasses, neither will your Father forgive your trespasses." Matthew 6:15

3. AN UNWILLINGNESS TO MAKE PAST OFFENSES RIGHT

If we have wronged someone in the past and are not willing to ask their forgiveness and make any necessary restitution, doubts about salvation often result. The very guilt of the situation causes us not to have an open fellowship with the Lord.

4. A PARTICULAR SIN WE ARE UNWILLING TO GIVE UP

When a person says, "I want to become a Christian, but there is one thing I don't want to give up," he is laying the foundation for all kinds of future doubts. Becoming a Christian means receiving and "confessing Jesus as Lord." If He is the Lord or "boss," then He decides what all our activities should be.

5. A POINT OF PRIDE IN BECOMING A CHRISTIAN

Many have experienced doubts about salvation and couldn't understand why. Upon questioning, it was learned that they had decided to become Christians their way. One purposed she would never "walk forward" in a meeting. If this has become a point of pride, it will cause doubts.

NOTES

STEPS OF PRIDE IN REACTING TO TRUTH

STEPS OF REACTION

1. KNOWING THE TRUTH

We are born with a sin nature, yet we are able to recognize truth and the conviction of the Holy Spirit. ". . . I will put my laws into their mind, and write them in their hearts . . ." Hebrews 8:10

2. DISCOVERING MORE TRUTH

"Because that which may be known of God is manifest in them; for God hath shewed it unto them. For the invisible things of him from the creation of the world are clearly seen, being understood by the things that are made, even his eternal power and Godhead; so that they are without excuse." Romans 1:19,20

3. REJECTING BASIC TRUTH

"And this is the condemnation, that light is come into the world, and men loved darkness rather than light, because their deeds were evil. For everyone that doeth evil hateth the light neither cometh to the light, lest his deeds should be reproved." John 3:19,20

4. SEARCHING FOR NEW IDEAS

"Beware lest any man spoil you through philosophy and vain deceit, after the tradition of men, after the rudiments of the world, and not after Christ." Colossians 2:8

5. DEVELOPING A PHILOSOPHY

"Let no man deceive himself. If any man among you seemeth to be wise in this world, let him become a fool, that he may be wise. For the wisdom of this world is foolishness with God. For it is written, He taketh the wise in their own craftiness." I Corinthians 3:18,19

6. REVISING THE PHILOSOPHY

"Having a form of godliness, but denying the power thereof: from such turn away. Ever learning, and never able to come to the knowledge of the truth." II Timothy 3:5,7

EACH STEP INCREASES PRIDE AND REDUCES THE POWER OF GRACE

AN ILLUSTRATION

A certain young man sensed a growing conviction for his many sinful ways.

One day a friend invited him to attend a Gospel meeting. For the first time he listened to the realities of hell and judgment which God has pronounced on evil. With fearfulness, he responded to the invitation to become a Christian.

A few days later, he began to consider the changes that would have to come in his life as a result of being a Christian. He decided that the minister had used fear tactics to get him to make a decision. He then rejected both the minister and the message.

With awakened conscience, he now began to investigate other religions and philosophies. He was sure he could find one that was not so strict about evil.

After much studying of philosophy and religion, he devised his own views of God and moral decisions. He became very skilled in discussing these with others and debating their merits.

The conflicts of his immoral relationships convinced him that his philosophy was not as good as he had hoped it would be, so he looked around for new ideas to revise his philosophy. But whenever he heard someone speaking of the judgment of God on evil, he violently reacted to it.

NOTES

CONFIRMING SALVATION...

• BY CONFESSION OF THE MOUTH

One day a young man on a farm experienced a flood of doubts about whether or not he really was a Christian.

• "If you will confess with your mouth the Lord Jesus, and shall believe in your heart that God raised Him from the dead, you shall be saved.

"For with the heart man believes unto righteousness: and with the mouth confession is made unto salvation." Romans 10:9, 10

He walked outside behind the barn, knelt down, and prayed. His prayer contained the following:

> • "Thank you, God, for loving me and sending your son, the Lord Jesus Christ, to die for me, a sinner. Right now, I do receive Him and ask you to cleanse me by His blood and make me your child. Thank you for raising Him up from the dead as a living Savior, and thank you for hearing and answering this prayer."

He finished his prayer, pounded a wooden stake in the ground and wrote the date on it. About two weeks later, the doubts came back again. This time he had a ready and very effective reply, "All right, Satan. Come with me!"

He walked out behind the barn, pointed to the stake and said, "See Satan. Here's the date and here's the place I received Jesus Christ as my Savior. And God has promised that if I call upon the name of the Lord, I shall be saved." Romans 10:13

Since that time, the doubts never returned.

• BY CONFIRMATION OF THE HOLY SPIRIT

• "The Spirit itself beareth witness with our spirit, that we are the children of God." Romans 8:16

• BY CONFESSION THROUGH BAPTISM

When the early Christians were baptised, for many it meant being disowned, persecuted and rejected.

• "Therefore, we are buried with Him by baptism into death: that like as Christ was raised up from the dead by the glory of the Father, even so we also should walk in newness of life." Romans 6:4

Baptism is beginning life on a new basis. It is like living on borrowed time. It is dying to our rights, possessions, plans, etc., and being raised up to a new level of living. Everything belongs to God and Christ lives His life through us — one day at a time.

NOTES

6 EVIDENCES OF SALVATION

SPIRITUAL LIFE

↓

SPIRITUAL FOOD

↓

SPIRITUAL GROWTH

↓

TESTING OF FAITH

↓

FELLOWSHIP

WITNESSING

1. NEW AWARENESS OF RIGHT AND WRONG

There will be a greater awareness of words, thoughts and actions which do not please the Lord. ". . . He will reprove the world of sin, and of righteousness, and of judgment." John 16:8 "For I know that in me . . . dwelleth no good thing." Romans 7:18-25 "And we know that we are of God, and the whole world lieth in wickedness." I John 5:19

2. HUNGER FOR GOD'S WORD

Certain sections will begin to stand out to you with new meaning and understanding. "I have esteemed the words of His mouth more than my necessary food." Job 23:12 ". . . Thy word was unto me the joy and rejoicing of mine heart." Jeremiah 15:16 "But strong meat belongeth to them that. . . have their senses exercised to discern both good and evil." Hebrews 5:14

3. DESIRE FOR A CHANGED LIFE

There will be a genuine desire for a changed life and a new delight in the direct commandments of the Lord. "Therefore if any man be in Christ he is a new creature: old things are passed away; behold, all things are become new." II Corinthians 5:17

4. INCREASE IN TESTING

There will be an immediate increase in personal testing, often from those closest to you who do not understand salvation or from other Christians who have lost their first love. "Blessed are ye, when men shall hate you, and when they shall separate you from their company, and shall reproach you." Luke 6:22, "Yea, and all that will live godly in Christ Jesus shall suffer persecution." II Timothy 3:12

5. LOVE FOR OTHER CHRISTIANS

There will be sincere enjoyment in the fellowship of other Christians. "Beloved, if God so loved us, we ought also to love one another." I John 4:7-13

It is essential that every Christian become an active member of a local church. This church must be true to the Word of God and active in proclaiming the Gospel to others who have not yet heard it.

6. DESIRE TO TELL OTHERS ABOUT CHRIST

One of the first signs of a genuine born-again Christian is that he will want to share his experience with others. It is important to provide opportunities for him to tell others who will encourage him rather than discourage him. "Let the redeemed of the Lord say so . . ."Psalm 107:2 ". . . be ready always to give an answer to every man that asks you a reason of the hope that is in you . . ." I Peter 3:15

NOTES

2. THE CALLING OF SEPARATION

• One of the greatest causes of diminishing the potential of our life message is the failure to turn from all the thoughts, words and actions which we know grieve the Spirit of God.

• Either we separate ourselves from our sins, or our sins will separate us from fellowship with God.

"Your iniquities have separated between you and your God, and your sins have hid His face from you that He will not hear.

For your hands are defiled with blood (of not warning the wicked - Ezekiel 3:18); and your fingers with iniquity (moral impurity - Psalm 51:2); your lips have spoken lies (broken promises and vows - Ecclesiastes 5:4); your tongue hath muttered perverseness (wrong attitudes)."

Isaiah 59:2,3

• Many don't realize how far reaching the scope of Satan's realm of power really is:

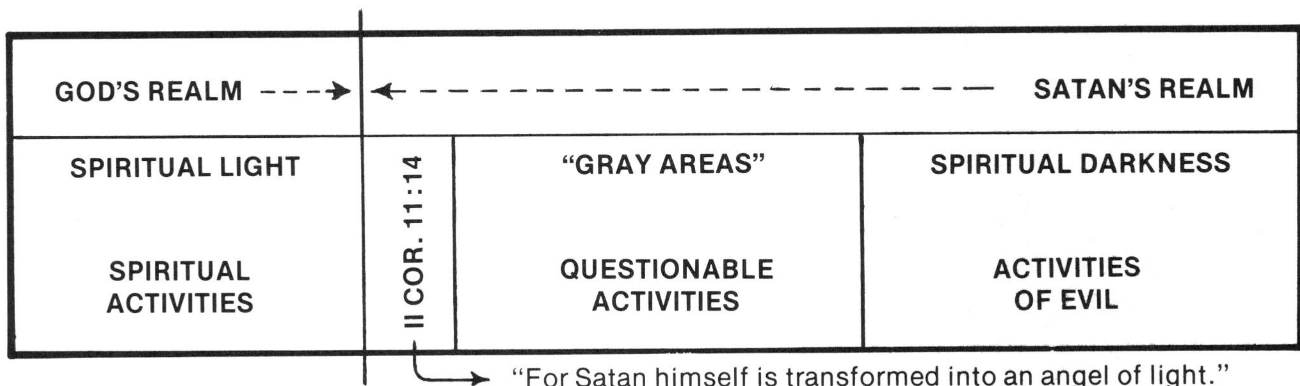

• We are not only to separate ourselves from those things which cause us to stumble but also from the practices which cause our "weaker brothers" to be offended:

"So then every one of us shall give account of himself to God. Let . . . no man put a stumblingblock or an occasion to fall in his brother's way.

"If thy brother be grieved with thy meat, now walkest thou not charitably. Destroy not him with thy meat, for whom Christ died." (Romans 14:12-15)

NOTES

3. THE CALLING OF DEDICATION

Dedication is the mature action of giving to God what really belongs to Him already. We are then free to set our affections on things above rather than on things of this earth.

- **It is not enough to turn from that which is evil. We must also turn to that which is good.**

" I beg you therefore, brethren, by the mercies of God, that you present your bodies a living sacrifice, holy, acceptable unto God, which is your reasonable service.

" And be not conformed to this world: but be transformed by the renewing of your mind, that you may prove what is that good, and acceptable, and perfect will of God." (Romans 12:1,2)

"Add to your faith virtue; and to virtue knowledge . . ." (II Peter 1:5)

As we dedicate ourselves to God's Word, we gain knowledge for greater dedication.

4. THE CALLING OF SERVICE

- **Add to your knowledge temperance** (enkrateia): **self-control; holding passions and desires in check. Self-control is the basis of fruitful Christian service. With self-control we do not serve ourselves, but we are morally free to serve one another in love.**

"For, brethren, ye have been called unto liberty: only use not liberty for an occasion to the flesh, but by love serve one another." (Galatians 5:13)

- **Service involves laying up treasures in heaven and building spiritual maturity in the lives of those around us.**

"Lay not up for yourselves treasures upon earth, where moth and rust doth corrupt, and where thieves break through and steal: but lay up for yourselves treasures in heaven where neither moth nor rust doth corrupt and where thieves do not break through and steal: for where your treasure is, there will your heart be also." (Matthew 6:19-21)

- **Men keep looking for better methods and God keeps looking for better men.**

NOTES

5. THE CALLING OF SUFFERING

"Add to your temperance endurance . . ." II Peter 1:6

• "Beloved think it not strange concerning the fiery trial which is to try you as though some strange thing happened unto you: but rejoice ..." I Peter 4:12

Suffering is essential in order to experience the final three callings.

• Suffering will usually come from people you would least expect.

Our Lord was rejected by the very people whom He had taught and fed and healed. He was put to death by those who were more familiar with the Scriptures than anyone else.

• Suffering is designed to open up new sections of scripture to us.

We don't fully appreciate scripture until we experience it. When we do, new insights are revealed that we will need in our life message.

After being turned upon by friends, the following verses take on new meaning: "I behaved myself as though he had been my friend or brother . . . but in my adversity they rejoiced . . ." (Psalm 35:14,15) "For it was not an enemy that reproached me: then I could have borne it: neither was it he that hated me that did magnify himself against me, then I would have hid myself from him:

"But it was thou, a man mine equal, my guide, and mine acquaintance. We took sweet counsel together, and walked unto the house of God in company." (Psalm 55:12-14)

Meditation will reveal new insights not only in these verses but in the chapters which surround them.

• Suffering is God's way of freeing us from that which hinders us from "setting our affections on things above." Colossians 3:2

When the three friends of Daniel were thrown into the fiery furnace, the only things that the fire burned were the ropes that tied them down. God's purpose is the same for us. He wants to free us from the multitude of cares which we think are essential, but which in reality only hinder us from true achievement.

• Suffering is most painful when we are partly at fault.

When we suffer after doing everything right, we are able to sing for joy as Paul and Silas did in prison. But usually most of our "fiery furnaces" are the result of doing the right things in the wrong way. God intends to use the fire to purify our lives from wrong motives, attitudes, words, or actions. For this purpose it is essential to spend much time in scripture.

NOTES

6. THE CALLING OF HUMILITY

When we humble ourselves through the suffering God allows, He gives us more grace both to respond to our offenders and to see new, rich insights in His Word. Humility is the basis of godliness.

"Add to your endurance godliness . . . " II Peter 1:6

- **Godliness** (eusebeia) **involves worth-ship or reverence paid to worth, whether in God or man.**

- **A godly response to those who offend us would be to recognize that God has only used them to put us through a "fire" that will be for our ultimate benefit if we respond to it and to them in the right way.**

- **God is far more concerned with our responses than He is with our experiences.**

  His purpose is that we "be partakers of His divine nature". (II Peter 1:4) Toward this goal "All things work together for good . . . " (Romans 8:28)

7. THE CALLING OF UNDERSTANDING

The reward of going through suffering and responding to it in the right way is a new ability to understand the real needs of those around us.

"Add to your brotherly kindness love . . . " II Peter 1:7

- **Brotherly kindness** (philadelphia) **involves love of the brethren, alertness to their needs, and gentleness in meeting them.**

- **Before we go through the "fire" we may tend to regard Christian work on the basis of its being merely an organization and people functioning as a part of it. But when the fire burns away the stubble of human achievement, we have a new ability to sense the real needs of the people around us.**

- **We can sense when they have been hurt, and they are able to sense that we would understand if they told us about it.**

  This is the reward of suffering. "If you be reproached for the name of Christ, happy are you; for the Spirit of glory and of God resteth upon you." (I Peter 4:14)

NOTES

8. THE CALLING OF SPIRITUAL MATURITY

"Add to your brotherly kindness love . . ." II Peter 1:7

When others sense that we would understand if they told us about their problems, and if we gained insights from scripture through our suffering, we have the basis of leading many to spiritual maturity.

- **God does not want our work for Him to be in vain or to lack lasting results.**
  "I have chosen you and ordained you that you should go and bring forth fruit, and that your fruit should remain." (John 15:16) "For if these things be in you, and abound, they make you that you shall neither be barren nor unfruitful in the knowledge of our Lord Jesus Christ." (II Peter 1:8)

- **Lasting results will not occur unless we respond to all eight callings.**
  "But he that lacketh these things is blind, and cannot see afar off, and hath forgotten that he was purged from his old sins." (II Peter 1:9)

- **God allows us to go through "fires" so that we can build in others what we learn through them.**
  "The God of all comfort (counsel) comforts us in all our tribulation, that we may be able to comfort them which are in any trouble, by the comfort wherewith we ourselves are comforted of God." (II Corinthians 1:3,4)

- **Before we go through the "fire" we can go and tell others about the Christian life, but after we respond properly to our "fire" they come to us for this information.**
  "If you suffer for righteousness' sake . . . sanctify the Lord God in your heart: and be ready always to give an answer to every man that asks you for a reason of the hope that is in you with meekness and reverence." (I Peter 3:14-15)

- **Those we lead to Christ will be far more faithful if we prepare them for suffering and if they see that we have gone through that same suffering.**
  Before Christ died His disciples forsook Him and fled in the face of suffering. Afterward they endured it with joy.

- **Each time God takes us through these eight callings our understanding of them grows deeper, and our ability to lead others to spiritual maturity grows greater.**

NOTES

LEARNING PRINCIPLES OF LASTING RELATIONSHIPS

GENUINE FRIENDSHIPS

- DEVELOPING LEVELS OF FRIENDSHIP

- PREREQUISITES FOR DATING AND ENGAGEMENT

• Knowing how to detect and terminate unwholesome friendships and learning how to develop genuine friendships are two of the most important skills we must have for lasting happiness.

NOTES

DISCERNING LEVELS OF FRIENDSHIPS

• Many fail to achieve meaningful friendships because they do not have a clear understanding of the levels of friendship. There are specific freedoms and responsibilities on each level.

LEVELS OF FRIENDSHIPS	DISTINGUISHING CHARACTERISTICS	ACCOMPANYING RESPONSIBILITIES
1. ACQUAINTANCE	• Based on occasional contacts • Freedom to ask general questions: Public information	**1.** View each acquaintance as a "divine appointment." **2.** Design appropriate general questions for new acquaintances.
2. CASUAL FRIENDSHIP	• Based on common interests, activities and concerns • Freedom to ask specific questions: Opinions, ideas, wishes and goals	**3.** Learn to identify and praise positive qualities. **4.** Design appropriate specific questions for children, youth and adults.
3. CLOSE FRIENDSHIP AND FELLOWSHIP	• Based on mutual life goals • Freedom to suggest mutual projects toward reaching life goals	**5.** Visualize achievement in each other's life. **6.** Discern and develop appropriate projects to gain this achievement.
4. INTIMATE FRIENDSHIP AND FELLOWSHIP	• Based on commitment to the development of each other's character • Freedom to correct each other	**7.** Have open honesty with discretion. **8.** Discern basic causes of character deficiencies and suggest solutions.

NOTES

1. VIEWING ACQUAINTANCES AS "DIVINE APPOINTMENTS"

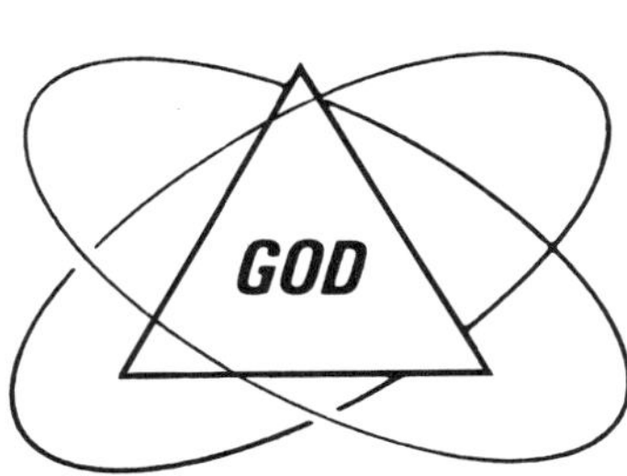

• A "divine appointment" involves two individuals whom God created and whom He loves meeting each other with potential benefit to each other.

• Whomever we meet we can be confident that God created them and loves them:

• In order to have the right attitudes toward each one we meet, it is important to have the following questions in the back of our mind:

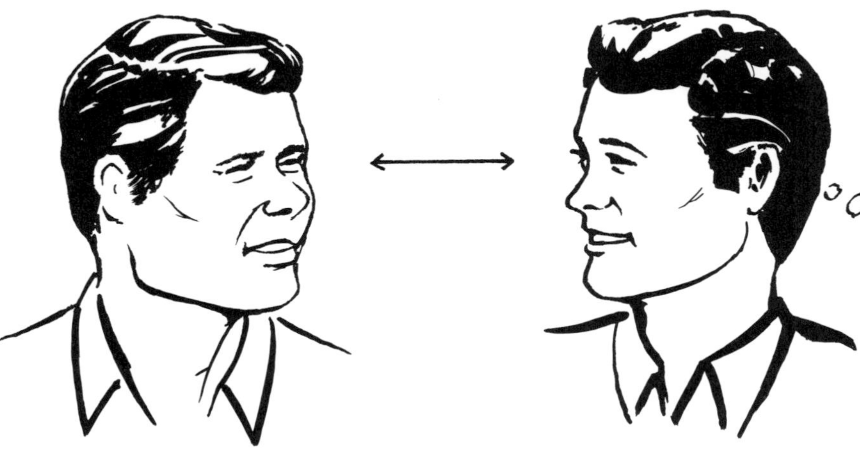

1. **WHAT ARE GOD'S PURPOSES IN HIS LIFE?** What responsibilities and opportunities has God given to him?
2. **HOW FAR HAS HE COME?** Has he achieved what he could have?
3. **WHAT HAS HINDERED GOD?** Bitterness, temporal values, or moral impurity?
4. **HOW CAN I COOPERATE WITH GOD?** Can I visualize achievement for him and assist in removing root problems?
5. **WHAT CAN I LEARN FROM HIM?**

• Many friendships are built or destroyed at the first meeting. The reason for this is that each person is very aware of the attitudes which the other one is projecting.

• **WRONG ATTITUDES:**

Fear: Will he accept me?
Selfishness: How will I gain from this friendship?

• **RIGHT ATTITUDES:**

Worth: He is important to God.
Interest: I want to learn from this friendship.
Acceptance: I want to help him reach God's potential for his life.

NOTES

2. DESIGNING APPROPRIATE GENERAL QUESTIONS

• Questions are to friendships what food is to living. It is both practical and advisable that we take time to design good questions ahead of time which can be used when we are introduced to new people.

By doing this, we gain a greater measure of self-confidence and are able to listen more carefully to what the other person is saying.

AREAS OF GENERAL QUESTIONS:
Information that is public knowledge

• FAMILY	• How many brothers and sisters do you have in your family? • Which number child are you in your family? • In what type of work is your father? • Do you know what the meaning of your name is? • Have you lived in quite a few different places? • Do you know much about your family heritage? • __________ • __________
• SCHOOL	• What school do (or did) you attend? • In what course are (or were) you majoring? • What is (or was) your favorite subject? • __________ • __________
• CHURCH	• What church do you attend? • How long have you been connected with this church? • Does your whole family belong to this church? • __________ • __________
• INTERESTS	• What sports do you enjoy? • What are some of the hobbies you have? • Do you play any musical instruments? • What are some of the organizations to which you belong? • __________ • __________

NOTES

3. IDENTIFYING POSITIVE QUALITIES

• One of the most important purposes of a friendship is to assist one another in developing Christ-like character qualities. In order to do this we must be able to know and distinguish between specific qualities.

1. Truthfulness vs. Deception
2. Obedience vs. Willfulness
3. Sincerity vs. Hypocrisy
4. Virtue vs. Defilement
5. Boldness vs. Fearfulness
6. Forgiveness vs. Rejection
7. Persuasiveness vs. Unreasonableness
8. Alertness vs. Unawareness
9. Hospitality vs. Loneliness
10. Generosity vs. Stinginess
11. Joyfulness vs. Withdrawal
12. Flexibility vs. Resistance
13. Availability vs. Dominance
14. Endurance vs. Giving Up
15. Accuracy vs. Carelessness
16. Reverence vs. Disrespect
17. Diligence vs. Slothfulness
18. Thoroughness vs. Incompleteness
19. Dependability vs. Inconsistency
20. Security vs. Anxiety
21. Patience vs. Restlessness
22. Wisdom vs. Natural Inclinations
23. Discernment vs. Unperceptiveness
24. Faith vs. Presumption
25. Discretion vs. Simple-mindedness
26. Self-control vs. Self-gratification
27. Creativity vs. Underachievement
28. Enthusiasm vs. Apathy
29. Resourcefulness vs. Wastefulness
30. Thriftiness vs. Extravagance
31. Contentment vs. Covetousness
32. Punctuality vs. Tardiness
33. Tolerance vs. Prejudice
34. Cautiousness vs. Impulsiveness
35. Gratefulness vs. Pride
36. Neatness vs. Disorganization
37. Initiative vs. Unresponsiveness
38. Responsibility vs. Irresponsibility
39. Courage vs. Cowardice
40. Decisiveness vs. Double-mindedness
41. Determination vs. Faintheartedness
42. Loyalty vs. Unfaithfulness
43. Attentiveness vs. Unapproachableness
44. Sensitivity vs. Callousness
45. Fairness vs. Partiality
46. Compassion vs. Indifference
47. Gentleness vs. Harshness
48. Deference vs. Rudeness
49. Meekness vs. Anger

NOTES

DISCERNING POSITIVE QUALITIES THROUGH NEGATIVE TRAITS

• Every negative trait is a positive quality misused. A person who is careless with money is misusing the quality of generosity. A person who is critical and judgmental is misusing the quality of discernment. Here is a further list of misuses.

POSITIVE QUALITIES	POSITIVE QUALITIES MISUSED (NEGATIVE TRAITS)
1. ALERTNESS	Jumpiness; quick criticism; presumptuous inquisitiveness
2. AMIABILITY	Gullible; status-seeking; socially preoccupied; spineless
3. ANALYTICAL	Pickiness; fussiness; pettiness; over-attention to detail
4. ASPIRATION	Selfish competition; vain ambition; scheming
5. COMPASSION	Gushy sentimentalism; undiscerning empathy; taking up offenses
6. CONFIDENCE	Conceited; cocky; overbearing
7. COOPERATIVENESS	Compromising; conniving; lacking initiative
8. COURAGE	Recklessness; brashness; brazenness
9. COURTESY	Self-consciousness; social stiffness; superficial flattery
10. CREATIVITY	Mischievous; crafty; day-dreaming; devious
11. DECISIVENESS	Inflexibility; ruthlessness; dominance
12. DILIGENCE	Slavishness; one-track mindedness; selfishly industrious
13. DISCERNMENT	Snoopiness; judgmental; critical; fault-finding
14. DISCIPLINE	Rigidness; harshness; overbearing; tyrannical
15. DISCRETION	Over-cautiousness; secretiveness; timidness; undue carefulness
16. EARNESTNESS	Nervous meticulousness; over-conscientiousness; over-seriousness
17. EFFICIENCY	Perfectionism; fussiness; rigidness; impatience
18. ENTHUSIASM	Fanatical; over-bearing; over-wrought; aggressive
19. EXPRESSIVENESS	Wordy; glib; vociferous; melodramatic
20. FAIRMINDEDNESS	Indecisive; indiscriminate; undiscerning
21. FLEXIBILITY	Wishy-washiness; indecisiveness; spinelessness
22. FORGIVENESS	Irresponsible leniency; permissiveness; irresponsibility; weakness
23. FRANKNESS	Tactless; insensitive; undiplomatic; disrespectful
24. FRUGALITY	Stingy; miserly; penny-pinching
25. GENEROSITY	Extravagance; spend-thriftiness; wastefulness; squandering
26. GRATEFULNESS	Flattery; gushiness; extravagant generosity
27. HONESTY	Outspokenness; bluntness; brutality; indiscretion
28. HOSPITALITY	Ingratiating; social climbing; cliquish
29. HUMILITY	Self-abasement; extreme self-criticism; lack of self-confidence
30. LOYALTY	Possessiveness; idol worship; blind obedience; undue attachment
31. NEATNESS	Perfectionism; over meticulousness; intolerance; stiffness
32. OBJECTIVITY	Insensitivity; cold calculation; unloving
33. PATIENCE	Indifferent; permissive; disinterested
34. PERSISTENCE	Stubbornness; inflexibility; self-willed; headstrong
35. PERSUASIVENESS	Smooth talking; high pressure tactics; pushiness
36. PUNCTUALITY	Intolerance; impatience with tardiness
37. PURPOSEFULNESS	Single-mindedness; intolerance; inflexibility
38. RESPECTFULNESS	Idol worship; debilitating subservience
39. RESOLUTENESS	Hardheadedness; closed mindedness; stubbornness
40. RESOURCEFULNESS	Over-independence; manipulating; scheming calculation
41. SENSITIVITY	Touchiness; easily offended; emotional
42. SINCERITY	Gullibility; over seriousness; impulsiveness

NOTES

4. DESIGNING APPROPRIATE SPECIFIC QUESTIONS

• After getting acquainted with a person and asking general questions, we can determine by his openness in responding to the questions whether we are free to go to the next level of friendship and ask specific questions.

AREAS OF SPECIFIC QUESTIONS:
Information on ideas, opinions and goals

• **FAMILY**	• To what do you look back as your happiest childhood memory? • What do you feel is the most important factor to having a happy family? (or marriage) • Did your parents have any special wishes for your life? • What were the childhood goals of your parents for their own lives? • How did your parents come to choose the name they gave you? • __________ • __________
• **FUTURE**	• What are some of the goals you have for your life? • What to you is the most important thing in life? • How did you happen to get interested in your present work? (if employed) • If you could have one wish right now, what would it be? • __________ • __________
• **FAITH**	• What do you think God's purpose was in making you? • What were the events which led up to your becoming a Christian? (His answer may reveal the need to explain salvation to him.) • God gives each Christian a spiritual gift. Do you know what yours is? • Have you ever dedicated your life to God's will? • What do you see as the greatest difficulty in living the Christian life? • __________ • __________

NOTES

5. VISUALIZING CHARACTER ACHIEVEMENT

• The third level of friendship involves the responsibility of visualizing character achievement for your friend and then designing practical projects to reach those goals with him.

A. OVERCOMING FEAR OF FAILURE

When most teen-agers are asked, "What do you plan to do when you get all through school?" the normal inward response is one of fear. "Will I find my place in life?" "Will I get into the right job?" "Will I be happy and successful?"

For this reason they will usually be immediately interested when a friend says to them, "Do you know what work you'd be good in?" or, "You'd make an excellent — (teacher, pastor, etc.)."

B. VISUALIZING VOCATIONAL DIRECTION

At one of our first ministers' workshops, I asked each minister if he could think back to some human motivation toward the ministry in addition to being called into it by God's Spirit.

Fully 25 percent of those men immediately recalled a person who had said to them in youth, "You'd make an excellent minister," or, "You'd be a good youth director." These statements started them thinking about the ministry.

C. INSTILLING A SENSE OF DESTINY

One of the first and most essential tasks of a parent is to instill a sense of spiritual destiny in each child. God made each of us for an important purpose, and it is the wise parent or friend who can emphasize this fact. A statement by John Wesley's mother did this for him when he was saved from death in a fire: "Thou art a brand plucked from the burning. God must have some special purpose for you to perform."

D. VISUALIZING CHARACTER ACHIEVEMENT

Even more vital than visualizing vocational direction is the ability to visualize character development. One of the first ways to do this is to know the character meanings of names. Most people are quite interested and pleased if you know what the meaning of their name is and can translate it into character. For example, Wayne means, "Burden Bearer." Cynthia means "Reflector of Light."

NOTES

6. DESIGNING CHARACTER PROJECTS

• By visualizing achievement for a close friend we prepare the way to design projects with him in order to reach that which we visualized.

Scripture commands us to "Consider one another to provoke unto love and good works." (Hebrews 10:24) As genuine Christians we are to be unique in that we are "zealous of good works" (Titus 2:14)

A. PROJECTS MUST BE PRACTICAL, MEASURABLE AND ACHIEVABLE

A good project is the result of much careful thought. It must be quickly recognized by your friend as something he would want to do and something that would help him fulfill the goals he has already decided to reach. The project must not be too big for him to accomplish in a given period of time and he must be able to measure the progress he is making on the project.

B. PROJECTS SHOULD BE DESIGNED TO STRENGTHEN CHARACTER QUALITIES

A young boy was easily led by his friends to do things that were wrong. He needed to develop the character qualities of discernment and courage to stand alone. He was given the project of reorganizing the book of Proverbs around all the types of people in it, such as, a fool, a strange woman, a slothful man, a scorner, etc. After a very short time this boy began discerning the types of attitudes his friends were revealing and was able to withstand their promptings to do evil.

C. PROJECTS SHOULD BE THE BASIS FOR MEANINGFUL DATING

Dating is actually a relationship which involves the third level of friendship, and as such, it carries with it the opportunity and responsibility to design projects for one another which will help each one come closer to the Lord.

It was suggested to one young couple who had difficulty maintaining a conversation during dates to memorize a section of scripture prior to the date and then quote it and discuss it when they got together.

Some excellent sections would be I Corinthians 13 on genuine love and Colossians 3, I Thessalonians 4, Galatians 5, etc., which emphasize moral purity.

NOTES

7. CORRECTING "BLIND SPOTS"

• One day I listened as a young couple argued. The wife was accusing her husband of flirting with other girls. He was vigorously denying it. After talking with the husband, I could see what the problem was. He had a "blindspot" and was not aware of it.

1. God has a "norm" or standard of behavior for each one of us in every area of our life.

NORM OF BEHAVIOR

- In morality
- In obedience
- In gratefulness
- In humility
- etc.

"BLINDSPOT"

He couldn't see it because his focus was on what he used to be rather than on what he should be.

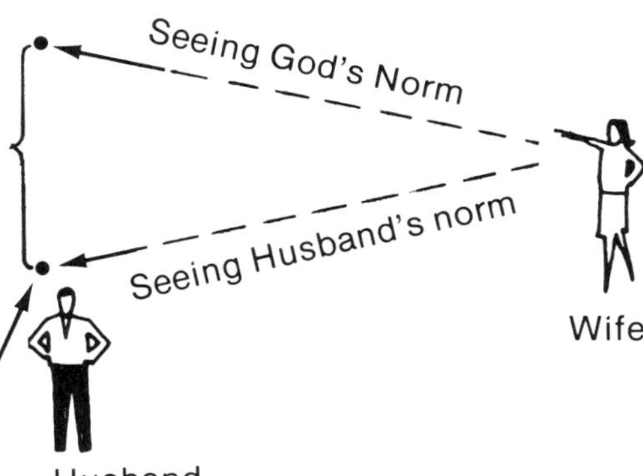

Violating God's Norm

"Great Improvement"

LOWERED NORM OF MORALITY

2. When the husband mentioned above was in high school, he greatly violated God's norm in his moral life.

3. Following his schooling, he repented of his immoral way of life and purposed to live a godly life. He looked back on what he used to be and was encouraged with his improvement.

• Every one of us has blind spots, and it is essential that we have various intimate friends who have the freedom to tell us what they are. "Faithful are the wounds of a friend." Proverbs 27:6 "Iron sharpeneth iron; so a man sharpeneth the countenance of his friend." Proverbs 27:17

NOTES

8. GIVING DIRECTION WITHOUT JUDGING

• At what point does a sincere concern for another person become a judgment of him? How does judgment differ from discernment? Here are important steps of comparison.

DISCERNMENT I Corinthians 12:10	**JUDGMENT** Romans 2:1-3
anakrino - to distinguish (I Corinthians 4:3) diakrino - to investigate (I Corinthians 11:31; 14:29)	krino - to give a verdict (with no intention of personal involvement) Matthew 7:1; Romans 4:13
1. Discernment asks questions until all important factors are understood. ". . . the honor of kings is to search out a matter." Proverbs 25:2	**1.** Judgment accepts hearsay at face value and forms opinions of motives on a few known factors. "The simple believeth every word: but the prudent man looketh well to his going." Proverbs 14:15
2. Discernment studies all important factors in order to discover root causes for the present problem. ". . . he shall not judge after the sight of his eyes, neither reprove after the hearing of his ears:" Isaiah 11:3	**2.** Judgment openly shares conclusions with those not related to the solution of the problem. "He that answereth a matter before he heareth it, it is folly and shame unto him." Proverbs 18:13
3. Discernment looks for a comparable problem in personal experience. II Corinthians 1:4	**3.** Judgment avoids personal self-evaluation by projecting hostility toward the offender and his offense.
4. Discernment carefully reviews the steps taken to overcome a similar problem.	**4.** Judgment has not yet overcome the same personal problem.
5. Discernment accepts the offender as he is and waits for the right opportunity to approach the problem.	**5.** Judgment fails to differentiate between the sin and the sinner and, therefore, reflects a rejection of both.
6. Discernment gains the confidence of the one in need and then shares the steps taken to overcome a similar problem.	**6.** Judgment tells a person where he has been wrong without providing direction for a solution.
7. Discernment assumes the responsibility for restoration. Galatians 6:1	**7.** Judgment reminds God of the shortcomings of the offender.

NOTES

DEVELOPING LEVELS OF FRIENDSHIPS

A. ACQUAINTANCE

A. Be alert to each new person around you.
B. Have a cheerful, friendly countenance — smile.
C. Learn and remember his name.
D. Greet him by his name.
E. Ask him appropriate questions which reflect interest and acceptance.
F. Be a good listener.
G. Remind yourself of the interest God has for him.

B. CASUAL FRIENDSHIP

A. Discover his strong points.
B. Learn about the hopes and desires he has for his life.
C. Develop and ask him appropriate specific questions.
D. Show interest and concern if he shares problems with you.
E. Be honest about yourself and acknowledge your faults to him when appropriate.
F. Reflect interest and trustworthiness in being his friend.
G. Talk with God about him and his needs.

C. CLOSE FRIENDSHIP

A. See potential achievement in his life.
B. Discover and discuss the specific goals he has.
C. Assume a personal responsibility for the development of his goals.
D. Discern the conflicts which hinder the development of these goals.
E. Be creative in designing projects which would help him achieve these goals.
F. Learn how to build his interest for the projects you have developed for him.
G. Be alert to Scripture which would encourage or guide him.

D. INTIMATE FRIENDSHIP

A. Learn how to give comfort to him through his trials and sorrows.
B. Assume personal responsibility for his reputation.
C. Be sensitive to traits and attitudes which need improvement in yourself and him.
D. Discern basic causes of character deficiencies.
E. Build interest for correction of these deficiencies. Ask him to tell you about your faults.
F. Search the Scriptures for keys to a solution.
G. Be committed to faithfulness, loyalty and availability.

NOTES

EVALUATING PRESENT FRIENDSHIPS

• Most teen-agers don't realize why it is true that in order to have the right friends, we must be willing to have the right enemies. God warns ". . . whosoever therefore will be a friend of the world is the enemy of God." James 4:4

A. WHAT HAPPENS WHEN A WRONG FRIENDSHIP IS CONTINUED? WE LOSE MANY POTENTIAL FRIENDS FOR THE FOLLOWING REASONS:

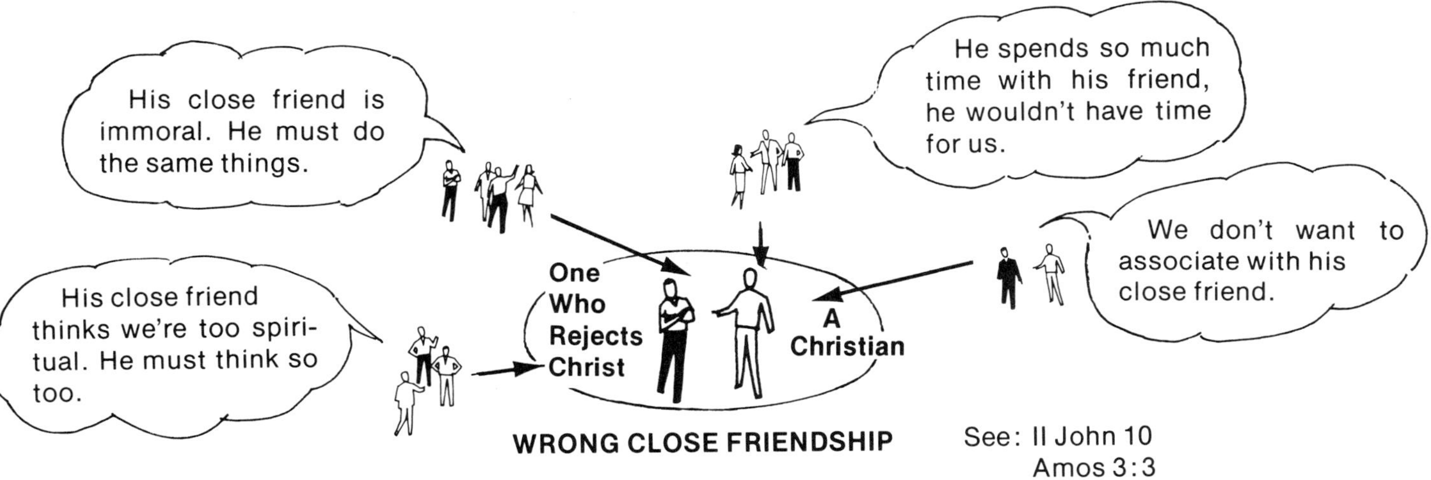

WRONG CLOSE FRIENDSHIP

See: II John 10
Amos 3:3
II Corinthians 6:14-18

B. STEPS TO APPLY TO A QUESTIONABLE CLOSE FRIENDSHIP

1. Find out if he ever has experienced a spiritual re-birth and if he has dedicated his life to the lordship of Jesus Christ.

2. Design character-building projects which will assist both of you to come closer to the Lord. If he decides not to do these with you, it will be he that leaves you, rather than you leaving him. "They shall separate you from their company." Luke 6:22 "They went out from us, but they were not of us, for if they had been of us, they would no doubt have continued with us." I John 2:19

C. BASIC COMMITMENTS FOR FRIENDSHIPS:

1. Purpose that those who reject Jesus Christ must also reject you (for close or intimate friendships), and those who love Jesus Christ should also love you.

2. Purpose to verbally explain your relationship to Jesus Christ whenever you are asked to compromise your standards.

3. Purpose to let God choose your friends on the basis of their needs and their desire for God's help through your life.

NOTES

• The principles of friendships must be the basis upon which dating is built if it is going to accomplish the greatest benefit in the life of each partner.

DATING AND ENGAGEMENT

• The far-reaching importance and effects of patterns in dating cannot be overemphasized. Here are basic considerations essential to achieving successful dating patterns.

NOTES

PREREQUISITES FOR SUCCESSFUL DATING

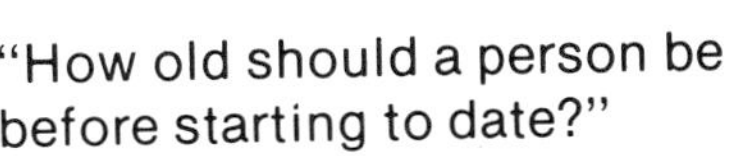

• After checking into the tragic accounts of many marriages, it soon becomes obvious that decisions and patterns that were made in dating have a far more serious effect on the success or failure of a marriage than most teen-agers or adults realize. Because of this, it is essential that certain prerequisites be established in order to determine when a teen-ager is old enough to date.

• One day during a youth discussion on dating, a teen-ager glanced up at her father who was sitting next to her. She noticed that he had his eyes closed. Then she quietly raised her hand and asked:

"How old do you have to be before you can start to date?"

Her startled father quickly woke up and glared at his daughter. Then he folded his arms and settled his eyes on me as if to say, "You'd better not double-cross me on the rules I've laid down for my daughter!"

Meanwhile, the daughter's pleading eyes were asking for some relief from the regulations which she apparently felt were too strict on her dating privileges.

The following response caused both the daughter and the father to do some re-evaluating:

"YOU ARE OLD ENOUGH TO DATE WHEN YOU HAVE ACHIEVED THE FOLLOWING THREE PREREQUISITES."

1. **When you are aware of both the benefits and the dangers of dating**
2. **When you have personally worked out from Scripture a set of God's dating standards**
3. **When you have purposed that you will not lower these standards, even if it means losing dates**

NOTES

THE BASIC PURPOSE OF DATING

• TO EVALUATE DATING STANDARDS, WE MUST DETERMINE HOW THEY WILL AFFECT A FUTURE MARRIAGE—TO BUILD IT OR DESROY IT.

• Most teen-agers have little comprehension of the seeds of success or failure which are sown during their dating years.

A prerequisite for successful dating is an understanding of the requirements for a successful marriage.

• Until recently, marriage counselors have appeared to be chiefly concerned with physical harmony and intimacy in building happy marriages. However, in view of a disproportionate increase in divorces among those who have been married twenty years or longer, many new studies have been made on what makes a successful marriage.

• A significant account has been given of a woman whose 19-year marriage came to an end. She was attractive and explained to her best friend that none of the standard problems of sex, money or children had ever really troubled her marriage. Nevertheless, a gulf had slowly opened between her and her husband.

• Why had their marriage failed? They had neglected to understand or achieve marriage's deepest and most subtle test—the test of genuine intimacy.

• For most people, intimacy is associated only with the physical. But to the wise marriage counselor, intimacy involves far more than the physical. It is not an act. It is a state of existence in which both partners in the marriage trust the other with more and more of their innermost thoughts, wishes and emotions. This relationship is the key to a successful marriage.

• Most modern marriages fall far short of genuine intimacy. This occurs because in our distorted age of romanticism, each partner expects instant intimacy. They feel that intimacy can be achieved by means of physical or emotional methods, but they fail to see that true intimacy begins and is maintained by a oneness of spirit.

• The chief purpose of dating is to develop a oneness of spirit which when achieved can be the basis of a continuing third or fourth-level friendship, or the basis of engagement and marriage.

NOTES

REQUIREMENTS FOR A TOTAL MARRIAGE

GOD'S ORDER	OBJECTIVES TO ACHIEVE	RELATIONSHIPS	CONFLICTS FROM VIOLATIONS
SPIRIT **SPIRITUAL**	**COMING TOGETHER IN ONE SPIRIT:** Spiritual intimacy is achieved when two Christians are able to fully and freely share with one another God's dealing in their lives on salvation, total dedication and victorious Christian living. Genuine love heightens a delight in Scripture, witnessing and Christian work.	**DATING**	When physical involvement is entered into on this level, there is an inability to share one's faith after marriage to the same degree that would have been otherwise possible.
SOUL **INTELLECTUAL** **VOLITIONAL** **EMOTIONAL**	**MENTAL AND EMOTIONAL ONENESS:** Intimacy of soul is achieved as plans are made for a future together. There is a sharing of likes and dislikes as they relate to living and working together. A focus of expectation and delight is centered on the definite time when these plans can be fulfilled.	**ENGAGEMENT**	There is a struggle to keep the original emotional feelings intact as the "romance" wears off. The real personality of each is unknown to the other.
BODY **PHYSICAL**	**PHYSICAL UNION:** Physical intimacy is consummated in marriage. "For this cause shall a man leave his father and mother, and cleave to his wife; and they twain shall be one flesh . . ." Mark 10:7,8	**MARRIAGE**	There is a breakdown in communication and the feeling that each is a stranger to the other. Self-condemnation and roots of bitterness develop. A coldness develops as memories are reviewed. Feelings of guilt bring frustration.

NOTE: Satan seeks to reverse this order by having teen-agers begin their dating with physical involvement. This produces emotional involvement along with guilt. Spiritual development, therefore, is often put off until after marriage.

NOTES

INTIMACY OF SPIRIT IN DATING

• The chief purpose of dating is to achieve spiritual oneness. When this is accomplished, there will be a greater love for God, a new joy in the Scriptures, a new desire to tell others about Christ, and a deepening fellowship with other Christians in these areas.

• DEVELOPING SPIRITUAL ONENESS

He is responsible for the spiritual leadership in dating.

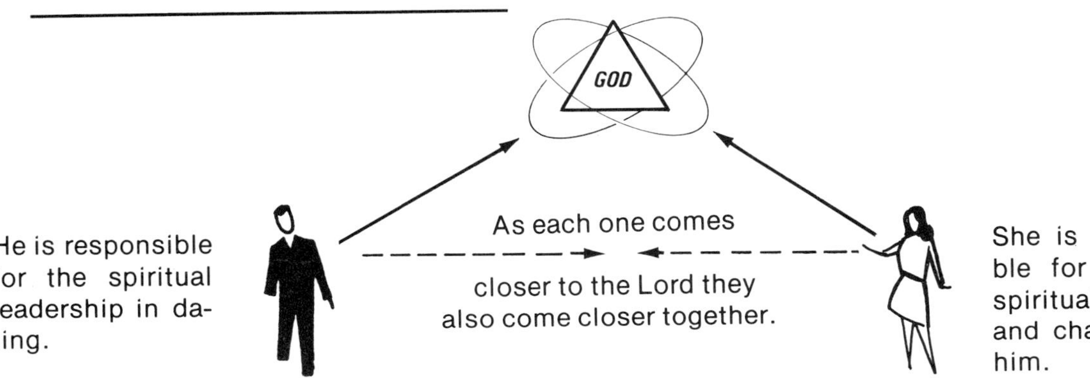

She is responsible for being a spiritual example and challenge to him.

• A oneness of spirit is accomplished as both seek to get as close as they can to God in their own personal lives. As each one develops his spiritual responsibilities and opportunities, a deepening fellowship exists and a greater ability to communicate with each other develops.

• DESTROYING SPIRITUAL ONENESS

• When the purpose of dating is not to encourage and help the other person in his spiritual development but is rather on the level of physical involvement, a sense of guilt develops and a growing awareness that their desires are contrary to God's desires. This also destroys communication between them.

NOTES

DISCERNING THE RIGHT LIFE PARTNER

	IS HE A CHRISTIAN ?	WHAT IS MY LIFE GOAL ?	SELF-CONTROL ?	HARMONY AT HOME ?	PROPER TIMING ?	WHAT IS MY GIFT ?	RESULT:
DECISIONS	**1** **I will only date and marry a growing Christian**	**2** **I will relate dating and marriage to God's purpose for my life**	**3** **I will not "defraud" the one I date**	**4** **Both of us must be in harmony at home**	**5** **I will wait for God's timing in our marriage**	**6** **I yield my right to date and marry to God**	**God's fulfillment of deepest needs**
RATIONALIZATIONS AND GOALS	II Cor. 6:14 "He's not a Christian but he's sure a nice guy." "He's a better gentleman than most Christians I've dated." "He's not a Christian because he doesn't want to be a hypocrite." "We have so much in common other than religion." "He wants our children to go to my church." "I think he's open. Maybe I can witness on our dates." "I told him he had to be a Christian so he accepted Christ."	Col. 1:28,29 "He's a little shy about religious things." "It never seems in place to talk about God or pray on dates." "After marriage we'll get active in church work." "We're only young once." "Another Christian wronged him so he's not active at church." "I don't want him to think I'm a religious fanatic."	I Thess. 4:6 "What's wrong with 'proving' that we love each other?" "He's got a few bad habits, but no one's perfect." "He thinks some Christians are too strict." "Dating standards are different today." "I should break up, but I don't want to hurt him."	Num. 14:18 "He says I'm the only one he can talk to." "I think his parents are too strict." "He's got a real temper, but he holds it around me." "When he leaves home things will be much better."	Gen. 29:20 1. Parent's Consent "We're old enough to make our own decisions." 2. Financial Preparation "We'll manage somehow." 3. Basic Education "We'll finish school together."	I Cor. 7:32 Matt. 6:33 Lam. 3:24-40 **GOAL:** UNDISTRACTED CONCENTRATION ON CHRIST AND HIS WORK	I Cor. 7:36 THE ONE GOD BRINGS INTO YOUR LIFE IF HE KNOWS YOU WILL BE HAPPIER AND MORE EFFECTIVE.
CONFLICTS	INCOMPLETE MARRIAGE The most essential aspect of a "total marriage" is lost when there is no spiritual union or basis for spiritual intimacy. The man must be the spiritual leader.	GOAL FRUSTRATION Without clearly-defined life goals there is little basis for making important decisions in dating or marriage.	SELF-CONDEMNATION Guilt and blame over wrong standards in dating carry into the marriage and become the source for many petty arguments.	CONFLICT TRANSFERENCE A man tends to treat his wife as he treated his mother. A wife tends to respond to her husband as she did to her father. The way each kept his room is the way each may keep house.	TENSION AND WORRY Dangerous stress is added to the marriage. Impatience is a sign of self-love or immaturity, since love can always wait to give.	SPIRITUAL IMMATURITY Essential training and experience are lost when the responsibilities of a premature marriage crowd out significant Christian activities.	

NOTES

THE EFFECT OF DEFRAUDING IN DATING ON:

COMMUNICATION BREAKDOWN IN MARRIAGE

<table>
<tr><th></th><th>HIS INNER CONFLICTS</th><th colspan="2">VISIBLE SYMPTOMS</th><th>HER INNER CONFLICTS</th></tr>
<tr><td rowspan="3">DATING</td><td>Lasciviousness.
He becomes interested in her through physical attraction.</td><td colspan="2">They come together on a physical level and disregard the need for spiritual oneness.</td><td>Defrauding.
She seeks to attract him through dress and actions.</td></tr>
<tr><td>Wrong moral standards.
He feels the need to prove his love and fears losing her affection.</td><td colspan="2">Each rationalizes lowering standards. They withdraw from the group, desiring to be alone more.</td><td>More concerned with his evaluation of her than with her own moral standards. Guilt is suppressed.</td></tr>
<tr><td>He equates love with sexual attraction. Expresses his love to gain physical involvement.</td><td colspan="2">Each is unable to discover the real self of the other. Arguments, frequent breaking up and redefining moral standards may occur.</td><td>Seeds of doubt and distrust are bred in her response toward him.</td></tr>
<tr><td rowspan="4">MARRIAGE</td><td>He views marriage as an acceptable way to meet his physical drives.</td><td>Tells of his love for her only when they are physically involved.</td><td>Develops frigidity. Communication breakdown.</td><td>She begins to internally question her husband's love. "The only reason he loves me is for what he can get out of me."</td></tr>
<tr><td>He becomes angry as her coolness threatens the fulfillment of his physical drives.</td><td>Becomes more argumentative and demanding.</td><td>Withdraws. Worries. Loses self-confidence or becomes dominant.</td><td>Senses inner guilt which comes from her inward concern that she has been unable to fulfill her role as a wife.</td></tr>
<tr><td>He becomes concerned about the need to regain her affection. Tries to prove his love to her.</td><td>Buys material things. He attempts to appear happy. Financial problems result.</td><td>Begins to substitute love of children, friends, possessions for husband's love.</td><td>Accepts the situation as it is. Feels God is punishing her because she isn't submissive, or because she married the wrong person.</td></tr>
<tr><td>Entertains thoughts that he married the wrong one. Begins to breed seeds of unfaithfulness.</td><td>Goes his own way. Attempts to find fulfillment in his work.</td><td>Becomes deeply hurt. Is condemning, critical, suspicious of others.</td><td>She doesn't care. Gives up.</td></tr>
</table>

NOTES

DISCERNING GENUINE LOVE

I CORINTHIANS 13:4-8	AMPLIFICATION
1. **LOVE SUFFERETH LONG** It is slow to lose patience	Doesn't demonstrate irritations, or reflect anger, or have a quick temper. Has fully accepted the character of the one being dated.
2. **IT IS KIND** It looks for a way of being constructive	It is actively creative. It is able to recognize needs. It discovers successful methods of improving or contributing to the other's life.
3. **IT ENVIETH NOT** It is not possessive	It does not hold exclusive control where one is allowed little or no freedom to fulfill himself apart from the one dating him.
4. **IT VAUNTETH NOT ITSELF** It is not anxious to impress	Doesn't seek to make an impression or create an image for personal gain.
5. **IT IS NOT PUFFED UP** It does not cherish inflated ideas of its own importance	It is not self-centered. It has the ability to change and to accept change. It is flexible. It doesn't allow or expect life to revolve around itself.
6. **IT DOES NOT BEHAVE ITSELF UNSEEMLY** It has good manners	Has respect for others which results in a set of Christ-centered standards. Has discretion. Knows what is proper and when.
7. **IT DOES NOT SEEK ITS OWN** It does not pursue selfish advantage	Does not have primary concern for personal sexual appetites or social status but concern for the needs of the one being dated and the families involved.
8. **IT IS NOT EASILY PROVOKED** It is not touchy	Is not hypersensitive or easily hurt. Does not take things too personally. Is not emotionally involved with personal opinions so that to reject ideas is to reject the one giving them.
9. **IT THINKETH NO EVIL** It does not keep account of evil	Doesn't review wrongs which have been forgiven. Doesn't dwell on past evil. Destroys evidence of past mistakes when possible.
10. **IT REJOICETH NOT IN INIQUITY** It doesn't gloat over the wickedness of other people	Doesn't compare self with others for self-justification. Doesn't use other's evil to excuse personal weakness. Doesn't say, "Everyone is doing it."
11. **IT REJOICETH IN THE TRUTH** It is glad with all godly men when truth prevails	Is in active fellowship with dedicated Christians. Is occupied with spiritual objectives.
12. **IT BEARETH ALL THINGS** It knows no limit to its forebearance	Has the ability to live with the inconsistencies of others. Has empathy for the problems of others.
13. **IT BELIEVETH ALL THINGS** It knows no end to its trust	It believes in the person and the person's worth without question. It has no reason to doubt the person's integrity.
14. **IT HOPETH ALL THINGS** It knows no fading of its hope	It is not fickle. It has perfect peace and confidence that God is primarily responsible for introducing the right partner at the right time.
15. **IT ENDURETH ALL THINGS** It has unlimited endurance	It is able to outlast anything. It is able to endure all obstacles and even love in the face of unreturned love.

NOTES

INDEX

NOTES

F

G

H

I

J

K

L

M

N

O

P

NOTES

Q

R

S

T

U

V

W-X-Y-Z

NOTES

SCRIPTURE REFERENCE INDEX

NOTES

NOTES

NOTES